D0875723

Famine in Africa

Other Books Published in Cooperation with the International Food Policy Research Institute

Famine in Africa

Causes, Responses, and Prevention

JOACHIM VON BRAUN, TESFAYE TEKLU,
AND PATRICK WEBB

Published for the International Food Policy Research Institute

The Johns Hopkins University Press
Baltimore and London

© 1998 The International Food Policy Research Institute
All rights reserved. Published 1999
Printed in the United States of America on acid-free paper
9 8 7 6 5 4 3 2 1

The Johns Hopkins University Press
2715 North Charles Street
Baltimore, Maryland 21218-4363
www.press.jhu.edu

Library of Congress Cataloging-in-Publication Data will be found at the end of this book.
A catalog record for this book is available from the British Library.

ISBN 0-8018-6121-7

HC
800
.Z9
F388
1999

Contents

Tables and Figures

Tables

Figures

Foreword

As the twenty-first century dawns, it is a sad reality that famines are still with us, especially in Africa. And despite the speed with which telecommunications can spread news around the globe, famines in remote places are sometimes silent, virtually unnoticed on the world scene until they are irrevocable. Droughts, conflicts, or other short-term disasters are generally blamed for famines, but in truth, the fault lies mainly with enduring poverty. When a sizable portion of the population is extemely poor, many people do not have the resources to withstand the effects of severe setbacks, no matter how short-lived. As Joachim von Braun, Tesfaye Teklu, and Patrick Webb tell us in this comprehensive book on famine, "although political and military conflict and drought contribute to famine, they do so mainly where people are vulnerable and when resilience to external shocks has already worn thin."

This book sheds new light on both the theoretical and empirical bases for understanding famines and examines their diverse causes, which range from policy and planning failures to natural catastrophes, environmental degradation, overpopulation, market failures, and of course conflict. In the context of a comprehensive conceptual framework, the book confronts the reality of famine at the household level in Ethiopia and Sudan and considers programs in the field that have shown success in preventing or mitigating famine in, for example, Botswana, Ethiopia, and Zimbabwe.

It stresses that policies that prevent and mitigate famine can succeed only when both peace and participatory government prevail. Such policies must involve coordinated activity on the community, national, and international levels. What is especially important about this research is its multifaceted approach, which examines technical, economic, geographic, and political factors and combines theory, fact-finding, and policy analysis. And because of this, both scholars and decisionmakers will find this book particularly useful.

Per Pinstrup-Andersen
Director General, IFPRI

xiii

Preface

The research community's response to continued outbreaks of famine in Africa remains fragmented. Some researchers argue that the most serious issues have already been addressed, others lock themselves into sterile arguments over issues of causation—the "availability" versus "entitlement" debate, or the "conflict" versus "failed development policy" debate. Some analysts suggest that, at the turn of the twenty-first century, famines have become a transitory phenomenon that will eventually disappear even from Africa. If that be the case, only pessimists would plan long-term research on the topic. Others claim that famine has little to do anymore with agriculture, drought, or even policy— it is now only associated with political struggle and therefore lends itself poorly to conventional empirical research.

Yet too many of the arguments continue to be pursued in an empirical vacuum—informed by experience from Asia but misinformed by anecdotes from Africa. As a result, the limited body of empirical work undertaken on African famines in the past has not been much enhanced in recent years. Although acute famines appear to be similar across continents (at least in the media), their causes, their victims, and the policies needed to respond effectively to them differ immensely.

This book seeks to fill in just a few of the empirical and conceptual gaps that continue to hinder our analysis of such complex events. We try to strengthen the empirical basis for understanding household-level effects of famines. We also analyze drought and famine responses on the market, complementing existing work in Asia. And we attempt to assess selected famine mitigation, rehabilitation, and prevention efforts with a view to better informing future action.

The results presented here are the product of empirical research in numerous parts of Africa, but with a particular focus on Botswana, Ethiopia, Niger, Rwanda, Sudan, and Zimbabwe. It represents a collation of fieldwork results (some published, some not) in each of these countries combined with relevant findings from many reports, papers, and articles relating to each country individually.[1]

---

1. See the References for related works by the authors and others on these countries' experiences with famines.

We owe thanks to many people who have supported, encouraged, critiqued, and interacted with us in this work. The book is based on long-term collaboration with many researchers, policymakers, nongovernmental organizations (NGOs), and donors across Africa and elsewhere. The research in Sudan was undertaken in close interaction with and administrative support of the Ministry of Finance and Economic Planning (MFEP). The regional ministries of Agriculture and Natural Resources (MANR), Animal Resources, and MFEP; the Department of Forestry; and the El Obeid branch of the Agricultural Bank of Sudan (ABS) in Kordofan were very helpful partners. The Ministry of Health and Social Welfare, Nutrition Division, kindly provided original nutrition-survey data for further analysis. The Jebel Marra Rural Development Project in Darfur collaborated with us on analyzing survey data collected in the project area.

Work in Ethiopia was carried out in association with Ethiopia's Ministry of Planning and Economic Development (MPED—formerly the Office of the National Committee for Central Planning), the Ministry of Agriculture (MOA), and the International Livestock Center for Africa (ILCA) (now the International Livestock Research Institute). Numerous Ethiopian agencies provided assistance in gaining access to secondary data: the Central Statistics Authority (CSA), Relief and Rehabilitation Commission (RRC), National Meteorological Services Agency (NMSA), Institute of Agricultural Research, and the Institute of Development Research (Addis Ababa University). We are also indebted to the following international organizations and NGOs for their cooperation in Ethiopia: the Food and Agriculture Organization of the United Nations (FAO), World Food Programme (WFP), United Nations Emergency Preparedness and Prevention Group, United Nations Children's Fund (UNICEF), European Community (EC), Redd Barna-Ethiopia, Save the Children Fund (United Kingdom), Lutheran World Federation, OXFAM-America, OXFAM-United Kingdom, and CARE-Ethiopia.

In Niger, research was carried out in collaboration with the Sahelian center of the International Crops Research Institute for the Semi-Arid Tropics (ICRISAT) and the Département d'Economie Rural (DECOR) of the Institut National de Recherches Agronomiques du Niger (INRAN). The International Food Policy Research Institute (IFPRI) is particularly grateful to Sahirou Bawa, Samba Ly, and Bokar Moussa of INRAN and to the Government of Niger for supporting the research. Special thanks also go to the following national institutions for their assistance during the project: the Ministère des Finances et du Plan, Ministère d'Agriculture et de l'Elevage, Système d'Alerte Precoce (SAP), Office des Produits Vivriers Nigeriens (OPVN), and the Agence Nigerienne de Travaux d'Intérôt Public pour l'Emploi (NIGETIP).

The research work in Botswana was made possible through research and administrative support of the ministries of Finance and Development Planning, Local Governments and Lands, Agriculture, and Health. We owe special thanks to Ms. T. C. Moremi and Mr. N. J. Manamela of the Ministry of Finance and Development Planning, Mr. B. Dintwa and Mr. G. R. L. Tidi of the Ministry of Local Governments and Lands, Mr. H. K. Sigwele of the Ministry of Agriculture, and Ms. Maribe of the Ministry of Health.

In Rwanda, our research collaborators were the Ministry of Agriculture and the Enquète Agricole-Project. Serge Rwamasirabo and Bernard Mutwewingabo provided considerable personal guidance and support.

In Zimbabwe, research was conducted in partnership with the Zimbabwe Institute of Development Studies (ZIDS). Special thanks are also due to the Ministry of Labor, Manpower Planning, and Social Welfare; the Agricultural Technology and Extension Division of the Ministry of Agriculture (AGRI-TEX); and the Ministry of Health.

The authors would like to express their gratitude to Hermann Eiselen, whose individual commitment to ending hunger serves as an inspiration to many. Whereas countless individuals have helped us as thoughtful discussion partners during the research or as reviewers, the following few deserve special mention: Harold Alderman, Yisgedullish Amde, Judith Appleton, Melaku Ayalew, Abdel Razik el-Bashir, Shewangizaw Bekele, Leyla Omar el-Beshir, Jim Borton, Eshetu Chole, D. Layne Coppock, Christopher Delgado, Günter Dresrüsse, Jean Drèze, Hannan Ezekiel, Torsten Feldbrügge, Salvador Fernandez, Hank Fitzhugh, Stephen Franzel, Aklu Girgre, Michael Goe, Tesfaye Haile, Tsehaye Haile, Wolfgang Herbinger, Sarah Holden, Julius Holt, Nurul Islam, Bob Kates, Randolph Kent, Shubh Kumar, Sheik el-Mak, Simon Maxwell, Sharles May, John Mellor, Karen Moore, Penny Nestel, Jonathan Olsson, Rajul Pandya-Lorch, Richard Pankhurst, David Pelletier, Kurt Peters, Klaus Pilgram, Per Pinstrup-Andersen, Dessalegn Rahmato, Martin Ravallion, Thomas Reardon, William Renison, T. Edgar Richardson, Frank Riely, Jr., David Rohrbach, Barbara Rose, Mandi Rukuni, Stephen Sandford, Amartya Sen, Senait Seyoum, Hassan el-Sheik, Peter Svedberg, Kees Tuinenburg, Michel Vallee, Stephen Vosti, Peter Walker, Sudhir Wanmali, Graciela Wiegand, Timothy Williams, Mesfin Wolde-Mariam, Amde Wondafrash, Yisehac Yohannes, E. A. A. Zaki, Tesfaye Zegeye, and Hashim el-Zein.

We also thank Lynette Aspillera, Angela Hau, Peter Lohr, and Jay Willis for their contributions to the preparation of several drafts of the manuscript. On a personal note, Patrick's thanks are also due to Anna, Tristan, Julien, and Gabriel, whose love and support are priceless.

This research was made possible by grants to IFPRI from the Ministry of Economic Cooperation of the Federal Republic of Germany, with additional support from the U.S. Agency for International Development (USAID) and UNICEF in Ethiopia; the Rockefeller Foundation in Sudan; and USAID and the Deutsche Gesellschaft für Technische Zusammenarbeit (GTZ) in Botswana, Niger, Rwanda, and Zimbabwe.

Famine in Africa

1   Introduction

A famine is a catastrophic disruption of the social, economic, and institutional systems that provide for food production, distribution, and consumption. For a long time famines have been considered anomalies—crises that must be remedied by short-term relief activities so that the normal processes of development can be resumed. In this it was assumed that "development" represents a normative process of progress from fear and destitution toward security and well-being. Famines were seen as temporary phenomena that merely interrupted this progress, which would be restored once a crisis had passed.

We now know differently. Famines can destroy not just life, but also the hope of development. They can make progress infinitely more difficult than it had been before. Relief operations alone, even if successful in terms of saving lives, are not a sound basis for a sustainable future. More—much more—is needed.

Historically the eradication of famine has been achieved not merely by fine-tuning emergency response mechanisms, but also by elaborating development policies that sought to *prevent* crises, and upon which improved response actions could build (Watkins and Menken 1985; Kates and Millman 1990). What is more, it is now understood that prevention of famine is an essential building block for a sustained challenge to global hunger. This apparent tautology highlights the developmental aspects of famine prevention: namely, that improvements in nutrition and health, as well as greater social and economic integration and reduced risk, contribute toward long-term economic growth, which then makes overcoming hunger possible and sustainable (Fogel 1991).

At the beginning of the twentieth century, famine was still a global human tragedy. At the turn of the twenty-first century, famines are largely confined to Africa. This is not to say that the risk of famine has been eliminated from other parts of the world. Risk persists in countries undergoing badly managed economic transformation, often combined with social unrest, war, and other political crises. It also persists in isolated regions poorly integrated with global trade and aid, areas with limited public capacity to deal with emergencies and mass poverty, and in urban and rural settings where the collapse of public services leaves vulnerable groups without the means to cope under economic stress. However, while these various conditions can be found at different times in different places across the globe, today they are concentrated and most persistent in Sub-Saharan Africa (Table 1.1).

Is this a research issue? Can lessons learned elsewhere be applied to Africa in the twenty-first century? Can lessons from one African country be applied to others? This book argues that this is indeed the case. On the one hand, very important lessons are to be learned from South Asia and historical Europe (Drèze and Sen 1989). This book expands on the seminal analyses of Sen (1981) and Drèze and Sen (1991), who established cogent arguments for public action against hunger. Until the groundbreaking work of Sen (1981), economic research largely shunned the complex issue of famine. New empirical study may help expand the frontiers of our understanding and facilitate effective action for famine prevention in the future.

On the other hand, this book also seeks to delve deeper into the empirical relationships that exist within Africa. Learning from experiences within African countries may be at least as important as learning from outside the continent.

The latter hypothesis is based on three main premises. The first is that *famine is largely a function of institutional, organizational, and policy failure,* not just one of generalizable market- and climate-driven production failure. Strengthening institutional and organizational capabilities for policy and operational responses to crises is central for famine prevention, and a problem central to Africa's development crisis. Central, local, and community governments play key roles in famine causation as well as prevention. So do the characteristics and capacities of households affected by famine. Households— with their diverse internal organizations and external community linkages— must figure prominently in any such research precisely because institutional and organizational capabilities remain weak across Africa. The absence of effective systems of government can be both a cause and a consequence of famine. Thus, this book examines the constraints of the "weak state," as well as the limitations of market-dependent private actions for dealing with famine.

The second premise on which this book is built is that *famines in Africa must be explained in a long-term context.* They are seen here as a function of long-term developments associated with (1) increased location-specific concentrations of poverty, (2) often operating within a fragile, degrading resource base, interacting with (3) economic, (4) agricultural, and (5) social and demographic policies. These interactions make certain segments of society and regions highly vulnerable to even minor climatic shocks. Armed conflicts and other civil unrest (often related to institutional and organizational failures) may become partially endogenous to the determinants of vulnerability over time.

A third premise is that, just as the causes of famine are diverse, *there is immense diversity in policy responses to famine*—there is no one optimal

TABLE 1.1 Selected famines of the twentieth century

Country/Area	Year
India[a]	1899–1900
India (Darbhanga)[a,b]	1906–7
Russia[c]	1913–15
Russia[c]	1921–22
China[c]	1929
Russia/Ukraine[c]	1933–34
Russia (Leningrad)[c]	1941–43
India/Bengal[a,b]	1943
Russia/Ukraine[c]	1946–47
China[d]	1958–61
Nigeria (Biafra)	1968–69
Bangladesh	1971–72
Cambodia	1973
Sahel region (West Africa)	1969–74
Ethiopia	1972–74
Bangladesh	1974–75
Angola	1974–76
Zaire (Bas Fleure)	1977–78
Uganda	1980
Mozambique	1982–83
Sahel region	1982–85
Sudan	1984–85
Horn of Africa region	1983–85
Mozambique	1985–86
Sudan	1988
Somalia	1988
Ethiopia (Horn of Africa)	1989–90
Liberia	1992–93
Somalia	1992–93
Sudan	1993
Angola	1993–94
Liberia/Sierra Leone	1995–98
Zaire	1997
North Korea	1996–98
Sudan	1998

SOURCES: Lettered notes give sources for identification of famines up to the 1960s.

NOTE: The mortality effects of famines are not statistically well documented. In several of the listed cases, famine and war-related mortality are inseparable (for example, Biafra; Cambodia; Sudan, 1988). The list includes particularly large famines, such as China in 1958–61 (up to 30 million deaths) as well as smaller, more recent famines, such as in Liberia.

[a]Bhatia 1967.
[b]Loveday 1944.
[c]Dando 1980.
[d]Ashton et al. 1984.

solution. Strategies for famine prevention, centered on the key role of institutions and recognition of long-term forces, must differ in time and space. This is not to say that some generalizations should not be attempted. However, generalizations must build on an analysis of the diversity of famines in African settings. Many famine prevention and early-warning efforts in Africa are built on too few facts and unspecified conceptual frameworks. This book emphasizes that a fact-oriented analysis of famine (its impacts on production, markets, consumption, and nutrition) provides a better basis for policy action, but only if set in an appropriate conceptual framework. The protracted debate over famine concepts can be overcome by concentrating on empirical study that allows constructive feedback among theory, concept, and policymaking.

The above three premises lend a structure to this book. The following chapters represent a synthesis of findings, experiences, and insights from numerous African countries applied to current thinking on famine. It is both a summary of work in each country and a distillation of ideas that may lead to future operational and research work on famines. Thus it is not only a culmination, but a beginning as well. Chapter 2 describes the conceptual basis that underlines the analysis. This is followed in Chapter 3 by an assessment of policy failures and conflicts as famine symptoms and causes. The production side of famine causation is discussed in Chapter 4 through an analysis of food trends, shocks, and the role of drought. Population pressure and the demographics of famines are discussed in Chapter 5. How markets behave during famines and what role exists for market-oriented policies in famine prevention are discussed in Chapter 6. Chapter 7 deals with household and community coping mechanisms. It seeks to shed light on the potential of private and informal public actions to mitigate and prevent famines in rural areas. Chapter 8 reviews policy instruments and program experiences in a number of contexts and draws generalized conclusions.

The conclusions of the book are grounded in empirical material. Information was gathered at several levels: First, at the country level, where diversity in policy and history comes into play. A wide number of different country case studies is drawn upon in Chapter 3, which addresses policy failure issues. Second, from the climate and agro-ecology dimension—at the supranational level—Ethiopia's and Sudan's diverse agro-ecologies characterize many of the potentials and constraints faced by other African countries. They cannot of course represent every context in Africa and further research will need to broaden the scope of this work and compare the Horn examples with other parts of the continent. Third, policy- and market-level issues are addressed in Chapter 6 at the subnational level, again using the basis of Ethiopia and Sudan.

The degree that household and community data are representative for Africa as a whole is a question that cannot easily be answered. Local institutions are particularly diverse in Africa (Watts 1983; Iliffe 1987). While the empirical work in Botswana, Ethiopia, Niger, Rwanda, Sudan, and Zimbabwe covers a variety of community and household situations, we do not claim that the results presented are comprehensive or fully representative; case studies never are.

Finally, there is policy. Certainly, Ethiopia and Sudan, upon which so much is drawn, cannot in themselves provide us with a complete set of experiences for famine mitigation and prevention across Africa. Therefore, policies are examined from other countries as well, such as Botswana, Mozambique, Niger, Rwanda, and Zimbabwe. This leads to suggestions for a policy agenda (implicitly also a research agenda) for the eradication of famine in the twenty-first century.

This book is aimed at scholars and students of development policy and economics, and at policy advisers and planners in Sub-Saharan Africa. The authors certainly do not claim a definitive voice on these crucial life-and-death issues. We do not pretend to offer final answers. However, we do hope that this work will stimulate more research, debate, and, most important, *action* in this crucial, yet neglected, area of development policy and practice.

2 A Conceptual Basis for Research on Famine in Africa

Overview

Before discussing concepts associated with famine, some terms need to be clarified. A distinction should be made between famine, undernutrition, and hunger. *Hunger*—largely an advocacy rather than a scientific term—is defined here as the condition resulting from an individual's inability to eat sufficient food to lead a healthy and active life. It comprises a series of feelings, emotions, and behavioral changes, not easily measurable in themselves, that result from disruption in an individual's access to food. Naturally, hunger is a recurring feature of food insecurity of households and their members in developing countries (FAO 1996). *Undernutrition,* by contrast, is defined as the measurable nutrient deficiencies in a diet that can lead to illness (lack of energy, retardation, blindness) or even death. The symptoms themselves may not be recognized as indications of nutrient deficiencies since interactions between undernutrition, care behavior, and diseases are complex. *Famine* is a widespread and extreme hunger that results for individuals in a drastic loss of body weight and an increase in morbidity, and, at the community level (as an interaction of these two symptoms), in a rise in the death rate and massive social dysfunction and dislocation.

Because of these conceptual complexities, any attempt to establish a universal theory of famine has limited use. Unless one deals in the abstract, a theory of famines cannot be independent of time, space, or contextual interactions. This is so because of the strong roles played by historical and institutional factors and because famine disasters are location specific. The debate over famine theory has generally suffered from three problems: (1) untestable hypotheses of broad generality, (2) the synthetic generalization of anecdotes, and (3) a lack of empirical analysis of the actual socioeconomic processes that occur during famines.

To complicate matters further, the conditions that breed famine within Africa are changing. Africa's dynamic economic and political systems, conflicts and civil unrest, declining productivity, rapid urbanization, and recent climatic trends have combined to generate new famine risks. As a result, both single-cause explanations and general theories of famines are equally unsatisfactory.

The systematic study of famines is relatively recent, especially in Africa. It was only in the early 1980s, with the publication of *Poverty and Famines* (Sen 1981), that analysis of famine received a substantial theoretical foundation through an explicit integration of household and market relationships with the role of public actions in support of "entitlements." Market failures and distortions that have led to famine have been studied in depth in some Asian countries (Ravallion 1987a). The demographic dynamics of famines have become a topic of increased attention beyond simplified Malthusian concepts (Watkins and Menken 1985). Aspects of the political economy of famines and nutritional impacts have also recently become a research concern (Downs, Kerner, and Reyna 1993; Pinstrup-Andersen 1993a).

However, the debate over complex concepts (that remain only partially elaborated) continues. In such discussions it is often argued that ending wars will end famine; that food supply has little bearing on food consumption; that lowering population growth will increase food availability for all; and that optimal early warning of conducive conditions will prevent famine. These simplistic propositions will only be laid to rest once empirical analyses are framed by well-defined concepts, those that refine our understanding of the problem and can henceforth better influence actions "on the ground."

A Conceptual Basis for Empirical Research

Figure 2.1 portrays relationships between causes and symptoms of famine. Poverty, including the associated vulnerability to natural or man-made shocks, is a root cause of famine. Yet poverty may be seen as an endogenous outcome of a lack of resources and flawed policies. Endogenous and exogenous relationships can be conceptualized differently, beginning with broad interactions between policy failures, resource poverty and disaster, and the population transition process. Cause-and-effect relationships are then distinguished, with some of the more important indications of feedback mechanisms between the four layers of analysis as follows:

1. The top layer of the diagram represents economic strategy and policy interacting with social discrimination, conflicts, and wars; resource endowments and their relationship to climate or disaster events influencing poverty and instability of the (food) system; and population pressure. Little comprehensive research exists on the interactions between these three clusters.
2. The second layer relates to organizational capacities and governance, which are critical to the choice and effective implementation of policy

FIGURE 2.1 Determinants of and relationships in famines

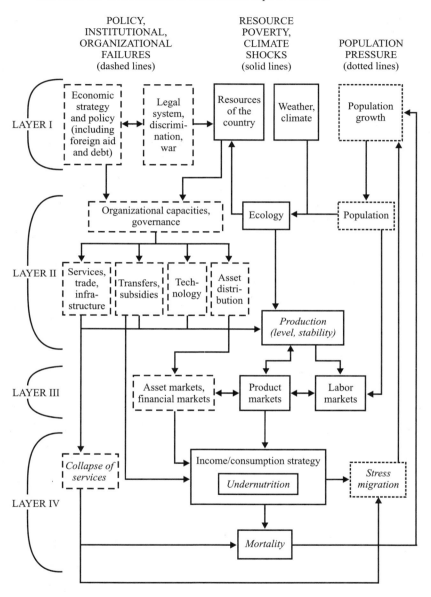

interventions, such as subsidies and distributional policies. Policy alternatives influence input/output relationships, such as production amounts and stability. The absorptive capacity of a country or region, in terms of emergency aid and its effective distribution, is determined in this sphere.

3. The third layer depicts policy interventions interacting with price formation and linkages among capital, labor, and output markets. The issue of market failures in famines arises at this layer.
4. The last layer relates to actual income and consumption failure (and resulting starvation and excess mortality) interacting with the collapse of services and distress migration. It is at this level of analysis that the failure of "entitlements" becomes evident.

Fruitful conceptual and analytical discussion of any one of the four layers in Figure 2.1 can be pursued if upstream and downstream linkages between layers are kept in perspective. However, there remains considerable controversy over the causes of famines. Some useful research has been pursued into one or more of the depicted linkages, but controversy often arises over *the* most critical relationships among related factors. Identifying a single cause of famine (such as drought or war) is ultimately of little help. Much of the controversy over allegedly comprehensive theories of famine results from a selective focus on individual layers of famine symptoms (as depicted in the above framework), which leads to misunderstandings between scholars (see, for example, exchanges between de Waal [1991] and Osmani [1991]). This is not surprising given that famine studies were only recently given a suggested theoretical foundation within the "entitlement concept" (which itself suffers from testability problems due to its generality). Discussion of the empirical value and relevance of concepts is part of a healthy, that is, critical theory-formation process. What follows is a brief discussion of key sections in the relationships portrayed in Figure 2.1, later revisited in the context of results from empirical studies at numerous sites across Africa (see Figure 3.1 for study sites chosen for this book).

Policy, Institutional, and Organizational Failures

Policy, institutional, and organizational failures—not only production and market failures—are arguably among the most important root causes of famines today. Legal insecurity, especially for the poor, and a lack of public preparedness to deal with shocks illustrate such failures. Famine risks posed by inefficient or irresponsible government and limitations on market-based private action suggest a continued need for improving the role of public action (Drèze and Sen 1989; Teklu, von Braun, and Zaki 1991; Webb and von Braun 1994). However, the call for public action—including state action—is complicated by governments that instrumentalize hunger as part of conflict acceleration, becoming part of the famine problem (Swift 1993). This then raises the issue of appropriate nongovernmental and possibly international public action.

Public-policy failures are also frequently associated with low agricultural productivity. Flawed policies, extensive environmental degradation, lack of rural and urban employment opportunities, limited access to education, and inadequate health and sanitation services lead to a high prevalence of poor nutrition within households. Resulting socioeconomic conditions impair the ability of households to "grow out" of poverty, thereby permitting production failures to develop into famines.

Policy failure of this kind is also revealed in inappropriate macro-economic policies and excessive state interference in economic activity. It can exacerbate inherent malnutrition, as is evident from the experiences of Ethiopia and Sudan. Exchange-rate regulations and export taxes historically have adversely affected rural economies in these countries, not only by undermining general rural growth trends but also by impacting directly on specific communities. One example of an inappropriate policy was Sudan's taxation of gum arabic—the product of an environmentally friendly export crop grown in the famine-prone provinces of Darfur and Kordofan—which eroded poor people's earnings potential in those areas (Teklu, von Braun, and Zaki 1991).

Policy failures are most dramatically highlighted where one finds a gross absence of legal remedies and the prevalence of domestic social/ethnic/political discrimination. To overcome these policy failures, more than short-term remedies are needed, including political changes. Physical and mental insecurity and discrimination may result in ethnic conflicts and protracted battles, such as in Angola, Ethiopia, Mozambique, Somalia, and southern Sudan. The impact of armed dispute is felt not only in the areas of actual conflict, but throughout an entire economy due to the drain on national resources. Production and employment opportunities are lost, making populations more vulnerable to food crises. The overexploitation of resources during war has a devastating long-term effect on national reconstruction by undermining the already limited growth potential of famine-prone areas.

Some conflicts are not independent of economic strategies employed by governments, such as the centrally planned economic policies used by the Government of Ethiopia in the 1980s. However, external factors may play a role, too, such as the postcolonial violent and racist systems transformations in southern Africa that had an impact on Mozambique. Effective national, regional, and international mechanisms for conflict prevention and resolution would go a long way toward famine prevention. These issues are discussed further in Chapter 3.

Organizational failures relate to the lack of initiative or authority in famine prevention and mitigation. For example, in the 1980s the Sudanese Relief and Rehabilitation Commission (RRC) was charged with the task but not provided the power: it had a limited capacity to coordinate line ministries or donor assistance. Another example of organizational failure is the vacuum of responsibility and numerous deficiencies in implementing international care for refugees and internally displaced peoples (IDPs). This contributed to nutrition-related diseases in refugee camps in several African countries (ACC/ SCN 1992).

Resource Poverty and Climate Shocks

Resource poverty and ecological stress are closely related in the conceptual framework depicted in Figure 2.1. That the two are so linked is demonstrated by empirical evidence reviewed in later sections. Drought-famine links remain highly important in Africa and are therefore relevant to the analysis of famine; access issues cannot be seen in total isolation from supply issues.

The agricultural environment of many African countries continues to be under major stress from droughts that occurred in the 1980s and 1990s. In some famine-prone countries, such as Ethiopia and Sudan, food consumption is closely related to domestic production, which in turn is closely linked to rainfall. This situation comes about because lack of domestic and international market integration (due to policy and infrastructure deficiencies) exacerbates already existing ecological distress.

Of course, a single year of drought rarely causes famine, but sequences of droughts may do so. Drought and other climatic shocks are powerful determinants of famine only if they occur in countries with limited resource bases (for example, those that have been undermined by war) and in those with a lack of social-policy preparedness. Some famine-prone regions do have inherent resource poverty problems, such as certain regions of Ethiopia and Sudan's Red Sea Hills. Long-term deterioration of the resource base contributes to the vulnerability of the local population in such regions.

Population and Famine

Most of Africa's famine-prone countries have high population growth rates and rapidly growing labor forces. There are strong links between policy failure and resource poverty and the nature and speed of population transition (Ruttan 1994). Furthermore, the negative feedbacks from migration by famine refugees, and from related population concentrations, are not only symptoms of current famine stress but also provide the foundation for future vulnerability (Zolberg, Suharke, and Aguayo 1989). Chapter 5 takes up these related issues in detail.

The conceptual discussion thus far has followed the three columns, focusing mainly on the two top rows (layers I and II in Figure 2.1). Linkages further downstream—at the market (layer III) and household and intrahousehold levels (layer IV)—of the framework are addressed next.

Market Functioning and Failure under Famine

In times of food shortages, how food, asset, and labor markets operate is critical in determining famine outcomes. The literature on market behavior during famines in Africa remains limited compared with related work on Asia (Sen 1981; Ravallion 1987a). An attempt to fill some of the gap is made in Chapter 6.

Food crises are characterized by the increased entry of the poor into markets for the direct and indirect exchange of food for assets and labor. Where markets are weak relative to total output, price fluctuations tend to be large. This is typically caused by high transaction costs (as the result of poor infrastructure and policy restrictions on interregional trade) and a weak capacity for public price or supply stabilization (due to limited domestic food reserves and a poor ability to import food). Such price movements typically have a relatively greater effect on the poor, and due attention to price developments in the context of famine theory is needed.

However, food prices alone cannot be the guiding yardstick for public intervention. State-controlled marketing and prohibitions on domestic trading often prevent market integration during times of famine, as is discussed in Chapter 6 concerning Ethiopia's experience. Lack of infrastructure—such as rural roads and other transportation facilities—make market-oriented and efficient public and private famine relief responses difficult, as has been the case in Ethiopia and Sudan.

Transaction costs (including market risk) and the asset base and purchasing power of the poor also require attention. Basic infrastructure deficiencies and government trade restrictions often impair interregional market exchange during famine years. A sudden collapse of purchasing power—in the context of production failure and a parallel decline in employment opportunities—may not necessarily force sharp price increases in an affected region, because of a simultaneous fall in effective supply and demand. The potential for relying on the market to mitigate repeated famines becomes increasingly limited, however, because the asset bases of many households become eroded.

Household Coping and Suffering

Famines also represent a failure of the response capabilities of households and individuals. Such failure relates to the deterioration of the quantity and value of assets under household command, and to social safety nets of families and communities. Any household-level analysis of famines must be context specific since resource endowments and agro-ecological and institutional settings vary so much.

Some of the household's resources (land and labor, in particular) go into crop production. In addition, part of the family labor generates nonfarm income to supplement crop income. Household income at any particular point in time is a combined product of these income sources. Exogenous changes, such as in climate, prices, or public policies (outcomes depicted in Figure 2.1), influence the amount as well as the sources of household income. Income generated from these sources is translated into consumption and asset accumulation. Food consumption is presumed to affect household nutritional status, which, in interaction with the sanitary and health environment, in turn influences the incidence of morbidity and mortality.

Various adjustments available to households include changes in production, labor, assets, transfers (individual, community, or public), and consumption. A large drop in crop production is likely to subject a poor household to severe stress because of strong production-income-consumption links. However, a production shortfall should not necessarily be translated into reduced food intake if other adjustments prevent large income and consumption declines.

Of course, the relative importance of these paths changes, depending on the source, persistence, and phase of the process that has triggered food distress, and will vary for households in different stages of demographic life cycles. Differences in endowments (skills and employment experience, resource access, asset accumulation, and access to steady outside-income sources or transfers) contribute to variation in response choices and coping success. Households with low income, particularly those that mainly rely on high-risk income and have few income sources and assets, are particularly vulnerable. The burden of coping thus falls on individuals within these households, unless community or public support reinforces their coping devices.

The literature on famine impact, and on the means adopted by households to minimize that impact, has become increasingly complementary and convergent. Reviews of existing research on household famine responses broadly conclude that, while conditions vary by locality, there are identifiable behavior patterns associated with the onset, progression, and climax of a crisis (Jodha 1975; Torry 1984; Campbell 1990; Bohle et al. 1991; Davies 1996). These responses are largely determined by the nature of the crisis—its speed, intensity, and duration—but also by the varying abilities of different households to cope. This variability in so-called coping capacity is widely believed to hold the key to an effective design of famine early-warning systems (EWSs) and appropriate interventions (Torry 1988).

Capacity for coping is making a series of adaptations until all choices are exhausted. This is, of course, not solely a function of income or asset base; it is also a function of human skills and resources. For instance, in Sudan, rural children whose parents had some formal education and especially those whose mothers had received some schooling, were significantly better off in terms of nutritional status than other children in the aftermath of the 1985 famine (Teklu, von Braun, and Zaki 1991). How successful households are in pursuing and attaining insurance against food security risks plays a large role in determining the outcome of subsequent crises.

The final stage in adapting and responding to stress, which may become inescapable if famine conditions persist in the absence of external aid, involves the crumbling of all normal systems of survival. At this point, the diet of most households is dominated by unusual "famine foods" (roots, leaves, rodents), and victims are obliged to sell their remaining assets, including homes, fields, and clothes. If still able to do so, many households break up and leave their residences in search of assistance from distant relatives or at a relief camp. This is not coping; it is despair (Davies 1996). It is important to point out that since households often break up at this stage, the empirical study of famine should not be restricted to the "household" as the aggregate unit of observation. The focus needs to be on individuals and on intrahousehold processes.

Conclusions Concerning the Conceptual Framework

The empirical analysis in the following chapters is structured along the lines of the conceptual framework shown in Figure 2.1. It should be noted that flowcharts of the kind presented may be helpful to get an overview and identify major pathways and structural relationships, but their limitations must be kept in mind also. They do not lend themselves to fully capture political economy issues; they neither show the relative importance of a specific factor, nor the particularly important dynamics of famine events (no time subscripts are shown); and the very collapse of institutions and organizational structures, such as the household, can only be hinted at. The ensuing analysis and policy and program review also emphasizes those issues. In the chapters that follow, an effort is made to remain (self-) critical of the limitations of any general framework. There are limitations to how much one can compress the realities of complex phenomena within a "comprehensive" framework or general theory. Such a simplification in the pursuit of clarification is not sought here.

3 Policy Failure, Conflict, and Famine

Most of Africa's recent famines have occurred within the context of armed conflicts (Figures 3.1 and 3.2). These may be wars between countries or civil conflicts within countries. The latter have often been associated with challenges to political regimes that show a disregard for civil and human rights and participatory governance. In such circumstances, religious, ethnic, or political groups that feel oppressed or the target of discrimination often form the basis of a civil uprising.

Some general tendencies can be discerned concerning the incidence of violent conflicts in the last several decades: More than 90 percent of all violent conflicts between 1945 and 1992 took place in developing countries, with Africa accounting for one-quarter of all wars (48 wars: North Africa, 9; West Africa, 8; central Africa, 10; East Africa, 13; South Africa, 8). The types and frequency of wars have changed over time in Africa; in the first half of 1960, wars of independence and secession dominated (first in North and East Africa), followed in the second half of the 1970s mainly by antiregime wars. Another increase took place in the beginning of the 1990s. With the exception of North Africa, internal conflicts dominated in all regions of the continent, although in some of these cases external parties were directly or indirectly involved, for example in Angola and Mozambique (Gantzel and Schwinghammer 1995).

In regions where food consumption is barely enough to subsist even under normal conditions, the use of food as a weapon is a dangerous option for repressive or aggressive governments. Events in Ethiopia, Mozambique, Somalia, and Sudan in the 1980s and 1990s are recent cases in point. So, too, is the Biafran famine associated with Nigeria's civil war in the 1960s. Even at the end of the twentieth century, there are standard calls in many international fora for more formal global opposition to the use of food as a weapon.[1]

---

1. Such as the "Rome Declaration" of the World Food Summit 1996 and the "Madrid Declaration" of December 1995.

FIGURE 3.1 Famine-affected countries in Africa, 1960s–1990s, and location of research sites for this book

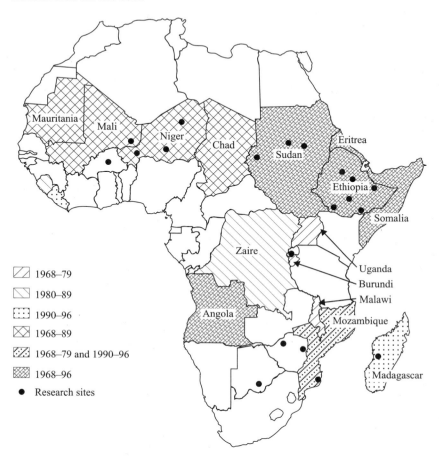

SOURCE: Authors' design.

Causality Issues

The direct consequences of conflict on production and distribution systems, as well as on human capabilities, are well known. However, to what extent do political systems, using diverted resources for wars and military machinery, influence famine? This question may be addressed first by taking account of the evolution of political systems in Africa and second by reviewing the use of resources for military expenditure. Both issues turn out to be closely related to the prevalence of famine in many countries.

FIGURE 3.2 Political systems of Sub-Saharan Africa, 1997

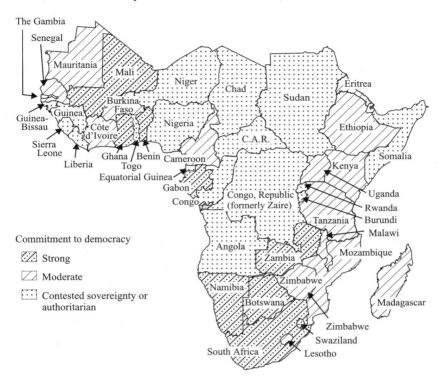

SOURCE: 1997 update by the author based on *Africa Demos* 1992.

NOTES: CAR = Central African Republic

In our conceptual framework, however, the consequences of the detrimental interaction between conflict and economic policy—represented by reduced resources and organizational capacity for public services—are important. Discussion of the theory of war and civil conflict goes beyond the scope of this study. Thompson (1992) provides a useful categorization of conflicts in post– Cold War developing countries. He divides developing-country conflicts into six categories.[2] Although such categorization offers some suggestions regard-

---

2. (1) Colony-colonizer; (2) postcolonial "sort out," including the related refugee flows of expelled people (Eritrea and southern Sudan are cases in point); (3) intrastate ethnic conflict (particularly relevant in several African conflicts, such as Rwanda); (4) interstate ethnic conflict (witnessed in the Horn of Africa between Ethiopia and Somalia); (5) ideological and religious conflicts, which have played important roles in Ethiopia and Sudan; and (6) superpower projection (again using examples from Angola, Ethiopia, and Somalia).

ing the causes of conflicts, the underlying patterns may be broadly classified into four groups:

1. Inequalities in the processes of development and modernization (for example, through marginalization of social groups, disregard of less dynamic regions, or fragmentation of traditional relations/kinships).
2. Political and economic transitions, with resulting tensions between winners and losers.
3. Growing demand on the environment and natural resources (conflicts of allocation and use).
4. Taking advantage of ethnic, cultural, and religious differences (sometimes amplified by the colonial heritage of artificial borders; economic, social, and political transformations during the development process; forced integration of minorities; or separatist movements of regionally concentrated ethnic groups) (OECD/DAC 1996).

Although conflicts fostered by political ideology may be on the decline, there is a danger that nationalist-, ethnic-, and religiously inspired wars are expanding (Hansch 1995). And a number of political conflicts in developing countries persisted during much of the 1990s despite the end of the Cold War. Discrimination and conflict are typically found in areas where the role of the military is paramount and civil rights have been curtailed.

Although it is argued that such sociopolitical processes are determinants of famine, there also exist some feedbacks from famine to resultant political crises. That is, some famines have brought down governments and contributed to conflict as well as major changes in political systems. There were such forward-and-backward linkages between famine and armed confrontation in some of the most notorious cases in Africa, such as Angola, Ethiopia, Liberia, Mozambique, Somalia, and Sudan. For example, the transition from authoritarian monarchy to communist regime in Ethiopia (1974/75) was largely fueled by the inept handling of famine in the north; the sucessor Mengistu regime's pursuance of extravagent war aims in spite of the 1984/85 famine in turn contributed to its own downfall in 1990/91.

Yet singling out conflict as an isolated cause of famine is misleading. Armed disputes do not necessarily lead to famine. However, its likelihood increases if warring parties fight in poor countries. As Sen (1991) points out, much depends on whether conflict leads to increased domestic divisiveness, reduced solidarity, and reduced efforts to protect the vulnerable. Civil (intrastate) wars and unrest are caused by and often exacerbate divisiveness, whereas wars between countries may actually increase domestic solidarity, evidenced by greater efforts for famine prevention and maintenance of basic services in some countries. The Somali invasion of Ethiopia in 1977 may qualifiy as one example. Most of Africa's recent conflicts have been of the first kind (within countries and typically increasing social divisiveness).

The relationship between famines and wars in Africa suggests that there could be a high payoff for famine prevention through greater emphasis on conflict resolution (Bardham 1997; UNSG 1995; WFP 1996a). This includes addressing protracted, and rapidly growing, problems of refugees and IDPs.

Governance and Famine

Africa's political landscape has been in constant flux during the final decades of the twentieth century. Fostered by evolving relationships among superpowers and by political change in South Africa, fundamental shifts occurred in the domestic power structures of many countries, leading to a diverse array of democratic and authoritarian systems (see Figure 3.2).

It should be noted that none of the countries marked as having a strong commitment to democracy in Figure 3.2 was prone to famine in the past two decades: Benin, Botswana, Ghana, South Africa, and Zambia. What is more, few of the countries characterized as moderately democratic were famine prone, with the exception of Angola, Eritrea, and Ethiopia, countries where violent clashes continue to erupt.

By contrast, most countries with repeated famine events in the past three decades can be categorized as "authoritarian" (for example, Niger and Sudan), with "ambiguous commitment to democracy" (the Republic of Congo [formerly Zaire] or Rwanda), or under "contested sovereignty" (Liberia, Sierra Leone, and Somalia).

What then is the nature of political transition (and related domestic struggles) in Africa, and has famine risk really increased during that transformation? Economic vulnerability certainly increases for households caught up in armed struggle. It affects others through an erosion of governments' ability to protect those vulnerable. In the early stages of political transformation, analysts focus on political issues. The problems of food policy and social-service provision tend to receive limited attention, at least until the political outcome is less ambiguous. This was the case in Ethiopia after the overthrow of the Mengistu regime in 1991/92.

However, if system transformation leads toward increased democracy (with the related outcomes of freedom of information and the investigative press), attention quickly turns to how the new government will ensure physical and food security for its constituents. Democratic South Africa continues to search for new operations to alleviate poverty and malnutrition in its townships. Democratic systems that give representative voting rights to the very poor clearly not only shift the balance of power but also raise the political costs of neglect. This lesson has been well learned by most countries in southern Africa. Botswana and Zimbabwe, with relatively strong participation in local government, are countries in which government action has indeed responded to public demands. The promotion of democratic government should therefore have a high priority, not only to ensure equity in representation, but also with a view to famine prevention. This is one of the lessons learned from Asia that most easily transfers to Africa (Sen 1991).

The Militarization of Famine

Military expenditure and social action compete for resources. In the early postcolonial era, Africa's militarization was largely a consequence of super-power politics on the one hand and South Africa's destabilization efforts on the other. Both influences have all but disappeared. And yet in the 1980s and 1990s, the flow of arms into Africa has continued. Military buildup in Africa occurred rapidly during the early 1980s. Armed forces increased from 1.3 million in 1978 to 1.7 million in 1988 (U.S. Arms Control and Disarmament Agency 1989).[3] In all of Sub-Saharan Africa, there are estimated to be about as many soldiers as teachers, and there are 76 soldiers per physician (UNDP 1992, p. 167). Military expenditures in the early 1990s still exceeded total combined expenditures for education and health in Africa, largely because of ongoing conflicts in Ethiopia, Somalia, and Sudan (Table 3.1).[4] Whereas Ethiopia and Somalia calmed down, fighting raged on in Burundi, Liberia, Sierra Leone, and Sudan during 1996.

What is more, these figures underestimate actual resources used for aggression and defense. The 1980s witnessed a dramatic militarization of large parts of rural Africa, unaccounted for by official government military expenditures. Weapons moved into villages far from actual war zones, paid for with meager resources by communities in need of self-defense against looters, cattle thieves, and other aggressors. For example, large ruminant herds in Somalia, western Sudan, and northern Uganda were sharply reduced in recent years, first by drought and famine, second by looting, and third by sales forced by the need to buy guns for self-defense. This vicious cycle hampers efforts to rebuild herds (see Chapter 7). And whereas "official" military conflicts can be brought to an end through negotiation, it is harder to encourage scattered gangs to support peace and the rule of law.

Despite conflicting official data on military expenditure, an interestingly diverse picture emerges: first, west African countries spend less on the military

---

3. It should be stressed that military expenditures by low-income countries were only part of the problem. Industrialized countries still spent a larger share of their income on military expenditures (4.9 percent) than Sub-Saharan Africa (3.2 percent)—for instance, the amount of Europe's military expenditure in 1988 was a mind-boggling US$530 billion. The point is, global, not just regional, resources are wasted by military expenditures.

4. In the second half of the 1980s, there was a decrease in military buildup; military expenditure as a percent of total government expenditure declined during the period 1984 to 1988. In the year of the major African drought (1984/85), this expenditure dropped from 16.6 to 14.4 percent and thereafter continued to decline to 13.6 percent in 1988 (U.S. Arms Control and Disarmament Agency 1989, p. 32). Also, in real constant dollar terms, military expenditures in Africa as a whole dropped from US$17 billion in 1984 to US$14.3 billion in 1988.

TABLE 3.1 Indicators of military expenditures for selected African countries and famine events

Countries	Famines in 1980s, 1990s	Government Military Expenditure[a]		Arms Imports as Percent of 1989 National Imports	Change in Military Expenditure, 1982–90, in Constant US$[b]
		as Percent of GDP, 1989	as Percent of Education and Health, 1989		
Angola	x	21.5	n.a.	n.a.	+
Cameroon		2.1	51	1.3	=
Côte d'Ivoire		1.2	14	2.1	=
Ethiopia	x	13.6	239	n.a.	+
Ghana		0.6	13	3.9	=
Kenya		2.6	31	8.8	=
Madagascar	x	1.3	34	n.a.	−
Malawi	x	1.6	31	4.6	−
Mali		3.3	83	5.2	+
Mozambique	x	10.4	n.a.	2.8	+
Niger	x	0.8	21	1.4	−
Nigeria		1.1	65	12.0	−
Somalia	x	3.0	500	32.3	+
Sudan	x	n.a.	n.a.	13.6	=
Tanzania		5.2	108	n.a.	+
Togo		3.2	46	15.7	+
Zaire	x	1.2	67	1.4	+
Zambia		3.2	43	n.a.	−
Zimbabwe		7.9	65	26.1	=
Sub-Saharan Africa		3.2	108	4.7	n.a.
All least-developed countries		4.1	146	7.8	n.a.

SOURCES: UNDP 1992, p. 167; U.S. Arms Control and Disarmament Agency 1989.

NOTES: GDP = gross domestic product; n.a. = not available.

[a]Nongovernment expenditures for weaponry, which probably are an important use of national resources in some war-torn countries, are not included.

[b]+ indicates an increase of 50 percent or more; − indicates a decline of 50 percent or more; = indicates a change of less than 50 percent in either direction.

than do most east and south African countries. Most west African countries in the early 1990s were spending between 1 and 3 percent of gross domestic product (GDP) on the military sector. Many states in East Africa, however, far exceeded that amount, and not only in the war-prone countries of Angola, Ethiopia, and Mozambique. High amounts were also spent in Tanzania and Zimbabwe, partly related to those countries' simmering conflict with the apartheid regime of South Africa (see Table 3.1).

The regional impact of war in southern Africa, in terms of physical destruction and lost output, has been estimated to be over US$60 billion from 1980 to 1988 (UN Inter-Agency Task Force 1989). Countries that increased their expenditure by more than 50 percent between 1982 and 1990 were Angola, Ethiopia, Mali, Mozambique, Sudan, Togo, and Zaire. It is striking, yet not surprising, that five of these seven are among the most famine-prone countries (see Table 3.1 and Figure 3.1). There are also indications that long-term military engagements tend to perpetuate themselves. Even a single incidence of violence in a disputed border area can quickly cause fighting to resume, as in Eritrea and Ethiopia in 1998.

Arms imports represent a heavy drain on foreign exchange reserves and compete with development-enhancing imports. In more recent years, foreign exchange crises have led to a substantial decline in arms imports. For example, between 1982 and 1988, total arms imports were steady at around US$2 billion (in constant 1990 prices). However, a decline occurred between 1989 and 1991. Some countries, such as Ethiopia and Sierra Leone, relied on valuable gold, diamond, or other reserves to finance arms purchases. Most merely drew on already limited foreign exchange reserves derived from agricultural and other exports.

The militarization of famine-prone countries also has an international dimension. In several notorious cases in the Horn of Africa, the root cause of militarization can be traced to the politics of the Cold War. When government power is based on external support (such as Siad Barré's in Somalia), the loss of such support can lead to collapse of the regime with attendant negative consequences (Pettengill 1993).

Any humanitarian response to the plight caused by a regime's collapse can become a long-term endeavor—witness Afghanistan, Angola, and Cambodia. Even if international military forces become involved, the goals of saving life and reestablishing a semblance of normality are not straightforward. Confronted with legitimacy, credibility, and logistics problems, joint humanitarian/ military operations can be a nightmare, as demonstrated in Somalia in 1992–94, Rwanda in 1994/95, and the former Yugoslavia in 1994–97.

There are also large international costs to such responses, in terms both of resources spent on military action (rather than development) and the erosion of public support for international development assistance. It is notoriously difficult for policymakers to explain to taxpayers in donor countries how aid resources can be well spent to rehabilitate a country destroyed by civil conflict. However, a moral responsibility can be claimed—for countries that extended the Cold War into Africa and gained immensely from arms sales—to facilitate a transition to stability in the countries currently wracked by political and economic instability. A broader responsibility rests with the international community as a whole to support a strong and legitimate international arrangement for preventing and/or resolving local conflicts that result in larger humanitarian crises.

Microlevel Perspectives on Conflict and Famine

Conflicts have many direct and indirect effects on food security, many of which occur far from the fighting. Such effects include a long list of obvious and not so obvious implications:

- Requisitioning food from farmers, traders, or food aid donors, such as in Angola, Liberia, and southern Sudan in the 1990s (de Waal 1993b)
- Disruption of production, loss of local genetic resource stocks, and erosion of national resources (Green 1987; Stewart 1993)
- Looting for profit, including cattle and other assets and equipment, such as in Somalia before the famine in 1992 and repeatedly in southern Sudan (Gonda and Mogga 1988)
- War-related destruction of infrastructure (houses, roads, bridges) and the environment (forests, water sources), with lasting effects (Cliffe 1989)
- Forced conscription of young men into the army thereby disrupting the productive capacities of rural households, as in Ethiopia in 1990/91 (Webb, von Braun, and Yohannes 1992)
- Spread of diseases such as AIDS by armies, as in the case of the Tanzanian occupation of southern Uganda in 1979, and in Ethiopia where its incidence among recruited soldiers increased from 0.07 percent in 1985 to 2.6 percent in 1991 (Kloos 1991). (An important indirect effect is the decline of medical services and immunization coverage during war, as was seen in Ethiopia in 1991 [Kloos 1991].)

A particularly protracted issue is the use of land mines in Angola, Mozambique, and Somalia. Direct effects of their use are death and disability; indirect effects include the loss of cropping, herding, and trade long after the actual war. Moreover in Angola, for example, food relief operations were severely hampered by mined roads, making necessary the use of more costly airlifts. Antipersonnel mines are said to be responsible for some 2,000 deaths or maimings per month worldwide (Roberts and Williams 1995, pp. 99–100; ICRC 1996). More than 13 countries in Africa are heavily mined, with Mozambique accounting for 1 to 2 million antipersonnel mines and Angola 9–15 million (Roberts and Williams 1995). However, with respect to food security it is less the absolute number of land mines than their location that determines their negative impact on reduced agricultural production. Integrating loss of development potential in the cost calculation of land mines (through reduced production and trade opportunities or unrealizable refugee resettlement) largely increases the agricultural development costs of countries such as Mozambique (Human Rights Watch Arms Project/Human Rights Watch Africa 1994; Feldbrügge and von Braun 1997). This means an additional burden to the people most directly affected, as well as for the countries on the way to rehabilitation after famine.

A microlevel view of the direct and indirect costs of war in famine-prone Ethiopia gives an additional perspective. Although difficult to calculate and always open to dispute, estimates of war damage in Ethiopia are substantial. It has been estimated that the conflict within Eritrea (prior to its independence) cost between 65,000 and 95,000 tons of lost food production per year (Bondestam, Cliffe, and White 1988). Cliffe (1989) calculates that between 1986 and 1989, 23,000 hectares of land in Eritrea were rendered uncultivable and roughly 44,000 animals were lost to their owners. Outside of Eritrea, Gondar, and Tigray (and parts of Gojjam and Wollo), the structural impact of conflict has been considerably less.

Nevertheless, Ethiopia's conflicts have generally affected the country as a whole. The drain on its economic resources has been enormous, in 1988 reported as over US$700 million per year, representing 50–70 percent of total government revenue (Buchanan 1990; *Horn of Africa Report* 1990; Lancaster 1990). As for the drain on human resources, nationwide conscription drives dating from 1976 brought government forces up to almost half a million men by the end of the 1980s. Between 1976 and 1982, such drives were undertaken on an irregular basis, but the decision in 1981 to formalize national military service for the "entire working people" resulted in annual and biannual conscription campaigns across the country—probably deeply affecting labor markets and education systems (de Waal 1991).

A lesser, but still important, effect of the fighting in noncombatant zones is the question of its financing, including levying of special taxes on smallholders to support the war effort. In addition to an annual agricultural tax of 20 birr (2 birr equaled approximately US$1 at that time), a peasant association membership fee of 5–10 birr, and other association and social-service fees (often exceeding a total of 15 birr), beginning in 1988 a "voluntary" contribution of 15 birr was exacted to support the war effort.

In a number of African countries famine has been an instrument as well as a consequence of conflict (Macrae and Zwi 1992, 1994; de Waal 1993b). This has been the case in southern Sudan, Ethiopia, and—as widely recognized—in Somalia. In Somalia, armed opposition to the Siad Barré regime intensified from 1988 onward, and cattle, trade, and commercial farming became increasingly militarized. Powerful businessmen and politicians were able to acquire weaponry for themselves and their clansmen. Some marginal ethnic groups (such as the Bantu, Digil, and Rahanweyn) were unable to acquire armaments to match these clans. In the 1992 Somali famine, the victims were largely the Rahanweyn and, to a lesser extent, the Digil and Bantu (de Waal 1993b). Famine in Sudan also has to be understood within the context of long-term political oppression and slave raiding decades ago, and more recent religious divisiveness due to enforcement of the Muslim *sharia* law on non-Muslims has contributed to the spread of famine (Daly and Sikainga 1993).

Many African countries now face the task of dismantling large armies. The demobilization itself is often a risky undertaking. However, if employment and some political representation are offered, the task does not necessarily increase local insecurity, as demonstrated in Uganda (Collier 1993) and more recently in Mozambique. In sum, there is a strong relationship between famine, large military expenditure, and conflicts within and between countries. This brings us closer to the real political and economic causes of conflict and famine today.

Gross Economic Mismanagement and Famine

Policy failure reveals itself in the promotion of faulty economic concepts, resource programming in the absence of coherent strategy, and gross economic mismanagement. Some early efforts of "structural adjustment" policies may fall in the first of these categories, but this extensively researched topic is not elaborated on here since there are few examples of famines in African states *post*-macroeconomic reform (Helleiner 1992; Stewart, Loll, and Wangwe 1992; World Bank 1994). Economic policy in Zimbabwe nearly fell into this category during its 1991–93 drought, but timely and massive external intervention prevented a famine—and protected the still embryonic economic reform program (Webb 1995b). Policies in Sudan can be considered an example of the second category of failure—absence of coherent strategy—whereas those in Ethiopia are examples of the third—gross economic mismanagement. The latter two cases of economic policy failure deserve some explanation.

The Case of Sudan

In addition to the war in the south, economic deterioration in Sudan turned into famine in the 1980s and again in the 1990s as a result of a long series of mismatched programs. Although most of these had some useful elements, inconsistency and ill-designed sequencing led to misinvestment (Shepherd 1988). The process is briefly described here, as it includes features typically found in other countries of the region as well.

Following independence in 1956, Sudan continued the colonial policy of promoting production of export crops in the high-potential riverine lands of central Sudan. Irrigated agriculture continued to be organized along the structure set up along the Gezira River in 1925, where the sole priority was cotton production. This approach continued with the nation's first 10-Year Economic and Social Development Plan of 1961/62 (D'Silva 1985; Wohlmuth 1987). Concurrent with the expansion of irrigated agriculture, there was spontaneous growth in the use of farming technology in the dry eastern and central regions. Large-scale, privately financed mechanized farming was considered an important and quick means of promoting agricultural production in a country where land was assumed to be abundant (Elhassan 1988). The subsequent five-year plan maintained an emphasis on irrigated and mechanized agriculture to accelerate cash- and food-crop production in high-potential areas.

The pattern continued with good prospects of capital inflows from Arab countries prospering from the oil boom of the mid-1970s, and the government embarked on a drive to promote agricultural production and agro-industrial products—the "breadbasket strategy." Nearly two-thirds of the technological upgrade was foreign financed, largely from Arab funds. This strategy received further support in the six-year plan initiated in 1977/78. At this time the desire to attain self-sufficiency in selected food crops (particularly wheat and sorghum) was formalized in the government's Food Investment Strategy of 1977. An important departure of that six-year plan, compared with its predecessors, was verbal recognition of the importance of smallholder agriculture and the call for a parallel strategy that would continue development of irrigated and mechanized agriculture as well as stimulate traditional crop and livestock production. In practice, however, the process resulted in the establishment of modern ranches and large cooperatives (Adams and Howell 1979). The six-year plan was abandoned a year after its inception as the country's already existing economic crisis deepened and its growth targets became unattainable.

The government, hampered by low foreign exchange savings, borrowed from the Central Bank to finance its mounting deficits. Central Bank financing of the public deficit reached 97 percent in 1977/78. In the late 1970s, the mounting disequilibria in internal and external balances of trade and capital obliged the government to enter into a stabilization and adjustment program designed by the International Monetary Fund (IMF)/International Bank for Reconstruction and Development (IBRD). This program, which started primarily as a stabilization scheme in 1978, eventually became the Economic Recovery Program of 1980. The program continued for seven years, until 1985, when it was suspended by a new military government. It was replaced by the annual development plan for 1985. Abandonment of the recovery program resulted from the failure to improve the country's economic situation, a problem exacerbated by drought in 1984. Neglecting to implement comprehensive reforms—including moving to a market-oriented exchange rate—was an underlying cause of increased famine vulnerability in Sudan during the late 1980s (Atabani 1991).

The civilian government that came to power in 1986 introduced a new four-year plan that, like previous economic development efforts, had the objective of achieving sustained economic growth and effectively boosting real per capita GDP. The agriculture sector's role was given prime importance— increased agricultural production would spearhead the growth process. The new program also incorporated the goals of income and wealth redistribution and access to food for rural and urban populations. In contrast to previous economic development plans, the 1986 program, drawn in the aftermath of the country's bitter experience of the 1984/85 famine, recognized the need not only for adequate food production but also for an efficient food-distribution system (Maxwell 1991). The policy, however, fell apart, as Sudan increasingly shifted toward an ideology of self-sufficiency ("we eat what we grow").

In sum, successive Sudanese governments relied on partial solutions, macroeconomic programs, and economy-wide controls. The food and agricultural policies pursued by Sudan concentrated on the irrigated agricultural subsector; promoted large-scale mechanized farming, at the cost of common land of pastoralists; and neglected promoting technical progress in smallholder agriculture. This occurred against the background of continued conflict and war. The country has experienced protracted civil war from 1955 onward, despite a break of 10 years of peace from 1972 to 1983. As a result of warfare, millions of rural people were displaced and have gone from being agricultural producers to net receivers of food assistance.

The Case of Ethiopia

The nature of economic policy failure in Ethiopia was very different from that in Sudan. Whereas the latter displayed mismanagement through a series of rapid modifications of inconsistent short-term programs, Ethiopia did so through the grand, but faulty, design of a Marxist planned economy. The only similarities are that both countries adopted policies that were detrimental to food security and laid the foundations for famine by weakening the economy and fostering conflict.

During Ethiopia's attempt to redistribute income and stimulate agricultural output, private ownership of land was abolished in 1975. This move changed the face of farming. Although tenure arrangements, cropping patterns, and farm technology varied across the country, agriculture before 1975 was generally dominated by the needs of a landed gentry, the church establishment, and an overseeing aristocracy. The reform measures transformed this structure and laid the foundations of a three-tier system.

The largest component of this system was the smallholder sector. Individual households, which were responsible for at least 90 percent of national production, were granted access rights to a maximum of 10 hectares for private production (Brüne 1990). In practice, average holdings were between 1 and 2 hectares per household. Over 5 million households were organized into some 20,000 peasant associations. These associations controlled the allocation and use of land, each association being responsible for up to 800 hectares. Almost 40 percent of the peasant associations had been "villagized" (physically aggregated) by the end of the 1980s (IFAD 1989).

Reform did go some way toward equalizing land access and providing security for the landless. Yet this was just the first step in the new political agenda. Other elements were needed to support the evolution of the proposed collectivist agriculture. To create the second tier of the new rural system, peasant associations were "encouraged" to work toward the formation of cooperatives. The first step in this direction was the organization of service cooperatives. These interim organizations were designed to sell farm inputs, provide storage and processing facilities, offer low-interest loans, and facilitate the sale of local produce (including basic rations of certain foodstuffs) (Cohen and Isaksson 1987a). A total of 3,600 cooperatives were serving 4.4 million households by the end of 1988 (IFAD 1989).

The next stage in cooperativization was the formation of producer cooperatives. These pooled land, labor, and other resources in an attempt to capture economies of scale. One day of labor in communal fields was registered as one "point." The communal harvest was then divided according to the number of points held per household. In order to attract members, the cooperatives offered lower taxes, interest-free loans, and priority access to inputs and consumer goods. By 1988, almost 4,000 producer cooperatives had been founded, comprising 302,600 households (Walters 1989). However, in 1988/89, producer cooperatives were responsible for only 5.5 percent of national cereal production (Gutu, Lambert, and Maxwell 1990).

The smallest component of the farming system was composed of state farms. Of an estimated 750,000 hectares of commercial farmland under cultivation before 1974, 67,000 were converted to state farms that, beginning in 1979, were operated under the jurisdiction of a new Ministry of State Farms (Cohen and Isaksson 1987b). The remaining commercial farmland was reapportioned and used either for settling the landless or for assimilation into adjoining peasant associations. By 1989, state farms occupied a total area of 220,000 hectares (Walters 1989; Brüne 1990). However, despite large investments and operating costs, these grossly inefficient farms were responsible for only 4.2 percent of main-season cereal production in 1988/89 (Winer 1989; Wörz 1989; Rahmato 1990).

Another trend of the 1980s was a concentration of investment in Green Revolution-type inputs for selected farmers in high-growth-potential regions and state farms. The Mengistu government rejected pre-1974 strategies that focused resources on capital-intensive mechanized farming (Aredo 1990; Girgre 1991). As a result, the 10-Year Perspective Plan (1984–94) not only raised proposed agricultural expenditure to 30 percent, but allocated 37 percent of this to the smallholder sector (IFAD 1989). Although this was an improvement for the smallholder faction, state farms still received the major share of agricultural spending until 1990.

There is a broad consensus that, although the structures of rural society and production that existed before 1974 required fundamental change, the policies pursued between 1975 and 1990 did not succeed in raising either national or household production on a large scale (Wolde-Meskel 1990; Belete, Dillon, and Anderson 1991; Magrath 1991). A major part of the problem (aside from constricting centralized control of resources) was a lack of producer incentives. There were limited moves toward gradual liberation of the economy in the late 1980s, but it was the 1991 change in government and the end of the conflict in Eritrea shortly thereafter that removed many previous obstacles (such as the fear of conscription, military disruption, and production quotas) (Belshaw 1990). Nevertheless, the poor in Ethiopia remained (and still remain) highly vulnerable to famine, owing to severe resource constraints for public investment and for the provisioning of basic social safety nets. The economic distortions entrenched by almost 20 years of overcentralized government will take time to be rectified. Large changes in access to food supply do not, under such conditions, happen overnight, although progress in agricultural output was solid during the mid-1990s as a result of progressive economic reforms (ADE 1996).

Conclusions Concerning Policy Failure, Conflict, and Famine

Famines, economic disasters, and political upheavals feed on each other in mutually reinforcing ways. The economic, political, and military preconditions of famines, and the systems established in their aftermath, represent a vicious circle for low-income, food-deficit countries. New conflict resolution mechanisms are called for to break these cycles. The United Nations and (possibly) regional organizations both have a role to play in ensuring conflict prevention, or at least early resolution.

Violent conflicts undermine agricultural potential and general economic development. War economies are not conducive to either short-term stability or long-term investment. Already deficient infrastructures are destroyed, thereby undermining market integration and local access to food. In agriculture this has the effect of entrenching low-productivity farming, rather than encouraging market-oriented production patterns. Moreover, deteriorating infrastructures affect the nature of conflict in African countries. Famine has indeed been an instrument in some armed struggles. With limited infrastructure, military regimes may allocate already limited resources to arm local rival groups, thereby fostering ethnic conflict and banditry. Both have an impact on local economic activity when fields and food stocks are burned and livestock are seized. Such activities, largely targeted at civilians, are not reprimanded with sufficient vigor either by regional or international organizations.

The triangular relationship—famines, economic disaster, and political turmoil—must be kept in mind when famine prevention and mitigation strategies are designed. Isolated technical or short-term measures can only have a limited, nonsustainable impact in the absence of peace. Only when the failure of famine prevention policies increases the insecurity of a political regime will famine preclusion be expected to move to the top of the political agenda. Participatory government makes it harder for politicians to ignore concerns about famine; governments can and should be held accountable. The issue of national sovereignty has to be reviewed when that principle protects regimes more than people. Somalia in 1992, Rwanda and Burundi during 1994–97, and Zaire in 1997 have all been tests of international resolve to elevate human rights over government rights.

There remains, however, considerable scope for effective international action, even in the presence of violent conflicts in famine-prone countries. The foundations to forestall famine during nonwar conditions must be laid early on; famine prevention policies may sometimes also serve to prevent war. Famine mitigation should be based on a recognition of the boundaries of human suffering, rather than on those defined by politics and geography.

4 Production Failure and Climate Shocks

African countries facing acute short-term degradation in food security also tend to show a long-term decline in their per capita food production. Of course production does not necessarily mean availability, but the two are closely connected in Africa. In 1995/96 on average, famine-prone African countries displayed a per capita food production index of 86, versus 93 in other Sub-Saharan countries (1980 = 100; Table 4.1). This difference in food production trends between the two country groups is small compared with the variance within each of the groups and within countries over time. Table 4.1 shows 11 countries in the group without a noted famine that reveal a lower growth performance in food production per capita than the average of the countries affected by famine (for example, Botswana, Gabon, Lesotho, and Tanzania). The general food production growth of individual countries seems to say little about famine risks. However, the unsatisfactory performance of agricultural growth in the region as a whole remains a central problem for economic development.

The declining long-term production trends increasingly expose poor countries and households to external shocks. Such shocks may take the form of production failure or deteriorating import capacity due to adverse terms of trade. These acute adverse events and the need for policies to address them must not, therefore, divert attention from the fact that they are generally symptoms of other underlying negative trends. The relationships between trends and short-term shocks (with special emphasis on climatic shocks) are discussed in this chapter primarily in relation to Ethiopia, Sudan, and Zimbabwe.

Since the 1970s there have been no drought-related famines in West Africa's Sahel region. And the southern African drought of the early 1990s, despite its largely negative effects on agricultural production, did not translate into famine. (It is argued in Chapter 8 that there are many reasons for this, not the least of which was a public commitment to prevent a drought disaster from derailing an ongoing macroeconomic reform process.)

That said, where public determination and capabilities are weak, drought and other climatic shocks continue to take a toll. For much of Africa, drought is an ever present concern (Rochette 1989; Tucker, Dregnes, and Newcombe

TABLE 4.1 Indexes of per capita food production in famine-affected and not-affected African countries, 1961–95/96

Country	1961	1971	1981	1991	1995/96
Countries affected by famine at least once during the 1970s, 1980s, or 1990s[a]					
Angola	126	136	96	79	88
Burundi	100	104	102	91	82
Chad	111	103	99	102	110
Ethiopia	113	104	96	86	96
Liberia	91	99	102	66	n.a.
Madagascar	104	109	100	86	80
Malawi	86	108	100	75	70
Mozambique	117	125	99	77	82
Niger	112	99	97	78	80
Rwanda	80	93	102	84	80
Sierra Leone	95	108	100	84	81
Somalia	99	109	101	78	n.a.
Sudan	98	97	109	80	82
Uganda	121	126	102	98	102
Zaire	117	107	99	94	82
Countries without a noted famine during 1970s, 1980s, or 1990s					
Benin	97	99	95	119	136
Botswana	134	150	102	68	72
Burkina Faso	112	116	100	119	127
Cameroon	91	111	101	78	86
Central African Republic	90	95	102	94	92
Congo	117	107	101	92	84
Côte d'Ivoire	74	88	100	93	106
Gabon	99	114	96	82	76
The Gambia	160	163	116	90	58
Ghana	117	129	99	116	134
Guinea	101	101	101	90	95
Guinea-Bissau	36	108	102	107	110
Kenya	112	110	95	103	90
Lesotho	136	127	96	70	75
Mali	95	100	106	96	90
Namibia	114	127	93	98	67
Nigeria	129	135	97	123	135
Senegal	153	139	124	98	107
Swaziland	69	95	107	85	78
Tanzania	97	93	97	78	74
Togo	119	117	97	95	90
Zambia	101	105	97	96	81
Zimbabwe	101	127	119	78	67

SOURCE: FAO 1997b.

NOTES: 1980 index = 100; n.a. = not available.

[a]See also Figure 3.1.

1991). It is, for example, a perennial feature of the Sudano-Sahelian region and parts of the Horn. And, as witnessed in southern Africa in the early 1990s, the once-in-a-century drought can devastate whole economies. It was precisely that devastation wrought on the crippled political and economic systems of Ethiopia and Sudan that led to famine. Things, however, worked out differently in Zimbabwe and Kenya. The following sections examine such diverse country cases in more detail.

Famine Prevention in Spite of Drought in Zimbabwe and Kenya

Zimbabwe's drought of 1991/92 took national and international policy-makers by surprise. Having made great strides in its agricultural development during the 1980s, Zimbabwe has been widely applauded as "a rare African success story" (Rukuni and Eicher 1994). Average yields and total output of maize rose sharply from 1979 to 1983, allowing the country to export grain to its neighbors and enjoy economic growth exceeding 4 percent per year. Bumper harvests in 1989 and 1990 that generated maize supplies in excess of 1 million tons supported the general impression that the country's food stock was secure (Sachikonye 1992).

The nationwide drought cruelly exposed the fragility of those previous gains. Rainfall in 1990/91 was only 75 percent of the long-term national average, and still lower in the drought-prone regions of the south. In 1991/92, rainfall was barely 50 percent of the average, resulting in a 0.4 million-ton national harvest that was only 20 percent of normal (FAO 1992; USAID 1992). By mid-1992, over 4.5 million people were requesting food assistance and over 2 million tons of imported cereals were needed to meet emergency food requirements (USAID 1992). In other words a single—albeit serious—drought highlighted the lack of reliable food supplies for Zimbabwe's rural households.

Agriculture employs roughly 75 percent of Zimbabwe's population. The agricultural economy is divided into two major sectors: a smallholder sector that mainly produces maize for domestic consumption (maize accounts for almost 50 percent of total calories consumed by households) and a commercial farm sector that focuses more on cotton and tobacco production for export. The widely reported "agricultural miracle" of the 1980s was largely based on growth in maize production among smallholders (Rukuni and Eicher 1994). Between 1980 and 1985, national output of maize almost doubled, with production in the smallholder sector rising threefold. The major stimulus for this growth came from a postindependence restructuring of inputs and incentives that greatly increased the profitability of maize cultivation for small farmers.

Among the first important changes was a rise in the official price of maize (Takavarasha 1994). A second important change was the emphasis on disseminating high-yielding hybrid maize cultivars that had been developed during preindependence years. A third change was the improvement of extension organizations to facilitate adoption of the new cultivars. An effort was made to train female extension workers in order to reach women-headed households (which constitute a majority of farm households). Fourth, access for small farmers to fertilizer and credit was improved. Between 1980 and 1985, the Agricultural Finance Corporation (AFC) increased loans to communal areas. Fifth, real agricultural wages climbed from Z$38 per month in 1980 to Z$61 (deflated) in 1982 (von Braun, Teklu, and Webb 1991). As a result of these changes, the share of maize deliveries to the Grain Marketing Board (GMB) from the smallholder sector rose from 9 percent in 1980/81 to almost 60 percent 10 years later (Moyo et al. 1991).

Droughts in the mid-1980s compromised these production gains, forcing real wages back down to pre-1980s levels (von Braun, Teklu, and Webb 1991). Nevertheless, the 1980s as a whole witnessed production growth, and national food stores seemed relatively ample. A bumper harvest in 1990 took food stocks above 1 million tons, which cost the GMB over Z$20 million in storage and interest charges (Sachikonye 1992). There was consequently much debate on how to manage overflowing silos. Increasing exports was decided upon as one option. A large amount of grain was exported in 1991 in an attempt to boost foreign exchange to support liberalization policies that had been announced in October 1990. Domestic sales were also high during 1991, particularly in areas where drought had caused regional crop failures (USAID 1992).

However, only a few months into 1992 all thoughts of food security vanished. Food stocks in April of that year were below 60,000 tons, and with the 1991/92 harvest down by more than 70 percent from the previous year (at between 400,000 and 600,000 million tons) the government was forced to import over 1.5 million tons of food via commercial channels, costing more than US$600 million (USAID 1992). A state of emergency was declared in early 1992 in response to the rising number of people seeking food assistance. However, a famine did not occur, largely because of rapid, coordinated intervention at both national and international levels. Few people starved as a result of the catastrophic drought. This experience stands in marked contrast to similar drought-induced disasters in West and eastern Africa.

Downing, Gitu, and Kamau (1989) also reported how appropriate policy responses to drought warnings in Kenya helped the country to avoid famine. In 1984, a severe drought affected much of the country. The first rains of that year were almost 1.5 standard deviations below the national average. The worst-affected region was the central highlands (less than 25 percent of normal in Nairobi); rainfall in western Kenya and the coast was closer to normal.

Cereal stocks at the beginning of the food crisis exceeded 90 kilograms per capita, reflecting good weather and an agricultural economy that had been healthy since 1982. Food production for the 1984/85 agricultural year declined dramatically from 1981/82 to the 1983/84 average: down 35 percent for maize and 40 percent for wheat. Cereals availability throughout the country declined sharply to less than 10 kilograms per capita by September 1984, the height of the food crisis.

The government responded to the catastrophe in a timely and expeditious fashion. The initial government response was based on meteorological reports, the fact that the drought was readily apparent and centered in Nairobi, the rapid increase in maize sales by the National Cereals and Produce Board (NCPB), and accounts from district officials and field staff of nongovernmental organizations (NGOs). In June 1984, the government appealed to donors for assistance and a month later began ordering maize and wheat imports. Commercial maize imports first appeared at the end of September, whereas large food aid shipments did not arrive until the end of the year. The primary government strategy was to stabilize food prices and supplies within the country through commercial imports (Drèze 1988). Only 20 percent of the maize imports was used for food relief; the balance was distributed through normal market channels.

Downing suggests that the Kenyan experience with recent drought is a qualified success story. Given the lack of preparedness planning, the success was fortuitous and did not result in conditions leading to reduced vulnerability to future droughts. A different set of political, economic, and environmental circumstances could well have led to a catastrophe.

Droughts and Famines in Sudan

The historical 1888/89 famine is considered to have been the worst in Sudan's history, and was associated with two consecutive years of severe drought coupled with political instability (Slatin Pasha 1896; Churchill 1899; Duncan 1952; Farwell 1967; Holt 1970). The year 1913 also witnessed poor rains, but famine was averted by the colonial government through maize imports that were freely distributed (MacMichael 1934).

Droughts in Sudan have been concentrated in the western and eastern regions, and in parts of the south (Figure 4.1). Local surveys identified 36 separate years of severe drought between 1912 and 1974 in western Sudan (Ibrahim 1985). Ibrahim's research on historical records shows that 1913, 1914, and 1927 were drought years (Table 4.2). These droughts spread from the east of Sudan to the regions of Kordofan and Darfur. Although Sudan largely escaped the worst years of the Sahelian drought of 1968–73, it experienced a major drought and famine eight years later.

The severe drought of 1984–85 was the culmination of a prolonged period of low rainfall that intensified in the beginning of the 1980s. According to Nicholson (1985), rainfall deficits for 1981 through 1984 equaled or exceeded those of the early 1970s in all Sahel, Sahelian-Saharan, and Sudanese regions. Hulme (1984) also concluded, on the basis of observed rainfall data in the Sudanese arid zone, that the years 1979–83 were as dry as 1969–73. Recent research on western Sudan reveals that dry conditions

FIGURE 4.1 Famine-affected areas in Sudan, 1980s and 1990s

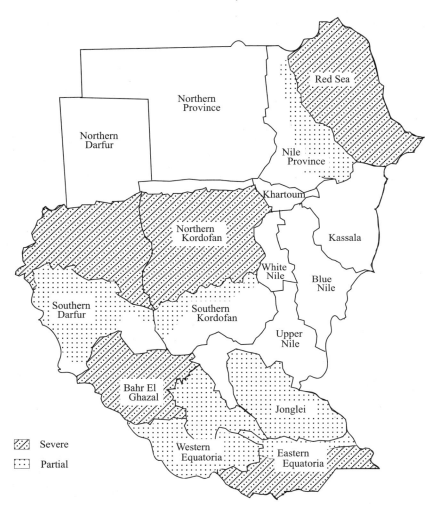

NOTE: Mapping of population groups by severity of food insecurity is based on a combination of ecological variation and measures of food gap by area.

have persisted in northern Kordofan and northern Darfur provinces since 1966 (Eldredge et al. 1987). The authors attribute the downward trend in annual precipitation to a decline in the days of rainfall in July, August, and September—months that account for at least 90 percent of annual rainfall.

TABLE 4.2 Selected famines and droughts in Sudan, 1880s–1990s

Years of Drought or Famine	Type and Damage, Cause (Drought or Other)	Areal Extent	Source
1885	Slight famine	Central and eastern Sudan	al-Gudal 1983
1888–89	Hundreds of thousands died	Central, northern, eastern, and western Sudan	Slatin Pasha 1896
1888–89	No rain for a year, crops failed and grain became increasingly scarce. People sold their children as slaves to save their lives and later bought them for higher prices	Central, northern, and eastern Sudan	Duncan 1952 Farwell 1967 Churchill 1899
1888–89	Thousands died of hunger and disease	Central, northern, eastern, and western Sudan	Holt 1970 MacMichael 1934
1890	Locust and mice consumed the products	Nile area	Farwell 1967 Duncan 1952
1913	Poor rain, corn brought from India and issued free of charge in distressed areas and cheaply elsewhere	Mainly northern Sudan	MacMichael 1934
1914	"The year of the flour" (flour brought from India because of poor rains)	Central Sudan	Henderson 1965
1927	Slight famine	Central and eastern Sudan	al-Gudal 1983
1968–73	Droughts in western Sudan	Mainly western Sudan, selected areas	
1984–85	Drought and famine; war related in south	Most parts of country	
1989–90	Drought, war	Mainly in south	
1993–94	Drought, war	South and west regions	
1995–96	Risk of famine as fighting escalated	South	ICRC 1996
1998	Famine, war	South	Bread for the World 1995

SOURCE: Based on Ibrahim 1985 and updates by the authors.

Drought and Famine in Eritrea and Ethiopia

A review of Ethiopia's history (including what is today the independent state of Eritrea) also yields a long list of crises (Table 4.3). Most famines have concentrated geographically within two broad zones (Figure 4.2). The first comprises the central and northeastern highlands, stretching from northern Shewa through Wollo and Tigray into eastern Eritrea. The second is made up of the crescent of low-lying, agro-pastoral lands ranging from Wollo in the north, through Hararghe and Bale, to Sidamo and Gamo Gofa in the south. Of the crises listed in Table 4.3, more than half were concentrated within these two zones.[1]

The rainfall records of these drought-prone regions show that for the nine provinces receiving precipitation below the national average, low mean rainfall over time combined with high interannual fluctuation. For example the coefficients of variation are highest for the provinces of Eritrea (48), Tigray (28), and Hararghe (27). By contrast, regions with the highest mean rainfall, such as Gojjam and Keffa, have coefficients of variation less than 12 (Webb, von Braun, and Yohannes 1992).

This does not mean that high rainfall areas avoid localized crises. Several droughts have occurred in Gojjam, Gondar, and Shewa during the past few decades. However, these and other drought-prone provinces did not always experience their "worst" years simultaneously. For example five of the country's provinces had their severest dry periods during the 1960s; only two (Wollega and Gondar) were worst affected during the 1970s; while four had their driest year during the 1983–86 drought. Precipitation rates in all worst years ranged from 18 percent below the long-term average to as much as 57 percent below. For Ethiopia as a whole, the worst year since 1961 was 1984, with rainfall amounts 22 percent below the long-term average. The crisis-prone areas closely correlate with present-day drought propensity, as calculated by Ethiopia's National Meteorological Services Agency (NMSA) (Degefu 1987, 1988). In other words, the regions most likely to succumb to drought in the next few years are generally the same as those that have suffered more in the past.

---

1. In such a compilation exercise, one faces the problem of defining parameters. The extent and causes of famines cannot be adequately described in a simple tabulation. Locally the areal extent and durarion of drought may differ substantially. Few food crises, for instance, in Ethiopia have resulted from catastrophic events such as floods or earthquakes (although some have certainly been associated with epidemics and warfare). Instead, as argued here, food shortages tend to take on famine proportions after their effects have become cumulative. Thus it is hard to say exactly when a food shortage ended and a famine actually started. Although some analysts refer to notable crisis years in Ethiopia, such as 1958 and 1973, others have stated that "during the 20-year period between 1958 and 1977, about 20 percent of the country was under famine conditions each year" (Fraser 1988, p. 20; see also Wolde-Mariam 1984).

TABLE 4.3 A chronology of major droughts and famines in Eritrea and Ethiopia, 1880s–1990s

Date	Regions Affected	Causes and Severity
1880	Tigray and Gondar	Much loss of livestock
1888–92	Ethiopia	Drought and spread of rinderpest caused loss of 90 percent of cattle and more than 30 percent of human population
1895–96	Ethiopia	Minor drought; loss of livestock and human lives
1899–1900	Ethiopia	Drought inferred from levels of Lake Rudolf and low Nile floods
1913–14	Northern Ethiopia	Lowest Nile floods since 1695; grain prices said to have risen 30-fold
1920–22	Ethiopia	Moderate drought, similar to 1895–96
1932–34	Ethiopia	Inferred from low level of Lake Rudolf in northern Kenya
1953	Tigray and Wollo	Severity unrecorded
1957–58	Tigray and Wollo	Rain failure in 1957; locusts and epidemic in 1958
1962–63	Western Ethiopia	Very severe
1964–66	Tigray and Wollo	Undocumented; said to be worse than 1973/74
1969	Eritrea	Estimated 1.7 million people suffered food shortage
1971–75	Ethiopia	Sequence of rain failures; estimated 250,000 dead; 50 percent of livestock lost in Tigray and Wollo
1978–79	Southern Ethiopia	Failure of Belg rains
1982	Northern Ethiopia	Late Meher rains
1984–85	Ethiopia	Sequential rain failure; 8 million affected; estimated 1 million dead; much livestock loss
1987–88	Ethiopia	Drought of undocumented severity in peripheral regions
1990–92	Northern, eastern, and southwestern Ethiopia	Rain failure and regional conflicts; estimated 4 million people suffering food shortage
1994	Northern, eastern, and southern Ethiopia	0.7 million people in need of food aid due to regional droughts

SOURCES: Wood 1977; Pankhurst 1984; Wolde-Michael 1985; Wolkeba 1985; Degefu 1987; Iliffe 1987; Gedion 1988; Gizaw 1988; Ethiopia-RRC 1990; FEWS Project 1991.

FIGURE 4.2 Famine-vulnerable areas in Eritrea and Ethiopia

SOURCES: Compiled from UNEPPG (United Nations Emergency Preparedness and Planning Group) 1990; Wolde-Mariam 1984; Gizaw 1988.

NOTE: The shaded areas are those regions most often affected by drought and famine. The country's former administrative boundaries are used because they related to conditions at the time of the IFPRI surveys.

Drought, Food Production, and Supply: Comparing Trends in Sudan and Ethiopia

Calorie consumption per capita declined in Sudan between 1978 and 1986 (Figure 4.3).[2] The annual growth rate was −1.4 percent. The trend diminishes (−0.7 percent) when the effect of the 1984 drought is controlled for, which

2. The absence of time-series data poses a problem for studying disaggregated Sudanese food consumption patterns over time. The best that may be done is to use an aggregate measure of food availability from food balance-sheet estimates. Available food consumption estimates are

FIGURE 4.3 Food production and consumption per capita in Sudan, 1969–92

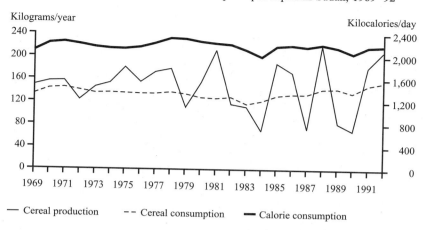

Kilograms/year

Kilocalories/day

— Cereal production   - - Cereal consumption   ▬ Calorie consumption

SOURCES: Compiled and computed from Sudan-MANR 1977, 1984a, 1984b, 1985a, 1987a; FAO, Office for Special Relief Operations, 1985, *Agricultural Trade Yearbook* various years, *Food Aid in Figures* various years, and *Food supply utilization data tape for Sudan,* 1996.

shows the strong impact of the drought-production effect on cereal consumption. Average per capita cereal consumption dropped to around 120 kilograms in 1984/85, down from approximately 140 to 150 kilograms in most years of the previous decade. The years 1985 and 1986 witnessed a marked recovery, with good harvests sharply narrowing the gap between domestic production and food needs. However, as noted earlier (in Table 4.1), per capita production continued its downward slide through the 1990s.

Ethiopia has also posted some good harvests in recent years (1994 and 1995). Nevertheless production is still not equal to demand, and national cereal production and food availability continue on a downward trend that was initiated in the 1970s. Per capita cereal production declined by an average of 4 kilograms per year between the early 1960s and the late 1980s (Figure 4.4). The same is true for food consumption. Cereal consumption per capita has been declining at an average of 3.3 kilograms per year, while per capita consumption of all foods (cereals plus pulses and roots) has been declining by 2.7 kilograms per year. The decline has not been smooth and uninterrupted for the entire period. Certain years, such as 1975, 1979, and 1995, saw large increases in cereal production that may have been associated partly with better than average rainfall and partly with policy changes.

---

derived from the aggregation of net domestic production available less net trade and net stock changes. These estimates, in general, set the upper bounds to actual consumption levels. UN Food and Agriculture Organization (FAO)-based estimates are used here to examine the behavior of aggregate food consumption over time.

FIGURE 4.4 Food production and consumption per capita in Ethiopia, 1969–92

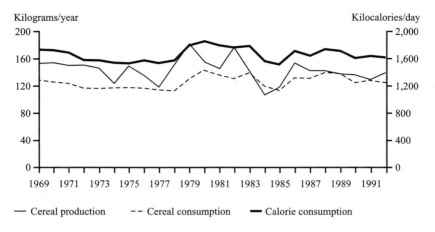

SOURCE: Per capita cereal production and consumption computed by the authors based on data sets compiled from FAO 1996; Ethiopia, Ministry of Agriculture 1979; Ethiopia CSA 1987a, 1987b, 1988, and 1989.

It seems evident that the large famines of the 1970s and 1980s in Sudan and Ethiopia coincided with food availability dropping below 140 kilograms per capita. This becomes clearer at the subnational level. The decline in Ethiopia, for instance, has not been smooth across all regions. Poor or good production in one province does not directly correlate with production levels in any other province (see Table 4.4). There is, therefore, variety within the country in terms of production variability and covariability.

Food availability in Ethiopia is to a large extent determined by the country's domestic production of cereals (availability and production correlate at 0.76). Although the relationship remained strong throughout the time series, the difference between the two widened during the 1980s. This points to the buffering role of food imports, food aid, and stock depletion. Imports (both commercial and food aid) compensated for some of the difference, but not all. Commercial imports contributed less than 15 kilograms per capita until 1985, when the imports of rice and wheat rose in response to the food crisis. However, they have remained low since that time.

Food aid, on the other hand, has increased since 1984 and remains high in Ethiopia, Sub-Saharan Africa's largest such recipient. Food assistance made an important contribution in the critical period 1983–85, and again in 1988. In overall terms, food aid contributed up to 20 kilograms per capita in these years. In 1988, emergency food aid exceeded 1985 amounts because severe drought occurred in many regions. Although the 1989 total declined to half a million

TABLE 4.4 Correlation of per capita cereal production in Ethiopia's six main provinces, 1979–87

Region	Correlation Coefficients						Average Per Capita Production
	Arssi	Gondar	Hararghe	Shewa	Sidamo	Wollo	
							(kilograms)
Arssi	—	−.02	.13	.17	.76*	.21	290
Gondar	—	—	.65	.66	−.18	.57	152
Hararghe	—	—	—	.91**	.31	.60	95
Shewa	—	—	—	—	.34	.73	153
Sidamo	—	—	—	—	—	.07	53
Wollo	—	—	—	—	—	—	151

SOURCE: Webb, von Braun, and Yohannes 1992.

* = 99 percent level of significance.
** = 99.9 percent level of significance.

tons, since 1990 food assistance has become the single largest form of resource transfer to Ethiopia, reaching more than $200 million per year in the mid-1990s (Fox 1996).

Food availability in Sudan is also to a great extent determined by domestic staple-food production. Domestic food production contributes, on average, 90 percent of total cereal consumption. There are, of course, marked variations among the individual cereal crops. Millet, the preferred crop in the west, is consumed solely from domestic production. The same applies to sorghum, which is largely consumed in the central, eastern, and southern regions. The contribution of imports and domestic stocks to millet and sorghum availability is minor. Years of large production shortfalls, such as in 1982–84 (when, in the latter year, production as a share of consumption fell to a low of 75 percent), are exceptions. To cope with the shortages, the government adopted a variety of measures, such as banning the export of sorghum, drawing down reserve stocks, and appealing for outside support (which came largely in the form of grants and concessionary imports). These policies are likely to remain in place in light of increased fluctuations in stocks as was observed in the 1980s.[3]

Drought and other climatic shocks clearly have complex and dynamic effects on production. It is from this interaction that broader economic, social, nutritional, and health effects result. The effects of drought on crop production impinge most heavily on crop yields per unit of land. It may, of course, also affect cropping patterns through farmers' responses to perceived risk of drought. In Ethiopia, this was seen by a decline in cultivated area during the severest drought years. A lack of imports led to a contraction rather than an

3. It should be noted that official stock figures are not all comprehensive.

expansion of cultivated area so that scarce resources could be invested in the most productive fields. As a result, a one-third reduction in cultivated area per household was reported in several parts of the country during 1988/89 versus 1984/85 (Webb and von Braun 1994). However, in comparing the 1970s to the 1980s there were no major changes in the proportions of land area allocated to various cereal crops. Only minor changes have been recorded, such as a reduction in the area share of sorghum since the late 1970s, paralleled by an upward trend in cultivated maize area (Webb, von Braun, and Yohannes 1992).

The relationship between rainfall quantity, distribution, timing, and resultant crop yields and output is complex. Nevertheless a simple relationship is expected between absolute rainfall amounts and production and yields. Although many other factors are important, such as economic incentives (output and input prices) and the ability of farmers to respond to actual incentives (functioning of supply systems, financing, labor availability, and so forth), the dominating role a large decline in rainfall plays in cereal production in the short run is assumed to limit the significance of such missing variables. Some of these variables may also be correlated with drought, as shown in the following modeling exercises.

Two models have been estimated for Ethiopia and Sudan. These have been simplified because of the lack of appropriate data (such as fertilizer use and response and price response) needed for more elaborate exercises. For Ethiopia, first an attempt is made to explain production and cereal yields for the years 1961/62–1988/89 by considering total annual rainfall:

$$Q_{it} = \alpha_0 + \alpha_1 \mathrm{RAIN}_t + \alpha_2 (\mathrm{RAIN}_t)^2 + \alpha_3 P_{(it-1)} + \alpha_4 P_{(jt-1)} + \alpha_5 T + u_t, \qquad (4.1)$$

where

Q_{it} = production or yield of crop i in period t,
RAIN_t = rainfall index in period t,
P_{it-1} = own deflated price in period $t-1$ (only in Sudan models),
P_{jt-1} = price of competing crop j in period $t-1$ (only in Sudan models),
T = time trend,
u_t = random-error term in period t, and
$\alpha_{0,1,2,3,4,5}$ are parameters to be estimated.

It was assumed that the effect of incremental precipitation on production would decrease at the margin (to be picked up by a rainfall-squared variable).[4] The results presented in Table 4.5 depict some of the actual variance in cereal production and yields over time. As expected, rising incremental rainfall beyond a threshold results in decreasing increments in national cereal production.

---

4. For Ethiopia, a dummy variable was also included that separates the time-series data into two portions: before and including 1978, and after 1978. This year is important because it saw the introduction of new methods for calculating farm yields and production.

TABLE 4.5 Regression analyses of rainfall-cereal production and rainfall-yield relationships in Ethiopia, 1961/62–1988/89

| Dependent Variable | Explanatory Variables | | Lag of Dependent $t-1$ | $DUMMY_t$ | Constant | R^2 | Ljung-Box (16)[a] | Effect of a 10 Percent Drop in Rainfall[b] |
	$RAIN_t$	$RAINSQ_t$						(percent)
$CEPROD_t$	25,426.3	−12.400	0.02	−1,443,193.7	−7,111,033.7	.77	10.15	−4.6
	(1.92)	(−1.76)	(−0.12)	(−5.65)	(−1.107)			
$CEYILD_t$	7.400	−0.0037	0.343	−233.8	−2,859.2	.81	14.09	−4.3
	(2.77)	(−2.64)	(2.35)	(−4.18)	(−2.236)			

SOURCES: Computed by the authors based on data from the Central Statistical Authority and National Meteorological Services Agency of Ethiopia.

NOTES: t-values are given in parentheses; N = 28.

Variables:

$RAIN_t$ = annual rainfall (country-weighted averages of regional rainfall using production shares as weights),

$RAINSQ_t$ = $RAIN_t$ squared,

Lag of dependent $t-1$ = lag of the respective dependent variable ($CEPROD_t$ and $CEYILD_t$),

$DUMMY_t$ = dummy variable for separation of production series before and after new statistics system (1978),

$CEPROD_t$ = total cereal production in metric tons in year t, and

$CEYILD_t$ = cereal yield in kilograms per hectare.

[a]The nonsignificance of Ljung-Box statistics for 16 lags indicates that residuals are white noise; Greene 1990, pp. 453–54.
[b]Below the long-term national average.

The second model is set up as a pooled, cross-sectional analysis for 1961/62–1988/89 across all Ethiopian provinces. It avoids the problem of including the different database used before 1979 (which required the dummy variable in the first model). A block of dummy variables separates each province from the other. In this model, an attempt is made to analyze the differential effects of rainfall variability on major cereal crops. Apart from barley yields, this approach depicts the rainfall-yield relationships reasonably well, as is shown in Table 4.6. These results suggest that a 10 percent decline in rainfall below the long-term national average results in an average drop in all cereal yields of 4.3 percent (see Table 4.5). As some substitution with area also occurs, a drop of 4.6 percent in total cereal production is found for a 10 percent decline in rainfall. The latter occurs as a result of disproportionately large declines in the yields of sorghum and maize. (The latter two crops are grown in the drier provinces of Bale, Hararghe, and Wollo.) The rainfall-production link is not perfect, however. Soil type, depth, location of plots, and soil temperature can all have a large effect on yields and total production, even within a limited area.

However, drought is found to be a very important factor contributing to food shortages in Ethiopia. The effects on yields and production show up quite strongly, but these effects vary considerably by crop and by region. Yield stability and yield amounts are clearly important considerations in setting agricultural policy for food availability, and the trade-offs between the two need to be better understood.

Similar model estimates for Sudan show comparable results (Tables 4.7 and 4.8). A 10 percent drop in annual rainfall results in a 5.0 and 3.7 percent drop in production and cereal yield, respectively (see Table 4.8). At the national level, the drought response of sorghum is higher (more sensitive) than that of millet (5.0 versus 1.6 percent for a 10 percent rainfall drop below the long-term national average). The sorghum drought response in Sudan is almost similar to the one found for Ethiopia (5.4 versus 5.0 percent).

In the case of Sudan, price response as well as drought response could be included in the model. Contrary to the situation in Ethiopia, government interference was low in Sudanese markets during the period of observation, and price information is quite reliable for sorghum. Short-term price response was found to be significant, as was expected for the much traded sorghum crop (Table 4.7, column 8). The elasticities also indicate that regional/provincial production was more sensitive to rainfall fluctuation than was aggregate production. There were also significant intercrop and interregional differences in drought-production elasticities (see Table 4.8).

Although further analysis along the lines of these models is clearly required, it can already be concluded that production–food availability relationships are strong at both national and provincial levels, since food aid, trade, and the drawdown of food stocks had a limited effect on reducing the gap between

TABLE 4.6 Crop-specific analysis on rainfall-yield relationships in Ethiopia, 1979–87

Yield	$RAIN_t$	$RAINSQ_{t-1}$	Lag of Dependent $t-1$	Constant	R^2	Ljung-Box (8)	Effect of 10 Percent Drop in Rainfall[a]
							(percent)
Barley	1.448	−0.0006	0.224	161.45	.36	12.174	−2.5
	(2.805)	(−2.348)	(1.958)	(0.469)			
Maize	2.410	−0.0008	0.064	−41.81	.41	14.102	−5.4
	(3.111)	(−2.080)	(0.625)	(−0.085)			
Sorghum	2.185	−0.0008	0.176	−172.69	.46	18.002	−5.0
	(3.105)	(−2.399)	(1.741)	(−0.395)			
Teff	1.048	−0.0004	0.384	−108.27	.45	3.766	−3.3
	(2.567)	(−1.900)	(3.749)	(−0.412)			
Wheat	1.859	−0.0007	0.164	−177.77	.44	7.792	−4.1
	(3.007)	(−2.293)	(1.343)	(−0.460)			

SOURCES: Computed by the authors based on data from the Central Statistical Authority and the National Meterological Services Agency of Ethiopia.

NOTES: Both yield and rainfall data sets are pooled across administrative regions; except for sorghum yield, the Ljung-Box statistics clearly show that the residuals are white noise; t-values are given in parentheses.

Variables:

$RAIN_t$ = annual rainfall (country-weighted averages of regional rainfall, using production shares as weight,

$RAINSQ_{t-1}$ = $RAIN$ squared, and

Lag of dependent $t-1$ = lag of the respective dependent variable ($CEPOD_t$ and $CEYILD_t$).

[a]Below the long-term national average.

TABLE 4.7 Parameter estimates of yield- and production-response equations for cereal crops in Sudan

Cereal	Region	Period	Dependent Variable[a]	Independent Variables						Log LF[b]	Degrees of Freedom
				$RAIN_t$	$RAINSQ_t$	$TREND_t$	$OPRC_{t-1}$	$CPRC_{t-1}$	Constant		
Cereals[c]	Sudan	1969–86	CRYLD	13.63 (2.48)	−1.10 (−2.32)	−0.02 (−2.85)	—	—	−4.93 (−0.26)	−82.94	14
			CRPRD	16.14 (1.82)	−1.30 (−1.70)	0.04 (4.11)	—	—	−116.41 (−3.80)	−131.86	14
Sorghum	Sudan	1969–86	SSRYD	17.59 (2.16)	−1.41 (−2.05)	−0.02 (−2.32)	—	—	−19.20 (−0.70)	−81.79	13
			SSRPD	33.12 (2.15)	−2.71 (−2.07)	—	0.52 (3.26)	−0.33 (−2.62)	−83.85 (−2.07)	−124.53	12
	Eastern (Gedaref)	1973–86	GSRYD	28.85 (3.92)	−2.21 (−3.38)	0.01 (0.21)	—	—	−88.44 (−3.44)	−65.88	9
	Central (Blue Nile)	1973–86	BNSYD	16.02 (2.34)	−1.18 (−2.18)	0.03 (1.54)	—	—	−51.05 (−2.38)	−66.74	8
Millet	Sudan	1969–86	SMLYD	10.61 (3.08)	−1.23 (−2.97)	−0.05 (−2.11)	—	—	−14.10 (−1.90)	−86.86	14
			SMLPD	12.56 (2.80)	−1.44 (−2.68)	−0.002 (0.17)	—	—	−21.60 (−2.26)	−104.96	14
	Kordofan (Northern)	1973–86	KMLYD	22.07 (2.98)	−2.02 (−2.84)	−0.04 (−1.65)	—	—	32.30 (0.56)	−64.71	10
	Darfur (Southern)	1973–76	DMLYD	9.78 (2.66)	−0.86 (−2.46)	−0.05 (−2.98)	—	—	85.94 (2.16)	−65.39	10

SOURCES: Based on data files of the Ministry of Agriculture and Natural Resources, Department of Agricultural Economics, Statistics Section, Khartoum; Teklu, von Braun, and Zaki 1991.

NOTES: t-values are given in parentheses; — = not applicable.

Variables:

$RAIN_t$ = Rainfall index in period t,

$RAINSQ_t$ = $RAIN$ squared,

$TREND_t$ = time trend,

$OPRC_{t-1}$ = Own price in period $t-1$,

$CPRC_{t-1}$ = Competing price in $t-1$,

$CRYLD$ = Sudan cereal yield per feddan in kilograms,

$CRPRD$ = Sudan cereal production in 1,000 metric tons,

$SSRYD$ = Sudan sorghum yield per feddan in kilograms,

$SSRPD$ = Sudan sorghum production in 1,000 metric tons,

$GSRYD$ = Gedaref sorghum yield per feddan in kilograms,

$BNSYD$ = Blue Nile sorghum yield per feddan in kilograms,

$SMLYD$ = Sudan millet yield per feddan in kilograms,

$SMLPD$ = Sudan millet production in 1,000 metric tons,

$KMLYD$ = North Kordofan millet yield per feddan in kilograms, and

$DMLYD$ = South Darfur millet yield per feddan in kilograms.

[a]Coefficients are adjusted for autocorrelation of error terms using the Cochrane-Orcutt procedure.

[b]Log LF is the value of the log-likelihood function at convergence.

[c]Cereals include sorghum and millet only.

TABLE 4.8 Response of yield and production of rainfed cereal crops in Sudan to a 10 percent change in rainfall index

Crop	Region	Response Variable	Rainfall Effect
			(percent)
Cereals[a]	Sudan	Production	5.0
		Yield	3.7
Sorghum	Sudan	Yield	5.4
	Eastern (Gedaref)	Yield	4.9
	Central (Blue Nile)	Yield	10.4
Millet	Sudan	Yield	1.6
	Kordofan (Northern)	Yield	5.3
	Darfur (Southern)	Yield	3.2

SOURCE: Calculated from the results in Table 4.7.
[a]Cereals include maize, wheat, sorghum, and millet.

production shortfalls and demand, particularly during the crucial 1982–85 period. Moreover, drought-production linkages are strong, albeit differentiated (as would be expected) by crop and region.

Conclusions Concerning Links between Drought Production and Famine

It has been argued that an isolated drought is rarely dangerous; only when a poor year follows others do droughts take on unmanageable proportions (Hay 1986; Corbett 1988; de Waal 1988). The disasters in Ethiopia and Sudan in 1984/85 certainly did not happen overnight. They were the culmination of a process that included successive droughts spread over many years. For example in Ethiopia, the time series for Hararghe and Wollo provinces show that the 1973/74 drought was merely the last and worst of a sequence of five to seven years of declining rainfall. Similar, although shorter, drought sequences preceded the crisis years of 1979/80 and 1984/85.

The same is the case with Sudan. The severe drought of 1984/85 was the culmination of a prolonged period of low rainfall that intensified at the beginning of the 1980s. According to Nicholson (1985), rainfall deficits for 1981 through 1984 were equal to, or exceeded, those of the early 1970s. Hulme (1984) also concluded, on the basis of observed rainfall data in the Sudanese arid zone, that the years 1979–83 were as dry as 1969–73. And dry conditions have persisted in northern Kordofan and northern Darfur provinces since 1966 (Eldredge et al. 1987). The 1984/85 drought season was the peak of the process set in motion in the late 1970s. However, the relationship between drought and famine is only strong where the resource base is poor, poverty is endemic, and public capacity for prevention and mitigation is weak. When these relationships are present, the drought-famine linkage becomes strong enough that it is no longer valid to argue that a single drought is not dangerous. In other words, the drought-famine relationship in resource-poor African countries is not necessarily constant nor perpetual. It takes other factors to tip the balance.

5 Rural Population Pressure and Urban Change as Famine Causes and Consequences

Population Pressure and Famine: An Aggregate View

Population growth has long been considered a prime cause of famine in low-income countries. As Africa is the region in the world with the highest population growth rates, the correlation between population growth and famine frequency seems to suggest a direct causal relationship. This is in line with Malthus's (1798) concept that a population's growth is unilaterally dependent on its potential to produce food, which is a direct and inelastic function of the given natural-resource endowment. Since a population ordinarily would increase geometrically, Malthus viewed famines as phenomena to keep the population/food supply ratio balanced.

Envisioning a scenario of future natural-resource constraints combined with continued population growth, neo-Malthusian ideas are found in a broad body of literature. Some of this literature focuses on the question of how many people the earth can sustainably feed, based on "carrying-capacity" studies (FAO 1996; Ehrlich and Daily 1993; Brown and Kane 1994; Engelmann and Leroy 1996). For estimates of potential limits to population growth, population numbers in these studies are generally reported as a function of a given amount of agricultural resource, for instance land; the resulting population/resource ratios usually reveal high population pressure. These studies often result in doomsday scenarios of rather naive circular linkages (Figure 5.1).

The following discussion sheds some light on the limited general validity of this perception for the Sub-Saharan African region as a whole. If one maps nutritional status data against cultivable land per capita—where land quality differences are approximated by yield—there appears to be an adverse relationship: undernutrition tends to be higher in countries with higher population pressure against agricultural land availability (Figures 5.2 and 5.3). The variance, however, is high. Obviously factors other than land influence the outcome. As seen by the reduced slope of the trend line in Figure 5.3 compared to Figure 5.2, the relevance of the rather weak relationship has declined even further over time. This might be explained by other factors including nonfarm

FIGURE 5.1 A vicious circle?

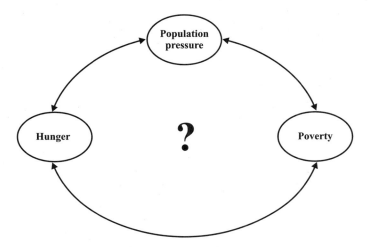

SOURCE: Adapted from von Braun and Qaim 1997.

FIGURE 5.2 Relation between cultivable land per person and undernutrition in selected African countries, 1970

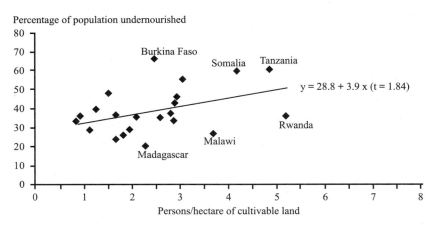

SOURCE: FAO data, various years.

NOTE: Undernutrition and person/cultivable land ratios are taken from FAO data. Only countries with more than 5 million inhabitants are included in this analysis. The more extreme country cases are named. Irrigated and rainfed land was weighted by yield differences.

FIGURE 5.3 Relation between cultivable land per person and undernutrition in selected African countries, 1992

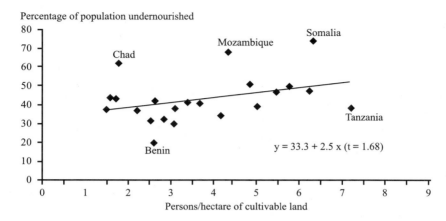

Percentage of population undernourished

$y = 33.3 + 2.5 \text{ x } (t = 1.68)$

Persons/hectare of cultivable land

SOURCE: Undernutrition data and person/cultivable land ratios are taken from FAO data.
NOTE: Only countries with more than 5 million inhabitants are included in the analysis. The more extreme country cases are named. Irrigated and rainfed land was weighted by yield differences.

income and the increased importance of nutrition-relevant public policies. Thus while the plotting of land/person ratios may hint at a general association of factors, more precise country-specific analyses are required to explore the nature of these relationships.

It is well known among scholars (but not among all relevant policy-makers) that food security is not merely a function of countries' food supplies. These are inaccessible if purchasing power is poor. Although for very-low-income countries and subregions increasing population pressure might indeed prove an obstacle to solving nutrition problems, they have to be seen in a broad context, and a wide range of policy options exists to prevent the (naive) vicious circle depicted in Figure 5.1 from evolving (see Figure 5.4). Such options should be based on country-specific problem assessments and on the responses available, which are influenced by institutional capacities. Just as poverty, hunger, and population pressure have reinforcing detrimental linkages, the measures to counter them need to be complementary and mutually dependent as well. Therefore, isolated actions might be ineffective and usually do not render sustainable solutions.

A simplistic concept of population pressure, understood in terms of accelerated person/cropped-land ratios, overlooks many potential resource substitutions. It also tends to be pessimistic about the rate of technological progress and underestimates the power of trade. Although there may not be much predictability in adverse global scenarios of population-food relationships, this does

FIGURE 5.4 Preventing vicious circles

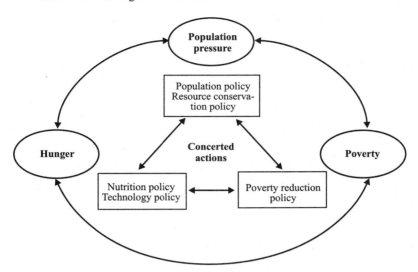

SOURCE: Adapted from von Braun and Qaim 1997.

not mean that population pressure plays no role at all in explaining famine. However, the relevance of the relationship seems location and time specific, rather than universal. It can be hypothesized that the impact of population pressure on the development of famine may be expected where

(1) rural population growth is particularily rapid, and technology is inaccessible, and
(2) population movements are constrained, or are headed toward mass urban poverty.

Following these hypotheses, one would need to study the more extreme patterns of population pressure and demographic change in Sub-Saharan Africa in order to identify their associations with famine. For example as population pressure grows in an area of limited land, households' marketable food surpluses may shrink, leading to increased reliance on risky, low-yielding, subsistence-food production (von Braun and Kennedy 1994). This can lead to increased exploitation of natural resources (resulting in erosion of the productive resource base), and also to more intense competition over factors of production. Where such constraints are not ameliorated, competition can turn into conflict. With this process in mind, the following discussion focuses on two examples where demographic changes to some extent have contributed to recent crises: First is the case of a densely populated rural area of the East African highlands in Rwanda. Second is the case of rapidly growing urban centers (such as in Khartoum and Addis Ababa) in famine-affected countries.

Rural Population Pressure and Famine Risk in Rwanda[1]

Famine and genocidal violence in the East African Great Lakes region during the mid-1990s must be seen in its complex historical, political, and ethnic context, which has been increasingly well analyzed (for example Sellström and Wohlgemuth 1996). The main event triggering the crisis was the invasion of Rwanda by the Rwandan Patriotic Front from Uganda in 1990. Peace accords that might have established a power-sharing arrangement collapsed in 1994 when a plane carrying Burundi's and Rwanda's presidents was shot down, killing them both. Genocidal violence and war ensued. Because of the fear of reprisal for the mass killings of more than 500,000 Tutsi, more than 1 million Hutu fled Rwanda. Most of the refugees settled just over the border in Burundi, Tanzania, and Zaire (Figure 5.5). Political destabilization followed in Burundi and Zaire, with a change of political leadership and country name in Zaire (to the Democratic Republic of the Congo).

Although Rwanda's acute situation is an important case in point for the study of famines in Africa, this is not the focus of this chapter. Rather, this section concentrates on long-term aspects of the development process that are relevant to changes in the "carrying capacity" of the regional economy and its implications for famine risks. A small region—Giciye *commune* (administrative district) in highland northwestern Rwanda, characterized by particularly high population pressure as well as very high population growth—is studied for the purpose. The *commune* comprises an area of roughly 185 square kilometers, approximately 120 square kilometers of which are suitable for agricultural production, the remainder being part of the forest of Gishwati.[2] In late 1984 the population of Giciye *commune* was about 52,000 and growing at more than 4 percent per year. The average population density was 435 persons per square kilometer of usable land, varying from approximately 270 persons per square kilometer in some higher-altitude *secteurs* (subdistricts) in the west to more than 900 persons per square kilometer on the volcanic soils at the border of the high plateaus in the east.

Changes in the relationship between population pressure and food production involve technical and socioeconomic feedbacks, some with long time lags. In brief, farmers' behavior patterns in economic environments such as this location typically reveal that food security usually has top priority in

---

1. This section is based on von Braun, de Haen, and Blanken 1991.
2. The following description of the study area is based mainly on the 1984 annual report of Giciye *commune*.

FIGURE 5.5 Refugees in the Great Lakes region of central Africa, November 1996

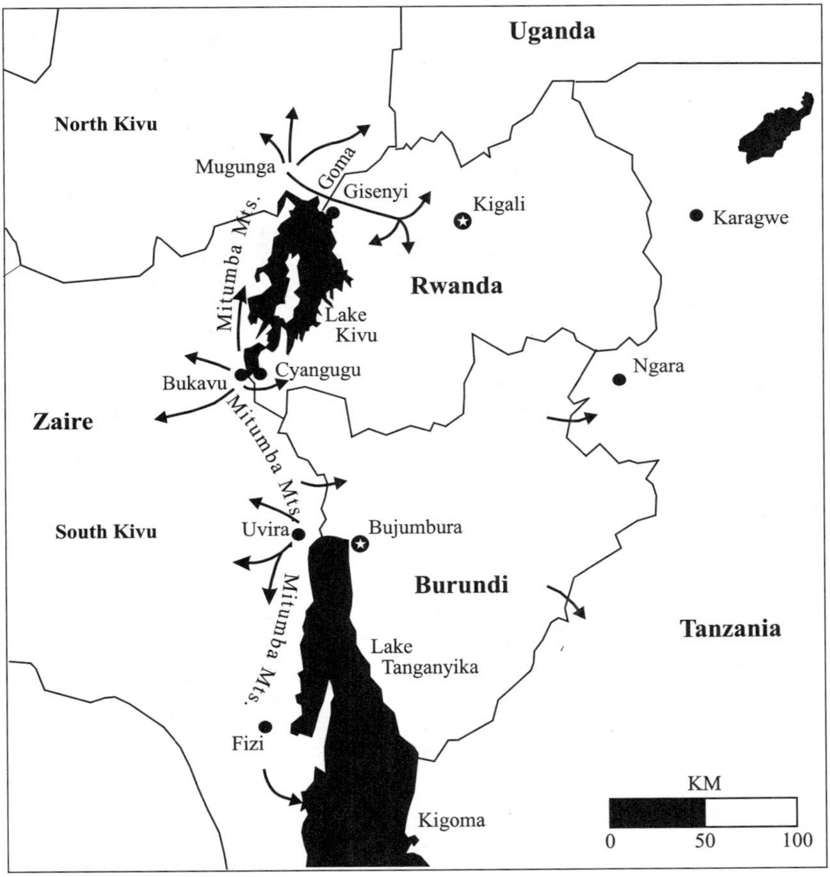

SOURCE: FEWS 1996.

production decisions; this implies that available land is allocated to crops used for home consumption until a desired degree of subsistence is reached (von Braun, de Haen, and Blanken 1991). This behavior is influenced by risks and uncertainties in the food and off-farm labor market and by an undeveloped system for credit. If the farm population grows and total available land remains static, proportionately more land is required for subsistence maintenance, at first to the detriment of remaining fallow, but later also at the cost of market-able surpluses. Thus the rapid population growth in the region imposes a limit to commercialization of agricultural production. This limit might be reached even sooner if the decline in fallow periods has a negative impact on soil fertility and yields. The reduction of marketable surpluses and the fallback into low productivity may be slowed down or avoided by means of either agricultural investment, technical innovation, or both. Yet the rate of technical progress in the region as a whole has been limited in the past and was halted by the war.

Analyses of detailed household surveys undertaken in Rwanda in the mid-1980s indicate that, as person/land ratios grow, farmers tend to intensify the labor input per hectare, enabling them to increase crop yields somewhat and to slow down the decline in per capita subsistence production that accompanies population growth (von Braun, de Haen, and Blanken 1991). However, significant and sustainable increases in the rate of productivity require a rising use of external inputs, particularly new seeds and mineral fertilizer. This need imposes a problem because the purchase of external inputs requires available cash, which becomes more and more limited by the decline of marketable surpluses.

Given these hindrances to growth in agricultural production, it is evident that nonagricultural employment becomes more important as population pressure grows. Theories of farm-household behavior suggest that such employment opportunities become more attractive as limited farm resources cause the marginal value of the agricultural product to decline relative to nonagricultural income opportunities (Singh, Squire, and Strauss 1986). This appears to have been the case in the Rwandan study area: households with larger person/land ratios spent a significantly higher share of their total labor capacity on nonagricultural activities, partly in home production for beer brewing (women) and partly in off-farm employment (men). Thus, population pressure may not lead farm households to fall totally out of the local market economy. Instead they may shift their emphasis from marketing agricultural produce to commercializing part of their labor force.

In order to explore the implications of population pressure for subsistence production and employment—two critical famine risks at the Rwandan study location—a simulation model was developed to describe typical household situations. It consisted of two components: (1) a demographic component that projected population change based on the current age structure and observed demographic variables (fertility, mortality); and (2) a resource allocation and production component that described likely responses of land use, production, and labor systems to projected population pressure.

The modeled results suggest that if the demographic parameters observed during the period 1978–83 were to continue until 2005, the population of the area in question would more than double.[3] This corresponds to an average

---

3. The demographic model assumed that neither immigration nor emigration will occur in the area represented by the sample households during the simulation period—that is, refugee flows

TABLE 5.1   Simulated person/land ratio in a Rwandan sample, simulations 1985–2005

| | | | | Lowest and Highest Person/Land-Ratio Quartile | | | | | |
| | Sample Average | | | 1985 | | 1994 | | 2005 | |
	1985	1995	2005	Low	High	Low	High	Low	High
Person/ land ratio[a]	5.51	7.93	12.01	1.97	10.87	2.68	15.76	3.72	23.94

SOURCE: von Braun, de Haen, and Blanken 1991.

[a]Adult-equivalent persons per hectare.

annual growth rate of 4.1 percent for the period 1985–95, and 3.9 percent for 1985–2005.[4] The average person/land ratio—the measure of population pressure—was assumed to increase from 5.5 in 1985 to 12.0 in 2005 (Table 5.1).[5]

The next step is to simulate the effects of these demographic developments on adjustments in the farming system. The results suggest that increasing population pressure causes households to shift from one crop subsystem to another; that is, to increasing the share of their labor-intensive crops, such as sweet potatoes. As farm households face increasing person/land-ratios, they reallocate their scarce agricultural land and adopt more labor-intensive cropping patterns. Input use is also adjusted and yields and output tend to respond positively as a result. In general, yields for potatoes and the crop system of maize/beans/potatoes increase with rising person/land ratios. However, yield-increasing effects (so-called Boserup effects) are limited by farmers' inability to finance external inputs (Boserup 1965).

Table 5.2 summarizes two scenarios of model projections for the production of major crops and total calorie production per consumer equivalent for 1985–2005. Scenario 1 is exclusively based on endogenous changes in agricultural labor input, overall land-use intensity, and changes in cropping patterns; in scenario 2, technological change effects at constant overall labor input levels are assumed.[6] Looking at the overall calorie supply from own production, Table 5.2 shows that in scenario 1, calorie production will increase by 11

---

are not endogenously considered—and that the land basis observed in 1985 will not change in 20 years. The relevant demographic parameters for the model have been taken from different sources (von Braun, de Haen, and Blanken 1991).

   4. According to the 1978 and 1983 censuses, the average population growth was 4.2 percent per year for Giciye *commune*.

   5. The person/land ratio is defined as the numer of adult-equivalent persons per hectare.

   6. The average yields of maize and sorghum are projected to remain more or less unchanged until the year 2000.

TABLE 5.2 Calorie production in a region of Rwanda, 1985–2005

	Scenario 1[a]			Scenario 2[b]		
Item	1985	1995	2005	1985	1995	2005
	(index: 1985 = 100)					
Total calorie production (all crops)	100	107	111	100	127	131
Total calorie production per consumer equivalent	100	73	56	100	86	66

SOURCE: von Braun, de Haen, and Blanken 1991.

[a]Projections are based on endogenous changes in labor intensity and cropping patterns, but not on other technological changes.
[b]Projections are similar to scenario 1, but include additional technological changes for beans, peas, potatoes, and sweet potatoes (2.75 percent a year).

percent, with a growth rate of 0.5 percent a year. In scenario 2, the average total calorie production will increase 31 percent by the year 2005. This corresponds to an average increase of 1.4 percent a year. Per consumer and per year calorie availability from own production will drop by 44 percent in scenario 1, and in scenario 2 by 34 percent. Average household self-sufficiency—expressed in terms of percent of own-produced food energy relative to requirements—will decrease from 73.8 percent to 37.9 percent in scenario 1, and to 44.8 percent in scenario 2. The need for imports into the region will thus increase substantially, but whether this need will be backed up by effective demand again depends to a great extent on available agricultural and off-farm employment opportunites as well as on prices and wage-rate development. To create this growth in effective demand, especially in those households that are food deficient at the outset, remains the major challenge for food security policy. Implications for employment are therefore derived from the simulations.

The labor force of the sample population will more than double during 1985–2005 (the index will rise from 100 to 211; see Table 5.3). On the other hand, the agricultural labor input, as derived from model scenario 1, will increase by only 21 percent over the 20-year period (1.0 percent a year). As a result, the potential nonagricultural labor supply will increase during the simulation period by 4.5 percent a year and, consequently, agriculture's share in the total potential labor force will decrease from 23 to 14 percent. Approximately 98 percent of the incremental labor force will need to be employed in nonagricultural work—possibly to some extent in home production, but primarily off farm (Table 5.3).

The conclusion from the simulation is that the study location in Rwanda will rapidly move toward a no-food/no-jobs situation—an untenable position given its high population growth. If not endogenous to these developments, the

TABLE 5.3 On- and off-farm labor allocation and distribution in a region of Rwanda under population pressure, 1985–2005

Item	Per Household, 1985	1985	1995[a]	2005[a]
(person-days/year)		(index: 1985 = 100)		
Agricultural labor input	201	100	112	121
	(0.23)		(0.18)	(0.14)
Labor force[b]	856	100	144	211
	(1.00)		(1.00)	(1.00)
Potential nonagricultural labor supply[c] (per household in 1985, and change for total population thereafter)	655[d]	100	154	239
	(0.77)		(0.82)	(0.86)

SOURCE: von Braun, de Haen, and Blanken 1991

NOTE: Figures in parentheses are the shares of the different labor input categories in the potential labor force capacity.

[a]The 1995 and 2005 figures are the labor supply of the households and their offspring in 1985 sample household averages.
[b]Computed from adult-equivalent persons × 300 days per year.
[c]Including home-goods production, such as beer brewing.
[d]This residual potential nonagricultural labor supply includes actual off-farm employment and unemployment time. On average, 96 days of actual employment per household were recorded in 1985 (66 days in the bottom quartile and 88 in the top quartile).

inherited tensions in the region will find fertile ground for a social explosion (Percival and Homer-Dixon 1995). The population pressure situation in the Great Lakes region had practically no outlet toward urban areas that could absorb rural migrants. In other famine-prone countries, however, the "urban option" played a more significant role among responses to famine. Therefore, the role of population flows in relation to famine and urbanization is addressed in the next section.

Rural-Urban Famine Links

Urbanization, Population Displacement, and Undernutrition

Rapid population growth in Africa is combined with even more rapid urbanization. Rural population pressure triggers food scarcity problems in urban areas. This is part of the link between rural famines and urban effects, which usually manifest in three specific ways: First, rural food crises result in accelerated rural-to-urban migration, only some of which is temporary. This influx has an impact on urban living conditions, including health, sanitation, education, and other services. It also has a poverty impact related to the rapid expansion of labor supply and decreased real wages in urban markets. Second, rural food shortages are not location specific. The price effects of reduced marketed surplus and food scarcity are often felt also in urban areas, the extent of which depends on market integration (as noted in Chapter 6) and on government interventions, such as subsidy and rationing schemes. Third, the national policy response to food scarcity in urban areas tends to be more active in countries where the political influence is concentrated in large cities. The regulation of food flows to those in urban areas with longer-term residence and formal employment tends to shield sections of the urban population from exposure to harsh, short-term adjustments in labor and food markets. However, although this has been true for extended periods of time in Sub-Saharan Africa, the ability of public policy to prevent rural famine from impinging on urban populations has diminished in the 1980s and 1990s due to fiscal restraints and an increase in the number of the urban poor.

Three major forces are spurring the rapid growth of urban populations: natural increase (the difference between births and deaths); rural-urban migration and, to a lesser extent, international migration; and reclassification of rural areas into urban ones. The contribution of rural-urban migration to population growth appears to be much higher in African cities (63, 62, and 59 percent, respectively, in Dar es Salaam, Yaoundé, and Lagos, for example) than in Asian cities (23 and 34 percent in Jakarta and Seoul, for example) (Stren and White 1988).

Africa's rapid urbanization has been taking place in the context of low or even negative economic growth.[7] Rural food crises and famines certainly have played their roles in contributing to this. The impact of slow or negative economic growth is felt severely by low-income, urban households. A large part of their budget is devoted to essential nonfood items, such as fuel and transportation, which limits their ability to meet basic food needs. During periods of economic contraction, there is a high likelihood that incomes of the urban poor will decline disproportionately, and that this decline will then be translated into reduced caloric intake.

Data from 13 African countries suggest that the nutritional status[8] of urban children is generally better than that of rural children (Table 5.4). In almost all of the countries with available data, the proportion of rural preschool children who are malnourished is greater than the respective proportion in

---

7. During the period 1980–89, GDP in Sub-Saharan Africa grew at 2.1 percent annually; industry, which is primarily an urban activity, grew at 0.7 percent annually; and agriculture grew at 2.0 percent annually (World Bank 1991). Annual population growth during this period was 3.2 percent.

8. Acute malnutrition or *wasting* occurs when there is a fairly rapid loss in weight. It is measured by comparing a child's weight relative to that expected for a child of the same height and sex from a reference population. The weight-for-age index thus developed is an indicator of the medium-term nutritional status of a child. Chronic malnutrition or *stunting* occurs over a longer period of time and is measured by comparing the height of a child relative to a population standard for the same age and sex. The height-for-age index thus developed is an indicator of the long-term nutritional status of a child.

TABLE 5.4 Prevalence of malnutrition in African children aged 0–59 months, by rural and urban location

Country	Year	Urban Population Share of Total (1990)	Prevalence of Malnutrition[a]		r/u[b]
			Rural	Urban	
		(percent)	(percent)		
Burundi	1987	25	38.9	20.2	1.9
Côte d'Ivoire	1986	47	13.7	10.3	1.3
Ghana	1987/88	33	31.4	22.8	1.4
Kenya	1978/79	24	n.a.	n.a.	n.a.
Lesotho[c]	1976	20	24.9	18.7	1.3
Madagascar	1983/84	25	36.9	28.4	1.3
Mali	1987	19	33.8	25.7	1.3
Mauritius	1985	42	26.6	20.2	1.3
Morocco	1987	49	19.7	8.0	2.5
Niger	1985	20	53.0	27.4	1.9
Nigeria	1983/84	35	n.a.	n.a.	n.a.
Senegal	1986	38	25.2	15.2	1.7
Sierra Leone[c]	1978	32	32.4	24.3	1.3
Togo	1988	26	27.8	15.9	1.7
Uganda	1988	10	24.3	12.8	1.9
Zimbabwe	1988	28	13.6	5.2	2.6

SOURCE: Derived from Carlson and Wardlaw 1990.

NOTE: n.a. = not available.

[a]Percent of population below -2 standard deviation of weight-for-age from the median of the reference population, unless otherwise indicated.

[b]The r/u ratio is the ratio of the prevalence of rural malnutrition to urban malnutrition. A ratio of 1.0 indicates equality, 1.5 indicates that the rural prevalence is 50 percent higher than the urban, and 0.5 indicates that the rural prevalence is half that of the urban.

[c]Malnutrition defined as population at < 80 percent of weight-for-age reference median.

urban areas. However, urban malnutrition rates are generally given for urban areas as a whole and do not distinguish between children living in slums and shantytowns and those in the more prosperous, middle-class areas. It is likely that malnutrition in many African countries is higher in urban slums than in the average rural area.

Large movements of refugees and internally displaced people (IDPs) are often found in the context of Africa's political and economic crises, and many of the refugees are malnourished or at risk (Table 5.5). Since the mid-1970s, the number of refugees worldwide has doubled approximately every six years, reaching a total of roughly 15 million in 1995; more than one-third of this number is found in Africa (ICRC 1996). In addition, the number of IDPs reached over 38 million in 1995, more than half of whom were African (ICRC 1996). In the mid-1990s the largest flows in Africa included refugees leaving

TABLE 5.5 Nutrition situation of refugees and displaced people in Sub-Saharan Africa, January 1994

Refugee/Displaced Population	High Prevalence of Malnutrition[a]	At High Risk[b]	At Moderate Risk[c]	Not Currently Critical[d]	Condition Unknown[e]	Total
Angola	560,000	1,040,000	1,600,000			3,200,000
Burundi Region	572,000	342,000				914,000
Central African Republic			11,000			11,000
Djibouti				32,000		32,000
East, central, and western Sudan			1,753,000			1,753,000
Ethiopia	45,000			200,000		245,000
Kenya				352,000		352,000
Liberia/Sierra Leone/Guinea/ Côte d'Ivoire	65,000	285,000		2,400,000	150,000	2,900,000
Mauritania/Senegal				60,000		60,000
Mozambique				1,866,000		1,866,000
Rwanda		240,000		330,000		570,000
Shaba, Zaire	33,000		257,000			290,000
Southern Somalia			160,000	1,280,000		1,440,000
Southern Sudan	49,000	100,000	1,821,000			1,970,000
Togo				235,000		235,000
Uganda		94,000		99,000		193,000
Zaire		75,000	87,600	264,000		426,600
Total	1,324,000	2,176,000	5,689,600	7,118,000	150,000	16,457,600

SOURCE: ACC/SN 1994, p. 21.

[a]And/or micronutrient disease and sharply elevated mortality (at least three times normal).
[b]Limited available data; population is likely to contain pockets of malnutrition.
[c]May not be available data; population may contain pockets of malnutrition.
[d]Population is not currently in a critical situation, nor is known to be at particular risk.
[e]Population is known to exist, but the condition is undetermined.

Rwanda for Tanzania and Zaire, Sierra Leoneans leaving for Côte d'Ivoire and Guinea, and hundreds of thousands of Burundians, Liberians, and Rwandese moving within their own borders. These population movements may entail a move into the cities, as in Ethiopia or Sudan, or a move away from cities because of urban violence, as in Liberia.

In many African famines, the distinction between economic and political displacement is blurred. In extreme cases internal conditions are so appalling as to create an overflow of needy people merely seeking basic security elsewhere, as in the case of people fleeing countries with tyrannical regimes. In these situations, the distinction between flight from violence and flight from hunger is, in practice, nonexistent (Zolberg, Suharke, and Aguayo 1989). The mass displacement of poor people therefore should not be considered an exogenous event to which some short-term relief response is the only appropriate action. As with famines, crises and conflicts (and resultant mass migrations) tend to result from longer-term developments (see Chapter 3). Treating them as short-term events focuses on the endpoint only, thereby missing the process leading up to it.

The following section discusses what has happened to urban poverty in the context and aftermath of rural famines, what are the living conditions of famine refugees and displaced people from rural areas when they move into town, and what are their sources of income and survival. Case studies from Sudanese and Ethiopian cities are used to assess the magnitude and nature of the problem.[9] In Chapter 8 experiences with public welfare programs and the recent policy shifts in Addis Ababa, Khartoum, Maputo, and the Republic of Niger are analyzed.

Urban Food and Nutritional Status within the Context of Famine

By 1992, greater Khartoum had a population of approximately 3.8 million. Estimates of the population of Addis Ababa range between 2.1 and 3.2 million (the 1993 official estimate shows a total population of 2.2 million). Official estimates for African urban population growth averaged 5 to 6 percent in the 1970s and 1980s, largely due to the influx of people from rural regions (particularly areas affected by war, drought, and famine). The rapid influx of refugees in 1992 and 1993 resulted in a much higher population growth rate in Addis Ababa in the 1990s.

---

9. The Sudanese study draws heavily on a 1990 survey of 1,100 households in Khartoum and surrounding areas (Abdou et al. 1991). The survey covered 440 households from three income-differentiated residential areas within Khartoum proper, and 660 households from the displaced camps on the outskirts of Khartoum. In addition, the data from 1986 and 1987 national surveys of child nutritional status are used to identify and establish determinants of child malnutrition in urban areas. The Ethiopian study draws largely from the 1990/91 survey of 1,688 households in the Addis Ababa metropolitan area. As with the Sudanese survey, the Ethiopian sample was drawn from areas that represented the city center and peripheral settlements, stratified by population density.

An income survey in Addis Ababa during 1990/91 (Gebre 1993) showed that at least 53 percent of the sample households were in the category of "urban poor." That is, no less than 53 percent of urban households in Addis Ababa could not afford to buy the minimum food and nonfood subsistence basket for 1992. The 1990/91 survey did not reflect developments since 1991, which have contributed to an increase in the numbers of those living in absolute poverty. These developments include new additions to the ranks of the underemployed due to the demobilization of about 326,000 soldiers, the displacement of 592,000 people from war-affected regions and areas in ethnic conflict, and the policy of reducing the number of civil service employees under the guise of economic reform. Given the already high underemployment in Addis Ababa, the limited private sector, and no access to formal pension funds, these recently unemployed constitute a class of "new poor." Rising food prices and the cost of other necessities further erode the purchasing power of already meager incomes. The occupational distribution of the Addis Ababa survey shows that 37.5 percent of household heads were employed either in government or private organizations. Among the self-employed, about 40 percent were engaged in low-income retail activities—selling *tella, kollo,* and *enjera* (local beverage and food items); newspapers; lottery tickets; and so forth. The bulk of these households was concentrated in low-income residential areas. And as poverty became worse, parents started requiring children to supplement their families' income: in the mid-1990s, a large number of children eked out a living in the streets of Addis Ababa begging, shoe shining, and selling all sorts of things.

An estimate of the poor in urban Sudan is based on scanty evidence. Farah and Sampath (1993) show an increase in urban poverty prior to the 1980s Sudanese famines; the famines themselves aggravated an already growing problem. The inflationary environment rendered the minimum wage inadequate for low-income urban workers to make a living. The problem of poverty was further aggravated among drought and war victims, particularly the displaced who moved to the fringes of towns and became highly vulnerable to food price increases and declines in real wages.

In the case of Khartoum, adjusting to an urban environment was very difficult for displaced families. The majority of the migrants were young families with large numbers of dependents. They had limited skills to cope with the nonagricultural labor market and services sector and, hence, faced a high rate of underemployment, as shown in a 1990 survey by Abdou et al. (1991). For the adult men who migrated from the nomadic areas, the high-paying jobs were found in the major Omdurman livestock market as brokers, guards, and animal herders. Women, young boys, and girls were often sent to work as house servants. Some also became "self-employed," selling tea, coffee, or traditional food. Others engaged in illegal activities such as theft, or brewing local beer or other alcoholic drinks. The resident poor within the towns followed similar income-supplementing strategies. Compared to the

TABLE 5.6 Sources of calorie and protein availability by type of residence and income level in Khartoum, 1990

	Calorie Availability				Protein Availability			
	Recent Migrant Familes from Kordofan		Resident Urban Families, Income		Recent Migrant Families from Kordofan		Resident Urban Families, Income	
Food Source	North	South	Low	High	North	South	Low	High
	(percent)							
Cereals	68.2	66.5	63.2	42.3	69.3	67.1	61.0	36.3
Meat, fish, eggs	5.1	6.6	7.3	12.4	11.8	19.1	16.7	29.6
Milk and milk products	2.8	1.7	3.5	6.1	4.7	3.0	5.7	12.3
Pulses	2.7	1.5	4.1	6.6	7.1	3.6	9.4	13.6
Sugar and honey	1.3	1.5	5.2	8.5	neg	neg	0.1	0.1
Vegetable oils	11.9	19.6	10.8	16.4	0.0	0.0	0.0	0.0
Vegetables and fruits	8.0	2.6	6.0	7.7	7.1	7.2	7.1	8.1

SOURCE: Abdou et al. 1991.

NOTE: neg = a negligible amount (less than 0.05).

temporary migrants, however, constraints were less tight on residents because of better access to jobs in factories, ownership of property such as housing, and better access to the public food distribution system.

A 1990 survey of urban households in Khartoum reveals that food accounts for a large share of total household outlays. Differences between migrant and resident families were notable in the types of cereal crops and animal products consumed. The migrant families largely consumed sorghum (millet as much as sorghum by migrants from North Kordofan), while the residents consumed more wheat and wheat products—the major subsidized foodgrain.

There is no evidence to suggest a change in consumption patterns of the migrant families from their traditional staples to the subsidized wheat cereal (Kibreab 1995). The low share of wheat in the diets of the migrant families presumably reflected the high cost of access to the official distribution of wheat. Anemia of various types was noticed among all groups. Intake of vitamin A was far below the requirements. Cereals represented a major source of energy and protein consumption across all income groups (Table 5.6).

There were some striking differences found in spending patterns between the migrant and the resident families. The migrant families mostly lived in simple, low-cost dwellings (huts made from sacks and cartons). Educational expenses were also low among the migrants. Limited access to schools and the need to have children work to supplement the family income contributed to low investment in human capital. Transport also accounted for a large share of their expenditures. Commuting costs for migrant families from their residence to the city center was substantial in proportion to their income level. A relatively high share of water costs in the migrant camps was an indication of water shortage in the outer areas of town, where migrants stayed and where a piped water supply was absent. Water was often purchased from water carriers by the bucket (Abdou et al. 1991).

According to a 1986–87 nationwide Sudanese nutrition survey, the prevalence of undernutrition was less for urban children compared to those from nomadic and sedentary rural families (Teklu, von Braun, and Zaki 1991). The relatively lower prevalence of undernutrition in urban areas should not be interpreted as there being no problem. It is largely a result of averaging quantifiers of undernutrition in medium- and high-income households with those found in poor households (where undernutrition is as prevalent as in poor rural households). The averages are thus misleading.

More detailed analyses of these individual and household data suggest that the education of parents helps to improve household nutritional status (because of higher income and a greater efficiency in the choice and preparation of food), particularly in the long term (Teklu, von Braun, and Zaki 1991). Also, regional and local price differences have a noted impact on nutritional outcomes in urban areas. Seasonality, meaning seasonal price, income, and health-related changes—typically considered a rural phenomenon—impacts also on the nutrition of poor urban communities.

Conclusions Concerning Population Pressure and Urban Change as Famine Causes and Consequences

The consequences of famines are increasingly spilling over into urban areas; urbanization rates in Africa increased quickly when the mass movement of people into cities was not prevented. Past famines have accelerated urban food and health crises because of the large flows of rural famine refugees and displaced people into urban areas. These problems need to be considered when designing new approaches to famine mitigation and prevention. In doing so, however, public policymaking must not lose sight of the root causes of famine, as well as the potential for sustainable famine prevention through rural economic growth, as evidenced by the Rwandan experiences.

Short-term improvements in the food security of displaced people in urban areas are merely a necessary treatment of the symptoms, not a cure. The costs of resources spent on urban programs must be compared with the potential for employment and growth stimulation in rural areas. One cannot, however, prescribe a policy that disregards famine refugees in urban areas. A balanced approach requires targeted public action, that is, programs that focus on the health and education of children of (famine) refugees, as well as those that provide incentives for voluntary relocation to rural areas. The long-term trends in the Rwandan case stress that rural crises usually evolve into a "no-food" situation, which is in large part a "no-rural-jobs" situation. What rural famine refugees bring to town is mainly labor. The two countries studied here as a basis for analysis of the urban famine consequences have not managed, so far, to address the employment problem effectively. These and other policy implications are discussed further in Chapter 8.

6 Market Success and Market Failure

In this chapter market and price effects in actual famine situations in Africa are discussed. It is of central importance for government policymakers to have a comprehensive understanding of the functioning of markets during food shortages. Understanding market relationships in famines can provide a key input into creating suitable policies for interregional trade, stockholding, and imports (including food aid). It also provides insights into the question of the relative merit of "free-market" versus "state-controlled" economies during times of economic stress. The latter remains a crucial and still much-debated policy issue in many famine-prone countries. It was a common debate during the nineteenth-century famines in Ireland and India, as well as within the context of this century's famines in Asia (Sen 1981; Ravallion 1987a; Drèze and Sen 1991).

Some of the drought-production relationships discussed in Chapter 4 have obvious price and market effects. Other price effects are not so obvious. Among the more apparent ones are the demand within drought-affected regions for market access to food from outside the region, and the interregional spreading of related price effects. Less obvious are factor price and capital goods price effects. Drought, for instance, reduces the demand for labor in agriculture and thus reduces returns to human time and real wages. The attempt to maintain an access to food at acceptable levels enforces distress sales of assets by the poor, which drives down asset prices. The amount of the asset base held by the poor will determine the relative outcome of those linkages.

At an aggregate level, the demand for food imports increases when food is locally scarce, which may raise exchange rates and further decrease the availability of import-dependent inputs. This can result in potentially depressing economy-wide effects as well as inflation. Food scarcity thus impinges on both local and national prices. It is these price and price-ratio changes (for example, between "low-value" food and "high-value" agricultural commodities; food and labor; food and capital goods) that determine outcomes within different population groups.

Market behavior and market outcomes are a function of upstream factors, such as policy failure or climate shocks (see Chapter 2). The literature on market behavior during famines in Africa remains limited, compared with the pioneering work done in Asia and particularly in Bangladesh. (Sen 1981; Ravallion 1987a). The following discussion therefore includes an assessment of policies and government interventions in Africa, focusing on price policies and underlying factors contributing to them. Ethiopia and Sudan represent different cases of government intervention in food markets; Ethiopia adopted a policy of detailed public management of cereal markets in the 1980s, whereas Sudan's policies were more general in scope.

The main elements of price development relate to the evolution of absolute and relative price movements, and regional price distribution. Shifts in the relative prices between cereals and nonfood cash crops and between cereals and livestock are important indicators of purchasing power erosion during food shortages. The pattern of price seasonality, which typically follows local production seasonality, may change during a period of drought, giving rise to a different timing of sales and to unexpected price changes. The extent to which deviations from normal patterns occur indicates the potential role of other sources of supply—imports, stocks, and food aid—in smoothing intrayear variations. Differences in interregional price variations hint at the key role of better market integration through improved rural infrastructure and market policies. The main objective at the present is to assess whether regional and local food shortages are alleviated by price changes across regions (as food flows toward regions of scarcity). Disconnected markets require public action. However, government policy can equally become a cause of market disruption, as illustrated by the Ethiopian example below. In either case, price and market information are fundamental to the analysis of vulnerability to and indicators of famine.

Prices during Famines

An evaluation of cereal price developments during the 1980s shows a dramatic increase in both the nominal and real (deflated) price of cereals in response to the production failure in both Ethiopia and Sudan. The national price index for cereals in Ethiopia, computed as the weighted average across all provinces, increased from 100 in 1981 to over 220 in 1985.[1] It rose again, though not nearly as sharply, in 1988 (Figure 6.1). Cereal prices in Sudan also rose steadily in the early 1980s, peaked in 1984, and then dropped in the 1985 and 1986 seasons. Between 1982/83 and 1984, cereal prices increased three-

---

1. The overall Ethiopian cereals price index is a weighted sum of prices for all 14 administrative regions. The regional prices are themselves weighted according to the relative production shares of individual cereals in each region. US$1.00 = 2.05 Ethiopian birr.

FIGURE 6.1 Ethiopian cereal price index during the 1980s famine

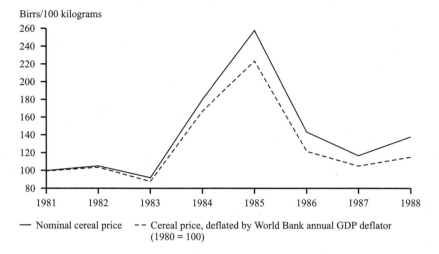

Birrs/100 kilograms

— Nominal cereal price   -- Cereal price, deflated by World Bank annual GDP deflator
(1980 = 100)

SOURCE: Computations based on data from Ethiopian-RRC.

NOTE: GDP = gross domestic product.

FIGURE 6.2 Sudanese cereal price index, 1970s and during the 1980s famine

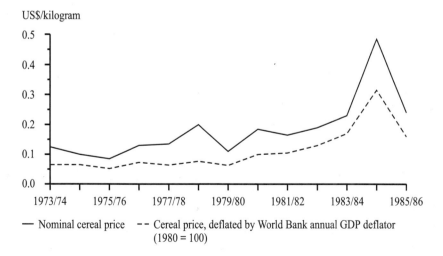

US$/kilogram

— Nominal cereal price   -- Cereal price, deflated by World Bank annual GDP deflator
(1980 = 100)

SOURCE: Computed from price series data compiled from various publications of Sudan-Ministry of Agriculture and Natural Resources, Department of Agricultural Economics.

NOTE: GDP = gross domestic product.

fold. The real price in the 1985/86 season was that prevailing in the 1970s (Figure 6.2). In Sudan, prices increased rapidly in the months preceding the 1984 harvest. The nominal price of sorghum in El Obeid, for example, increased by 320 percent between January and October 1984, reaching an amount nearly five times that of a year earlier. Cereal prices continued to increase and stayed high until the harvest of 1985. By the end of the 1985 harvest, however, prices had dropped to as low as 30 percent of the 1984 average.

For farm households that grow cash crops or raise livestock, purchasing power is largely determined by the terms of trade between food and the households' farm produce for the market. Although cash crops usually provide a reasonably reliable income source for farmers in normal years, their contribution to real income in food-crisis years, such as 1984–85, rapidly deteriorates. For example, the terms-of-trade index between sesame and sorghum in parts of Sudan fell from 0.73 to 0.32 between 1974–78 and 1984. This means that the same amount of sesame bought less than half (44 percent) as much sorghum in 1984–85 as in the 1974–78 period. The deterioration was similar for groundnuts. In Kordofan the price of groundnuts in terms of sorghum dropped from 1.1 in 1974–78 to 0.54 in 1984—that is, the same amount of groundnuts bought only half as much sorghum in the drought year of 1984.

A similar pattern emerged in the case of livestock. Livestock prices dropped significantly in 1984 in both Ethiopia and Sudan, particularly in months that coincided with the peak rise in cereal prices. In Sudan the price of cattle relative to sorghum deteriorated from the mid-1970s until 1985, when there was a turnaround (Table 6.1). In 1984, livestock herders could buy only about one-tenth of the sorghum per head of cattle that they could in 1979. In

TABLE 6.1 Terms of trade between livestock and sorghum as a ratio of price indexes in Sudan, 1974–85

Period	Central/Eastern Regions		Kordofan Region		Darfur Region	
	Cattle/ Sorghum	Goat/ Sorghum	Cattle/ Sorghum	Goat/ Sorghum	Cattle/ Sorghum	Goat/ Sorghum
	(price index: 1979 = 1.00)					
1974–78	0.63	0.96	0.47	0.61	0.85	0.93
1980–81	0.60	0.63	0.46	0.55	0.51	0.60
1982–83	0.32	n.a.	0.31	0.47	0.37	0.47
1984	0.12	0.14	0.09	0.17	0.11	n.a.
1985	0.68	0.67	1.06	1.02	1.39	n.a.

SOURCES: Sudan-MANR 1985b, 1987a, and 1988.

NOTE: n.a. = not available.

FIGURE 6.3 Terms of trade between food, livestock, and firewood in Dessie, Wollo region (Ethiopia), during the 1982–87 famine

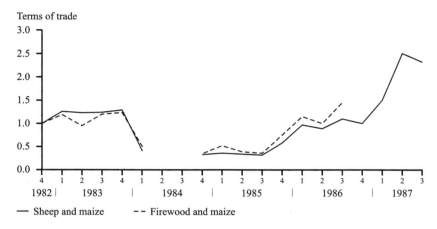

SOURCE: Ethiopia-CSA various years.

NOTE: Breaks indicate that no data are available for that period.

other words, herders had to provide about 8 to 10 times more cattle to acquire the same amount of sorghum in 1984 as in 1979. This situation applied to central Sudan as well as to the Kordofan and Darfur regions.

In Ethiopia, the protracted drought of the early 1980s also meant mass sales of livestock, which translated into a saturation of the market leading to a decline in the value of livestock relative to cereal prices. Figure 6.3 shows an example of this process from the Wollo region. The value of livestock (sheep) against the market price for maize fell by almost 75 percent from December 1982 to December 1984. However, it then returned to prefamine values by the end of 1986, only to climb to more than twice its 1982 value during 1987—the time when demand for livestock rose as part of the rebuilding of the post-drought economy. Similarly, the terms of trade between firewood and maize mirrored that between sheep and maize in Ethiopia (see Figure 6.3). Demand for firewood dropped during the crisis (because income was saved for food items), causing the price of wood to fall when the price of maize was rising. Firewood recaptured its position in 1986 and continued to grow in value in 1987 (possibly because many trees did not survive the prolonged drought of the mid-1980s or because of excessive wood cutting, or both).

The patterns of these price movements remained the same even when deflated to account for changes in general prices. It is evident that 1984, which witnessed large increases in cereal prices, was also a year of increases greater than general price trends of 1983. The increasing trends in general prices suggest that real commodity prices were lower than nominal prices, but followed a path similar to the movement of nominal prices. In sum, famine events in Africa were associated with large price movements. There seems to have been, at least in the short term, some flexibility for price stabilization through trade, aid, and stockholding.

Price Explosions Linked to Disrupted Production

Adjustments in stockholdings and trade permit a considerable degree of price stabilization during drought. The key questions are (1) the degree to which production fluctuations—which were determined to be very much influenced by the drought events above—result in price fluctuations, and (2) the extent to which trade (including food assistance) and stockholding is able to even out the fluctuations. The price formation process is certainly complex and, in principle, requires a simultaneous look at the supply and demand sides. Price is derived from the equilibrium condition as

$$CERS_t = CERD_t + \Delta STOCK_t, \tag{6.1}$$

where

$CERS_t$ = total supply of cereals per capita from domestic production ($CERP_t$), net imports (IMP_t), and food aid ($FAID_t$) in year t,

$CERD_t$ = consumption demand per capita in period t, and

$\Delta STOCK_t$ = change in stock of cereals per capita in period t.

The focus here is on explaining short-term price flexibility, particularly how much net supply of cereal availability ($CERS_t$ as defined in equation [6.1]) and initial stock ($STOCK_{t-1}$) influence price variability, taking the previous year's price as some indicator of expectations:

$$PICER_t = f(CERS_t, STOCK_{t-1}, PICER_{t-1}). \tag{6.2}$$

The effect of domestic production alone ($CERP_t$) can be tested on price fluctuations by excluding the import and aid components from equation (6.2); that is, setting the index of cereal price ($PICER_t$) as a function of current production per capita and the previous-year cereal stocks per capita:

$$PICER_t = f(CERP_t, STOCK_{t-1}, PICER_{t-1}). \tag{6.3}$$

The same model estimation exercise is then repeated for the cereal-livestock terms of trade ($CLTOT_t$) as:

$$CLTOT_t = f(CERS_t, STOCK_{t-1}, PICER_{t-1}) \tag{6.4}$$

and

$$CLTOT_t = f(CERP_t, STOCK_{t-1}, PICER_{t-1}). \tag{6.5}$$

TABLE 6.2 Determinants of price flexibility and domestic terms-of-trade flexibility in Sudan, 1973–88

Dependent Variable[a]	$CERP_t$	$CERS_t$	$STOCK_{t-1}$	Lag-Dep	Constant	R^2	F	Ljung-Box (16)[b]	χ^2 (.95)
(6.2) PICER		−3.314 (−4.03)	−4.33 (−2.44)	0.520 (2.63)	667.88 (4.32)	0.55	7.18	13.56	23.69
(6.3) PICER	−2.653 (−5.18)		−3.43 (−2.48)	0.235 (1.39)	563.00 (5.40)	0.67	11.35	19.82	23.70
(6.4) CLTOT	. . .	−0.026 (−5.68)	−0.044 (−4.58)	0.139 (0.92)	6.33 (7.36)	0.68	11.69	13.49	23.69
(6.5) CLTOT	−0.020 (−9.48)		−0.033 (−5.87)	−0.048 (−0.51)	5.17 (12.18)	0.86	32.12	12.32	23.70

SOURCE: Adapted (modified reestimation) from Teklu, von Braun, and Zaki 1991.

NOTES: *t*-values are given in parentheses.

Variables:

$CERP_t$ = cereal production per capita, in kilograms,

$CERS_t$ = total supply of cereals per capita from production, imports, net of exports, and food aid,

$STOCK_{t-1}$ = level of cereal stocks per capita at end of year $t-1$, or beginning-year stocks, in kilograms,

Lag-Dep = lagged dependent variable $(t-1)$,

PICER = Sudanese cereal price index (deflated, production-weighted mean of regional prices), and

CLTOT = cereal-livestock terms of trade.

[a]Figures in parentheses correspond to equation numbers in text.

[b]Ljung-Box statistics show that residuals are white noise for all of the models (Greene 1990).

The models hypothesize that the real price index of cereals increases with a drop in domestic cereal production in the same year, but decreases when the last year's ending stocks or current year's opening stocks, respectively, are increased. Similarly, it is hypothesized that the terms of trade between cereals and livestock commodities are largely driven by the same set of hypotheses. The determinants of the cereal-livestock terms of trade may, in fact, be even more complex than the determinants of cereals' real price development, because of the complex interactions between cereal markets and livestock markets, the differential effects of drought on cereal and livestock supply (distress sales of livestock drive prices down), and the adverse effects of increased cereal prices on the demand for livestock commodities by households. The results with respect to stocks must be treated with caution since those data are notoriously incomplete.

The parameter estimates and estimation results using Sudanese data are presented in Table 6.2. Price fluctuations are driven mainly by production fluctuations. The respective parameters estimated for *CERS* (total supply, including trade and food aid) change little in Sudan if production only is substituted (compare the *CERP* and *CERS* parameters in Table 6.2). With the help of the estimated parameters, the effects of a decrease in production of 10 percent, as well as a similar decrease in stocks, were derived for the cereal price and for the terms of trade. The results suggest that a drop of 10 percent in cereal production per capita raises cereal prices by 25 percent (Table 6.3). With a 10 percent drop in production, the order of magnitude is similar for the cereal-livestock terms of trade: they will increase by 19 percent (see Table 6.3). Holding other things constant, a decrease of 10 percent in cereal stocks would raise both prices and the terms of trade by 6 percent.

Results derived from a similar study of Ethiopia's production-price linkages point in the same direction. For example, the results from the regression computation suggest that a 10 percent decline in per capita cereal production would result in a 14 percent increase in price (Webb, von Braun, and Yohannes

TABLE 6.3 Effects of production and stock changes on cereal prices and cereal-livestock terms of trade in Sudan, 1973–88

Dependent Variable	10 Percent Decline in Production	10 Percent Decline in Stock
	(percent change)	
Cereal price	+ 24.9	+ 6.3
Cereal-livestock terms of trade	+ 18.7	+ 5.7

SOURCE: Computed from mean values of variables and parameters in Table 6.2, equations (6.3) and (6.5).

1992). This, however, is substantially lower than in Sudan, where a 25 percent increase was estimated. The main conclusion from this analysis is that as a drop in national production tends to lead to a large price increase in the short term, policies for production stabilization, stockholding, and facilitation of inter-regional trade are of critical importance. It may be most difficult to increase short- and medium-term stability in cereal production, given the dominance of the rainfed sector in this production in both countries. A new look at optimum storage levels, investing in rural infrastructure for interregional trade, and stabilization through international trade in cereals is warranted (Pinckney 1989). Research into the benefits resulting from these policies could have a high payoff.

Market (Dis)connection and (Dis)integration During Famines

Price increases during famines typically vary across regions within the affected country. For example Ethiopian data show that, between 1984 and 1989, the nominal price of the important traditional cereal—teff—was generally more than 100 percent greater in Dessie (the capital of food-deficit Wollo) than in Debre Markos (the capital market of Gojjam), a surplus-producing region enjoying stable production. During the 1984/85 famine, the Dessie teff price reached three times that of the Debre Markos teff price. While the picture is less clear for wheat and sorghum, similar differences in absolute prices were observed between the regions.

On the one hand, crop prices have been consistently higher in Dessie than in Debre Markos, with the price gap increasing during the major crises of 1984/85 and 1988. On the other hand, Dessie crop prices are lower than those of Nazret (the major market center of Shewa), except during times of crisis, when Dessie prices temporarily leap above those of Nazret.

There were also consistent differences in absolute prices for the major cereals within regions. Figure 6.4 illustrates that, despite similar price movements for teff across markets in Wollo during 1984–89, the prices in Mekane Selam were 100 percent more than Dessie prices in September of 1984. As expected, subregional markets were more closely integrated in surplus regions, such as Gojjam (Webb, von Braun, and Yohannes 1992). Nevertheless, while absolute prices were usually different between regions, the general pattern of price movements was similar in all regions during years of scarcity. A simple correlation matrix of regional aggregate cereal prices for Ethiopia—not presented here—shows that the great majority of markets correlate very closely, even if quite distant from, each other (Webb, von Braun, and Yohannes 1992). In only 27 out of a total of 91 correlations is the coefficient less than 0.65, and only 3 correlations are not highly significant. Similarly, Figure 6.5 compares the Sudanese total price index for cereals (computed as a weighted average using production shares by region as weights for prevailing prices) with local

FIGURE 6.4 Teff price variability in three main markets of the Wollo region (Ethiopia), 1984–89

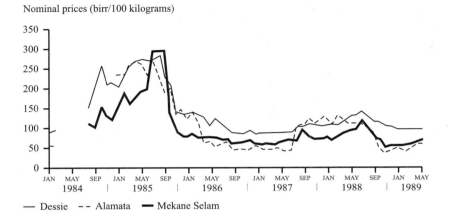

Nominal prices (birr/100 kilograms)

— Dessie   – – Alamata   ▬ Mekane Selam

SOURCE: Computed from price series data provided by the Ethiopia-Relief and Rehabilitation Commission, Addis Ababa.

NOTE: US$1.00 = 2.05 Ethiopian birr; breaks indicate that no data are available for that period.

FIGURE 6.5 Price indexes for sorghum, millet, and cereal during famines in Sudanese regions, 1973/74–1985/86

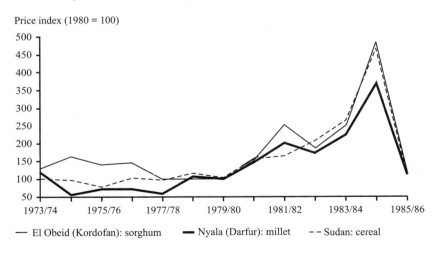

Price index (1980 = 100)

— El Obeid (Kordofan): sorghum   ▬ Nyala (Darfur): millet   – – Sudan: cereal

SOURCES: Computed from price series data compiled from Sudan-MANR 1985b, 1986, and 1987b.

price developments in Kordofan and Darfur. Although relative differences prevailed between regions when prices were not excessively high in the 1970s, the general price movement in 1984–85 was spread throughout the country.

Can we conclude from these patterns that the markets were highly integrated? This, in fact, cannot be concluded from simple correlations. If drought hit everywhere at once, one would observe a high correlation of prices even if markets were not integrated. Other factors may very well be at play, which may lead to price correlation without market integration. Still it is noteworthy that prices did move together in Ethiopia despite (or because of) heavy government interference in cereal markets, and despite poor infrastructure. One may derive a measure of the degree of integration (or lack thereof) between markets by using a statistical model. A model based on the work of Ravallion (1986) is applied to examine some elements of market integration in Ethiopia and Sudan during times of famine. The structure of the model is specified as

$$P_1 = f_1(P_2, P_3, \ldots, P_n, X_1) \tag{6.6}$$

and

$$P_1 = f_1(P_1, X_1), \tag{6.7}$$

where $i = 2, \ldots, n$ and where a central market price (P_1) is influenced by various local market prices (P_i) and market-conditioning factors specific to a central market (X_1). The local prices (P_i) are a function of central market price and a set of other influences (seasonality, drought) on local prices (X_i).

The dynamic structure of the model derived from the above (static) concept is defined as

$$P_{it} = \sum_{j=1}^{n} \alpha_{ij} P_{it-j} + \sum_{j=0}^{m} \beta_{ij} P_{it-j} + \gamma_i X_{it} + U_{it}, \tag{6.8}$$

where P_{it} and P_{1t} are the local and central market prices, respectively, and U_{it} is the error term. The empirical analysis below uses monthly prices.

Examination of the regional markets in Ethiopia and Sudan suggests that markets are directly linked with the central market in a "radial" configuration. That is, prices in each regional market are related to their own past values as well as current and past values of the central market price. An initial test for the order of integration shows that a one-period lag is sufficient for all price series to be stationary.

The specific equation chosen for estimation is

$$P_{it} = \alpha_{it} P_{it-1} + \beta_{io} P_{1t} + \beta_{i1} P_{1t-1} + \gamma_i X_{it} + U_{it}, \tag{6.9}$$

where α_{it} measures the effect of the one-period-lagged local market price on current local prices; β_0 and β_{i1} measure, respectively, the effect of current and one-period-lagged prices in the central market on local prices; and γ measures the effects of location-specific factors (X).

It is plausible that markets exhibit marked long-term price relationships. Following the work of Ravallion (1986), the hypothesis of long-term integration as tested by imposing a restriction as

$$\sum_{j=1}^{n}\alpha_{ij} + \sum_{j=0}^{m}\beta_{ij} = 1. \qquad (6.10)$$

Where long-term integration is accepted, equation (6.8) was reestimated by imposing the parameter restriction specified in equation (6.10). Then, the weak-form, short-run market integration was tested to see if, on average, the lagged effects of local and central market prices vanish:

$$\sum_{j=1}^{n}\alpha_{ij} + \sum_{j=0}^{m}\beta_{ij} = 0. \qquad (6.11)$$

In order to test the extent of integration in Sudan's sorghum and cattle markets, four principal regional markets were selected: El Obeid in the Kordofan region, Gedaref in the eastern region, Nyala in the Darfur region, and Omdurman in the central region. Omdurman is the main terminal market for cattle. Large supplies of cattle come from the western regions through the El Obeid and Nyala markets. Gedaref is both the main producer and the main market for sorghum. Even though the El Obeid market is largely supplied by the surrounding areas (particularly southern Kordofan), there is sizable competition for trading between the regions. A choice of one month as a time interval was considered a reasonable span for the flow of information and commodities in Sudan's case. All the variables are in logarithms. The parameter estimates of equation (6.9) are given in Table 6.4. The statistical significance of the β_{i0} and β_{i1} coefficients suggests that commodity markets are not segmented. In fact, the high β_{i0} coefficients for sorghum and for Nyala/Omdurman cattle show that the regional markets in the west have a strong long-term integration (see parameters for P_{1t-1}) with the principal markets in the central and eastern regions. In the short term, the cattle markets of Nyala and Omdurman do not appear integrated. The significance of the dummy variables for the 1984–85 months suggests substantive price movements for cattle markets, but not for cereals, over and above the general intermarket relations, during the famine period.

Traders have a well-functioning information network for following price developments in distant regional markets. Such information is not, however, complemented by strong connections in the short term. All the short-term integration tests show that none of the markets as connected for that period.[2] The connections were particularly poor for cattle markets.

---

2. Similarly, Timmer's (1974) index of market integration (IMI) ratios are greater than 1 for all markets, both in Ethiopia and Sudan.

TABLE 6.4 Regression coefficients for tests of Sudanese regional market integration during the 1980s famine

Commodity	Regional Market	Independent Variables				Constant	F	Ljung-Box
		P_{it-1}	P_{1t}	P_{1t-1}	D85			
Sorghum (feterita)	El Obeid[a]	0.612	0.707	−0.283	−0.032	−0.044	1,149.61	9.80
		(7.545)	(8.781)	(−2.715)	(−0.864)	(−0.660)		
Cattle	El Obeid[b]	0.772	0.231	−0.009	0.126	−0.160	1,586.69	25.77
		(11.426)	(3.739)	(−0.139)	(2.297)	(−1.601)		
	Nyala[b]	0.756	0.007	0.232	0.205	−0.251	771.48	5.04[c]
		(10.756)	(0.078)	(2.677)	(2.612)	(−1.692)		

SOURCE: Based on data files of Sudan, Ministry of Agriculture and Natural Resources, Department of Agricultural Economics, Marketing Section, Khartoum.

NOTES: The nonsignificance of Ljung-Box statistics indicates that residuals are white noise; t-values are given in parentheses; P_{it} = monthly wholesale price in market i in period t; and P_{1t} = reference market monthly wholesale price in period t.

[a]Reference market used was Gedaref.
[b]Reference market used was Omdurman.
[c]Ljung-Box statistics are significant for lags 1–6.

A similar model was applied to a deseasonalized series of local monthly prices for Ethiopia covering the period of famine in the mid-1980s (August 1984–October 1989). The analysis was conducted for six of the most important provincial markets compared to a reference market—Nazret in Shewa. While Nazret may not be the single most dominant central market for Ethiopia as a whole, its proximity to Addis Ababa allows its use here as an approximation of a central market situation.

The analysis was performed for three separate commodities: maize, teff, and an aggregate of cereals, where the latter was represented by an unweighted, compounded price index for major cereals by region (where applicable, barley, maize, sorghum, teff, and wheat). The model analysis of market integration sheds light on past relationships between markets (see Table 6.4). As discussed earlier, β_{i0} in equation (6.9) may reflect market segmentation when the parameter is insignificant.

Mixed market integration patterns were seen in Ethiopia during the famine years of the 1980s. In four of the six markets in the analysis for maize prices, the central market price is not significantly influencing local prices. The same is true for one out of four markets for teff, and for four out of eight markets for the aggregate of cereals price index this is found, too (Table 6.5). Thus segmentation was prevalent in many food markets in Ethiopia during the famine years. Infrastructure played a role here. Looking at the eight markets where the aggregate cereals price changes were analyzed in relation to the central market reveals that the distance of the first group of markets—the four segmented ones—from the central market ranges from 264 to 700 kilometers (average 461 kilometers), whereas it is between 76 and 357 kilometers for the second group (average 253 kilometers). Of course, distance alone does not influence communication flow between markets. However, many regional markets appear to have responded to price changes in the central market—even during the famine period—despite substantial government intervention.

Infrastructure and Government as Causes of Market Malfunction

The results so far confirm that regional markets transmit price signals to a widely varying degree. This holds true both in drought years (as in 1984–85), as well as in nondrought years. However, the extent to which commodities flow in response to price signals is unclear. Because of high market-transaction costs, such poor connections preclude markets from trading at efficient prices. Transportation alone accounts for, on average, 10–15 percent of consumer prices in Sudan. Ahmed and Rustagi (1987) also conclude, on the basis of their survey of African countries, that the share of transport in total marketing cost varies from 35 to 50 percent. Moreover they point out that the absolute transport cost in marketing is about twice as high in Africa as in Asia. This cost is

TABLE 6.5 Analysis of a market integration model on the Ethiopian famine, 1984–89

Commodity	Provincial Market[a]	Independent Variables				F	Ljung-Box
		P_{it-1}	P_{1t}	P_{1t-1}	Constant		
Cereals	Asela	0.527	0.612	-0.185	0.210	118.73	21.316
		(4.340)	(4.160)	(-1.161)	(0.891)		
	Awasa	0.670	0.346	-0.089	0.386	116.85	15.539[a]
		(6.364)	(2.631)	(-0.654)	(1.628)		
	Dessie	0.921	0.427	-0.406	0.235	187.02	20.873
		(12.253)	(2.524)	(-2.614)	(0.899)		
	Dire Dawa	0.683	0.199	0.001	0.575	99.156	17.304
		(6.254)	(1.614)	(0.005)	(2.201)		
	Gondar	0.715	0.218	-0.095	0.918	48.65	16.330
		(8.113)	(1.640)	(-0.697)	(2.527)		
	Harer	0.679	0.273	-0.016	0.218	227.10	22.359
		(7.566)	(2.967)	(-0.155)	(1.353)		
	Jimma	0.805	0.177	0.072	0.481	42.50	14.393
		(10.329)	(0.724)	(0.788)	(1.093)		
	Nekempte	0.796	0.240	-0.083	0.144	92.19	16.040
		(8.518)	(1.221)	(-0.436)	(0.474)		

Maize	Asela	0.360	0.288	0.215	0.215	46.22	21.968
		(2.793)	(1.474)	(1.115)	(0.715)		
	Awasa	0.809	0.255	−0.150	0.285	85.39	15.710
		(9.245)	(1.805)	(−1.079)	(1.233)		
	Debre Markos	0.615	0.334	−0.159	0.770	47.99	17.011
		(6.474)	(2.751)	(−1.222)	(2.835)		
	Gondar	0.648	0.187	−0.091	1.070	27.59	16.714
		(6.278)	(1.482)	(−0.726)	(2.974)		
	Jimma	0.825	−0.012	0.094	0.300	54.38	15.106
		(11.130)	(−0.056)	(0.447)	(0.848)		
	Nekempte	0.869	0.190	−0.143	0.310	97.91	9.069
		(10.656)	(1.141)	(−0.885)	(1.230)		
Teff	Awassa	0.475	0.471	0.063	−0.105	110.81	19.943
		(4.205)	(3.338)	(0.383)	(−0.387)		
	Debre Markos	0.630	0.059	0.212	0.231	56.32	8.103
		(7.327)	(0.403)	(1.328)	(0.740)		
	Dessie	0.677	0.551	−0.116	−0.506	128.30	13.278
		(6.074)	(2.745)	(−0.575)	(−1.217)		
	Gondar	0.777	0.370	−0.222	0.337	77.17	22.909
		(10.170)	(3.192)	(−1.767)	(1.178)		

SOURCE: Computed from price series data obtained from Ethopia RRC 1990.

NOTES: The nonsignificance of Ljung-Box statistics indicates that residuals are white noise; t-values are given in parentheses; P_{it} = monthly wholesale price in market i in period t; and P_{1t} = reference market monthly wholesale price in period t.

[a]Reference market used for all analyses was Nazret.

largely associated with poorly designed road networks, which is also evident from the comparison of transport shares in the sample of eastern and western Sudanese market areas in the present study. The transport cost share is higher in western market areas, where the rural road network is less developed.

A lack of adequate infrastructure also hindered market integration and a more equal sharing of scarcity and surpluses between localities in Ethiopia. The dearth of rural infrastructure in Ethiopia has been widely commented on (Iliffe 1987; Goyder and Goyder 1988; James 1989; WFP 1990). For example, Ethiopia has only 90 centimeters of road (all categories) per capita, compared with 930 centimeters per capita in Zimbabwe and 1,230 centimeters in Botswana (von Braun, Teklu, and Webb 1991). And within Ethiopia there remain wide disparities in coverage. The highest density of road coverage is found in the central and western grain-producing regions. Shewa has 3.14 kilometers of road per square kilometer, while Bale has only 0.11 kilometer per square kilometer (IFAD 1989). Thus almost 90 percent of the country's population still live more than 48 hours' walk from a primary road (WFP 1989). In Wollo, it is estimated that only 2 percent of the region's villages can be reached by all-weather roads, making the movement of food to remote markets extremely difficult (Ethiopia-OXFAM 1984).

Interregional market exchange during famine years has been impaired not only by basic infrastructure deficiencies but also by government trade restrictions, especially so in Ethiopia. Government intervention in food markets was considerable in Ethiopia, particularly after the establishment of the Agricultural Marketing Corporation (AMC) in 1976. The marketing corporation was responsible for grain procurement for public distribution, although the degree to which AMC influenced or substituted for private markets cannot be determined. Grain supplies for the towns and the army were secured via a quota system. The state farms played a major role in supplying grain to the AMC, particularly during famine years. Since 1978, when quotas began, they have provided over 50 percent of total quota requirements for maize and wheat. Also, peasant associations were obliged to deliver a minimum of 10,000 kilograms of their annual produce to the AMC at fixed prices. In 1981, this quota was raised to 15,000 kilograms, without an increase in producer prices.

Acting in tandem with the quota system (which permitted farmers to sell grain on the open market after procurement obligations had been met) was a policy that required licensed, private grain traders to make at least 50 percent of their purchases available to the AMC, also at fixed prices. In the high-production regions, this requirement rose to 100 percent of all privately purchased grain. The highest-producing regions in 1986/87 were Shewa (which provided 31 percent of all national cereal procurements), Gojjam (28 percent), and Arssi (20 percent) (Ethiopia-CSA 1987b). Private traders were paid 5 birr per 100 kilograms above the official farmgate purchase price. However, traders failing to fulfil their quota to the marketing corporation lost their license.

In order to control the operation of private traders, interregional cereals trade (and even the movement of labor) was strictly regulated. In 1973, an estimated 90 percent of marketed grain was handled by some 20,000–30,000 private merchants (Holmberg 1977). However, between 1976 and 1980, the spreading influence of the AMC was paralleled by the declining influence of traders, hindered by legal prohibitions on many small-scale commercial activities. Aside from the requirement of certified licenses (of which only 5,000 were issued in 1986), roadblocks were erected at the entrances to all towns and large villages, aimed at controlling (and taxing) grain and population movements (de Waal 1991). Individual farmers were normally permitted to move up to 100 kilograms of grain through roadblocks, as long as this did not involve crossing major administrative (provincial) boundaries.

Although information on actual marketing costs during famines is not available, it is clear that they were prohibitive in many instances. This was to be expected where people were prepared to move to find food, rather than to wait for food to come to those who still had purchasing power. A large share of interregional migration was due to drought and local food shortages, especially where there was a combination of shortage of food as well as a lack of local employment. It is interesting to note that liberalization of Ethiopia's grain marketing system in March 1990 has generally reduced cereal price spreads (the difference in wholesale prices) for major regional markets. In the periods comparing 1985–90 to 1990–96, average price spreads in 24 market pairs covering maize, teff, and wheat declined in 23 pairs after liberalization. Prices in surplus-producing areas have risen by 12 to 48 percent, while prices in cereals-deficient regions have declined by 6 to 36 percent in eight of nine cases (Ethiopia-Ministry of Economic Development and Cooperation 1997).

Conclusions Concerning Prices and Famine

The behavior of food, asset, and labor markets during times of famine is critical in determining famine outcomes. Often, emerging food shortages coincide with an increased entry into the markets by marginal farmers and increased assest sales and labor supplies. Price movements tend to be large and deviate from regular temporal and spatial norms where markets hold a small share in total supply; where transaction costs are high due to poor infrastructure, strict public control of trade flows, and associated risk premiums; and where public price stabilization is weak (due to low food reserves or limited capacity to import). The adverse effects of such price movements are felt most keenly by the poor, because of their resource and income constraints and the high proportion of their budget allocated to food and other essentials. Acute famine conditions are rarely the appropriate time for basic transformations of price regimes.

The principal market development during the Ethiopian and Sudanese famines of the 1980s was huge price increases. A decline in rainfall precipitated a decrease in cereal production. This translated into cereal prices that doubled in major regional markets. Moreover, there was a dramatic deterioration in the terms of trade between important income sources and commodities (wages, livestock, and cash crops, relative to food). However, it is theoretically plausible that a sudden collapse of purchasing power—in the context of production failure and a parallel decline in employment opportunities—may not necessarily result in sharp price increases, because a fall in effective demand would tend to keep prices low. In such circumstances, actual need would not be reflected in price changes, because effective demand would be lacking. In other words, with less purchasing power, less food could be purchased and prices would tend to remain stable. Although not a typical feature of African famines until recently, the increased asset depletion and vulnerability in the region make this scenario more likely in the future. Thus, local food prices alone cannot be the guiding yardstick for public intervention.

In a theoretical environment of well-integrated markets for food, labor, and finance, a local food production failure would result in interregional adjustments in product and factor prices. Food prices would increase and real wages decline everywhere, not only in the affected region but elsewhere because of a distribution of scarcity via price effects. Even under adverse famine conditions, market prices in the 1980s adjusted to the flow of information about scarcity. However, such information flows did not translate into needed physical flows of food, labor, and finance to mitigate the food shortages, particularly in areas that were poorly connected to main markets. Short-term market disruptions and price explosions were commonplace during the 1980s. The connection between regional markets and central markets was often weak; price developments in such markets were therefore largely driven by developments in the subregion. These cases of infrastructure- and policy-related market disfunction suggest that the monitoring of prices in one major market alone may not adequately reflect price movements in other parts of the region. It is therefore important for famine EWSs to consider prices not only in principal regional markets, but also those in secondary market centers.

The monitoring of market prices continues to be a mainstay of African EWSs, but data gathering alone will not provide definite answers. It is clear that prices are not an early predictor of famine; even in Wollo the steep price increases became apparent only in late 1984, long after the impending catastrophe had been detected by agents in the field. Thus price monitoring should be seen as a complement to production, stocks, employment, and health monitoring in famine early-warning policies and systems. Monitoring price ratios between food and assets and food and wages is most relevant in approximating entitlement risks. However, asset stocks (that is, livestock) movement by at-risk groups must also be more closely monitored; as was the case in previous famines, asset sales and price-ratio information may be only a partially relevant indicator. (Of course, there are other political and social implications for increased government control over and knowledge of the movement of its population's assets. These issues are not addressed here.) In sum, price monitoring systems must be part of larger information-monitoring systems. A set of indicators most appropriate to each vulnerable region needs to be determined in advance, prior to the next exogenous shock. In most cases prices will have some role to play; in few cases will prices alone serve to give adequate advance warning of a famine.

7 Household Food Insecurity and Famine

This chapter focuses on the issue of rural household and community responses to the threat or fact of famine, and the results of a failure to cope with that threat. Two key questions considered are (1) who are the worst affected by famine (and why); and (2) how do responses differ among individuals, household groups, and communities, and with what effect? This provides a basis for the study of appropriate policy actions that follows in Chapter 8.

Community and Household Coping Mechanisms: An Overview

There now exists a large, increasingly convergent, body of literature on the means adopted by households and communities to deal with famine. Most studies broadly conclude that, although conditions vary by locality, there are identifiable behavior patterns associated with the onset, progression, and climax of severe famines (Corbett 1988; Campbell 1990; Bohle et al. 1991; Riely 1991; Devereux 1993). These responses are largely determined by the nature of the crisis—its immediate cause, intensity, and duration—but also by the varying abilities of households to cope with stress.

The range of possible strategies, largely determined by the precrisis characteristics of individual households, is widely referred to under a composite heading called "household coping mechanisms." Coping patterns involve a succession of adaptations to increasingly severe conditions. This does not represent a sudden awakening to danger, but rather a movement in stages along a continuum of responses that runs from long-term risk minimization, through damage containment, to final household dissolution if catastrophe is not averted.

Care is taken here not to idealize the private coping capacity of poor households. Although much can be learned from indigenous knowledge concerning community support systems and alternative sources of sustenance during crises, there remains a danger of establishing a false dichotomy between private and public spheres of action. Yet where the production, distribution, or consumption systems upon which private actions depend are prone to break down, as they have been in countries such as Mozambique and Somalia, public intervention to protect and stabilize the food supply of poor households becomes vital. At its worst, "coping" can lead to destitution and death if not alleviated by appropriate public action (Davies 1993). Thus effective public intervention requires an understanding of how private actions are affected by, and respond to, famine.

A Framework

The close relationship between food production, prices, wages, and employment is critical when one looks at household responses to famine (Eele 1994). Such links can be analyzed within a framework that considers responses to fluctuations in food production, prices, and wages. For example, if we accept the basic proposition that consumption equals net income minus savings, then adjustments can take place in all three areas (Table 7.1). On the income side, households can adjust by changing their cropping patterns, intensifying their work in off-farm activities, supplementing their income through remittances or food aid, or by a combination of these responses. On the consumption side, households can adjust their nutritional intake as well as their consumption of nonfood items (which might create a conflict between calories versus diet quality and nonfood consumption). On the saving side, borrowing or accumulation are the possibilities.

Of course, such an analytical framework operates at an aggregate level and only includes parameters that represent adjustments by households as a

TABLE 7.1 A framework for analysis of famine response at the household level

$$C = Y - S, \tag{7.1}$$

with

$$C = C_{staple} (Q * P) + C_{nonstaple} + C_{nonfood}, \tag{7.1.1}$$

$$Y = [(Q_{staple} * P_{staple}) + (Q_{others} * P_{others}) - cost] \tag{7.1.2}$$

$$+ Y_{off\ farm} + Y_{remittances} + Y_{transfers}, \qquad and$$

$$S = S_{money} + S_{kind} + S_{durables} + I_{productive\ assets}, \tag{7.1.3}$$

where
C = consumption,
Y = net income[a],
S = savings (including I),
Q = quantity of (crop) output[b],
P = price[b], and
I = investment.

[a]Off-farm income includes wages and self-employment income.
[b]Others include collected bush and "famine" foods, such as leaves, roots, and rodents.

whole. It does not, for example, make explicit allowance for adjustments in activity level by individuals who reduce energy expenditure either by choice (to preserve productive assets) or out of necessity (Devereux 1993). Individual coping responses on the production/income side depend on preexisting means of access to the resource base and prior savings, as well as strategies adopted by households to protect their various resources. Nor does the analytical framework allow for households adapting their coping strategies according to community responses (household interactions) or for the sequencing of responses of other households.

The focus here is not on attempting to confirm the sequence of coping strategies (Watts 1988; Frankenberger 1991). Household responses involve trade-offs between and within various coping options. In other words, different households within the same community stand at different points along the coping continuum, and their response to a given threat will vary according to their endowment base, access to community support, and access to public interventions. Attention is paid more to the specifics of adjustments without implying that there exists an absolute chronology for such responses.

Such adjustments can be grouped into three broad categories: risk minimization, risk absorption, and risk taking to survive. The first stage involves taking steps to minimize the risk of crisis during a precrisis period, in an environment of limited credit and insurance markets. One of the unresolved questions about household coping is the extent to which responses relate to long-term expectations rather than being short-term adjustments to immediate events. Many millions of smallholders in Africa survive from one year to the next in harsh, semi-arid environments, constantly facing the threat of catastrophic disruption of production and consumption systems. Risk management (or containment) is inevitably a central element of the strategy of these smallholders (Anderson and Dillon 1992; Cleaver and Schreiber 1994).

Dynamics of Responses

Smallholders manage their resources in rational ways that allow for survival, a basic livelihood, and a chance to react to catastrophic events. At the core of such management is risk spreading and diversifying options (Reardon, Crawford, and Kelly 1994). Although the etiology of famine varies greatly, the main causes of devastation are relatively few: drought/flood, crops and livestock diseases/pests, human epidemic, armed conflict. The latter is not typically something that people prepare for, nor is human epidemic. Most households plan for the occurrence of climatic shocks or agricultural pest infestation every few years. Farmers do not necessarily aim either to maximize output in good years or minimize risk in bad—they tend to seek a balance of outcomes, representing a series of trade-offs, which forms the basis for the household's food security strategy (Mortimore 1989; Downing 1991; von Braun and Kennedy 1994).

There are four key elements to such a strategy. Vulnerable households make efforts to (1) protect agricultural productivity through intercropping, the spatial dispersal of fields, using a variety of seed types, managing mixed-species livestock, and preserving last-resort grazing grounds (van Lierre 1993; Campbell 1995; Unruh 1995); (2) accumulate assets by storing food and other commodities, storing cash, and investing where possible in valuable disposable goods (such as jewelry, farm equipment, and housing) (Corbett 1988); (3) build up social-support networks based on gifts, food sharing, and loan provision; and (4) diversify income by including nonfarm sources and, if available, migration remittances (Devereux 1993; Reardon et al. 1995). How successful households are in pursuing and attaining these goals plays a large role in determining the outcome of subsequent crises.

The importance of diversification of production, income sources, and social networks cannot be overemphasized. For example, households in the semi-arid region of Burkina Faso diversify their income base to such an extent that approximately 60 percent of income is derived from nonfarm sources—relatively more stable in drought years than farm income (Reardon and Matlon 1987). They were thus better able to cope with the severe drought of the mid-1980s than households in the less-drought-prone regions to the south, where households had not adapted to the risk of drought in as effective a manner. Similarly a survey of 400 urban and rural Niger households showed that urban respondents derived roughly 70 percent of their income from sources not related to agriculture—an outcome that one would not find surprising (Webb 1992). However, the rural households also derived an average of 60 percent of their income from off-farm sources, supporting the findings from other parts of Africa. This diversification of income base has been documented in many countries (Cutler 1984; Reardon, Delgado, and Matlon 1992; von Braun and Pandya-Lorch 1991). In The Gambia, for example, smallholders derive 23 percent of total income from nonfarm work (von Braun, Puetz, and Webb 1989). In Kenya and Rwanda, by contrast, the share of total income earned off farm represents 40 and 60 percent, respectively (Kennedy and Cogill 1987; von Braun, de Haen, and Blanken 1991).

Nonfarm income sources include petty trade, restaurant operation, and, of course, remittance income from urban migrants. Urban remittances are particularly widespread in much of southern Africa. Households in semi-arid regions of Zimbabwe, for example, typically migrate to towns in the same country, as well as to urban areas in neighboring countries. Zimbabwe's urban growth since 1980 has been roughly double that of total population increase (Moyo et al. 1991). Those family members left behind engage in craft work, food trading, brewing, and other nonfarm activities as means to diversify their incomes (Matiza, Zinyama, and Campbell 1989). And they also diversify their local and regional social networks. The importance of the latter is often overlooked. As documented by Adams (1993) for Mali, a wide array of social institutions and practices exists across Sub-Saharan Africa, many elements of which are essential to vulnerable households in their attempts to withstand the effects of external shocks. Based largely on kinship, patronage, and friendship, this so-called moral economy represents a veritable web of nonmarket relationships that allow for the sharing and exchange of favors (Platteau 1991; Fafchamps 1992). These relationships are established during the risk-minimization phase, though not just in areas where there is an expectation of crises. Are the networks more elaborate and broader based in crisis-prone regions? The answer is probably no because such regions tend, on the whole, to be poor regions with less dynamic economies. Thus one should be wary of equating well-integrated moral economies with poorly integrated market economies.

The second stage of coping—drawing down investments, calling in loans, and tapping more remote links in the social network—usually only occurs during a crisis. As consumption becomes more restricted, stores of food and cash are called upon, and the number and variety of potential income sources become crucial to survival.

One should include here the role of NGOs and other grassroots organizations, as well as internationally funded activities. In many ways local project interventions are part of the network of social and economic contacts; they are part of the informal safety net that is established by long-term presence in a locality. Project activities feed into the formation of rational household expectations. If an NGO is present in a community, the likelihood of relief in the event of famine is higher than if no such organization is established. When considering vulnerability, the presence or absence of any such grassroots partners should be taken into consideration.

Whereas the ability of the poorest households to protect investments (in farm or human productivity) declines, wealthier households obviously can handle this stage better than the poor; they generally have more assets to dispose of and more channels of credit to activate. Moreover, they can delay irreversible decisions longer. Poorer households may well have already decided to cut their food intake as part of an earlier coping response in order to protect their limited asset base and maintain a capacity for later economic recovery (Kelly 1992; Devereux 1993).

However, coping capacity is not just a function of the asset base; it is also a function of human resources. For instance in Sudan, rural children whose parents had some formal education—and especially those whose mothers had received some schooling—were (holding poverty indicators constant) significantly better off in terms of nutritional status than other children in the aftermath of the 1985 famine (Teklu, von Braun, and Zaki 1991).

The final stage in coping involves the collapse of normal systems of survival. The most prevalent response to worsening conditions is the consumption of unusual "famine foods" and the sale of remaining assets, including those ordinarily thought of as necessities such as the roof of homes and clothes.

If still able to do so, many people migrate in search of assistance from distant relatives or at a relief camp. If they are unable (or unwilling) to take the chance of a migration, many individuals are forced into a passive state of waiting that may ultimately result in starvation death.

This rough sequence of interlocking processes moves from the reversible to the irreversible. Earlier actions taken can often be counterbalanced by other actions once a crisis has passed. However, not all of the coping responses undertaken by households at each stage of the crisis are beneficial, either to the household or to its environment. Following Payne and Lipton's (1994) characterization of physiological adaptation to stress, a response should be seen as adequately "adaptive" if it increases the probability of a household's survival beyond the crisis. However, such adaptive behavior can only be considered morally and economically "acceptable" if it does not cause extreme pain, loss of function, or irreversible damage. In this sense, reducing basic food intake to minimal levels or breaking up a family to enhance individual members' chances of survival entails unacceptable suffering. Similarly, desperate actions such as the cultivation of marginal land or the wholesale felling of trees for firewood have unacceptable consequences for future environmental development and income generation.

In sum, responses to stress are not only diverse (according to time, place, and household characteristics), they also depend on the degree and duration of the stress. Some households form expectations of periodic crises and adapt their resource management strategy to take account of that risk. However, few households can prepare themselves for the extreme conditions faced during famine. At a given point in the process of risk containment, something snaps. Events take a feared but unavoidable turn for the worse. Subsequent household coping responses become just that: responses to things falling apart. This does not mean that people suddenly become "irrational." Rather the balance of trade-offs between longer-term and short-term concerns suddenly shifts toward the latter—and the "rational" response is simply to survive. Some households are fairly well equipped to ward off the worst effects. Many others succumb when all their options run out; there is nothing left to trade off. The specifics of a household's demographic structures obviously are an important factor in this process.

Empirical Data from Ethiopia and Sudan

The following sections examine the details of coping mechanisms as outlined above, drawing on empirical data collected in famine-prone regions of Ethiopia and Sudan.[1] The data presented here derive from detailed interviews

---

1. The survey designs are described in Webb, von Braun, and Yohannes (1992) for Ethiopia; and Teklu, von Braun, and Zaki (1991) for Sudan.

conducted in 1988 in Sudan and 1989/90 in Ethiopia. All information presented here in relation to household and individual behavior prior to 1988 is based on memory recall of interviewed participants. Where data from 1984/85 are compared in tables or text with data from 1988/89, both are based on information given by the respondents themselves.

The data were methodically pieced together through repeat interviews with respondents over many months. Although human memory is always imperfect, participants' recall was remarkably strong where catastrophic events were concerned. Questions aimed at confirming/contradicting previous answers given by the respondents rarely exposed major inconsistencies. This lends credence to the general picture presented here, if not necessarily to the specifics of numerical data offered for the mid-1980s period.

The Survey Settings

Questionnaire surveys were conducted among 550 households in 7 different locations in Ethiopia, and among 240 households in 10 villages of Bara and El Obeid districts in the Kordofan region of Sudan (see Figure 3.1).[2] These 17 survey sites were not chosen at random, nor were they designed to be "representative" of the two countries as a whole. For such to be the case, a massive survey covering all provinces and all categories of households would have been required. This was not possible. Instead, given the nature of gaps in our understanding of famine, the survey placed a greater emphasis on depth of analysis than on coverage.

The survey sites selected met two conditions. First, each location suffered problems (not caused by direct military disruption of production) of food supply, food availability, or both between 1984 and 1989. Indications of local crises were found throughout the district. The second condition was that each area received external assistance during their individual crises. We wanted to understand how households coped in their own manner, but also what public interventions were available to supplement private coping strategies. Prior to site selection many months were spent in both Ethiopia and Sudan reviewing project documents and donor reports, interacting with local university researchers, and visiting field locations. Relief and rehabilitation projects that kept good records of their activities, costs, and impact were identifed. The locations selected for study were found to be appropriate for the present analysis.

Methodology

At each site, a list of households that participated in relief interventions was drawn up from project records. A stratified, random sample of households

---

2. For further information on the details of survey sampling and methodology, please refer to Teklu, von Braun, and Zaki (1991); Webb, von Braun, and Yohannes (1992); and Webb and von Braun (1994).

was drawn from these lists to make up half of each site-specific sample. The other half (a control group) was drawn at random from local lists of community members or neighboring villages.

Not all samples were identical in size at each site due to variations in the size of communities across agro-ecological and ethno-religious regions. Given this difference in sample size across sites, a system of weighting was used for pooling data across multiple locations. The weights were derived from recent census data on the number of households in districts surrounding each survey community.

The variety of data available permits analysis at three levels of disaggregation: by agro-ecology, wealth status, and by gender. Such disaggregation allows for viewing the problem from many angles. It also avoids hiding diversity behind a mask of averages. Where location was used as a stratifying factor, three main subcategories were derived in relation to Ethiopia: highland, lowland, and pastoral.[3] Three of the communities surveyed in Ethiopia were located in highland areas at more than 1,500 meters above sea level, receiving an average of more than 1,200 millimeters of rainfall per year. The other four sites were located in the lowlands at altitudes of less than 1,500 meters above sea level, receiving an average of less than 700 millimeters of rain per year. One of the lowland sites was a seminomadic, pastoral community.

In Sudan, neither altitude nor rainfall played a major role in differentiating location. All 10 villages were located in the semi-arid Sahel environment, which receives only 400 to 600 millimeters of precipitation per year. Where "wealth" was used as a stratifier, three equal "income groups" were determined, representing differing amounts of wealth. These groups were based on postsurvey calculations of total net income per person for surveyed households based on the 1988/89 survey year. All income sources were considered in that calculation, including the value of home-produced crops and livestock, gifts and transfers, and nonfarm sources. Households were then separated into three equal groups and ranked according to their position on the local income scale. Given the real poverty found in all households in these samples, those at the very top of the income scale were still poorer than the poorest households in most other African countries. Thus the three groups were distinguished not as "rich" and "poor," but as "lower"-income tercile and "upper"-income tercile.

Finally, some data are reported using gender of the head of household as a stratifier. This is often important since female-headed households can be smaller, poorer, and more vulnerable than those headed by men—not necessarily *because* of their gender but because of what their gender signals in terms of other household characteristics. Where the household head was determined

---

3. This simple distinction between highland and lowland should not obscure the real problem of ecological zonation in Ethiopia. Highland and lowland categories can be subdivided further according to altitude, rainfall, and temperature. However, there is no authoritative classification of zones because of a lack of agreement on relevant parameters.

to be female, this constituted a de facto headship; that is, there had been no adult males present in the household for at least six months. The overall average share of households headed by women in the Ethiopian sample was 15 percent.

In the following sections, household data are examined for both countries within and across sites according to these three stratifiers. Following the stages of crisis response outlined above, the analysis focuses first on risk-minimization (ex ante) and risk-absorption (ex post) responses in relation to production, asset holdings, income, and food consumption. This is followed by consideration of the final (catastrophic) stage of risk taking, when households generally migrate or collapse.

Responses to Famine Risks

Adjustments in Crop Production

Regions and households most prone to food crises are typically characterized by low agricultural productivity that is not compensated for by strong markets or efficient public safety nets. Small farms (in higher-population-density regions) made up of scattered fields, with limited use of improved inputs, seasonal labor constraints, tenure insecurity, and high transaction costs are common features of stagnant, if not deteriorating, agricultural economies.

In Ethiopia, for example, the average farm size held by the 550 households surveyed in 1989/90 was only 0.15 hectares per capita. Of these households, very few had access to formal credit, improved inputs (seeds, fertilizer, or pesticides), or hired labor. None had ever opened a bank account, and only 17 percent reported membership in a community-based savings society (called an *equb* in Amharic).

Land and other natural-resource tenure rights were held by the state, which limited farmer investment in land-productivity enhancement and restricted potential productivity gains. As a result of such deterrents, yields and crop output were low even in the relatively good rainfall years of the 1980s. In a year of above-average rainfall, such as 1988/89, survey households obtained average yields of only 740 kilograms per hectare in highland regions (over 1,500 meters altitude), and 300 kilograms per hectare at lowland sites. This translated into an average of 111 kilograms of cereals produced per capita in this "good year" in the highlands, and only 50 kilograms per capita in the more arid lowlands (Webb and von Braun 1994).

The lowland sites of Ethiopia are in many ways comparable to the semi-arid regions of Sudan. In the northern province of Kordofan, for example, limited use of fertilizers, credit, and technology combine to produce low yields and output, despite rather more abundant land availability than in Ethiopia. In the relatively "good" rainfall year of 1988/89, millet output averaged less than

90 kilograms per capita among households surveyed in 10 Kordofan villages (Teklu, von Braun, and Zaki 1991). During the 1984/85 drought, the same households produced an average millet yield of only 4 kilograms per capita.

Given these harsh "normal" conditions, households attempt to cope with exogenous shocks as well as underlying constraints by spreading risks—both within agricultural products and across farm and nonfarm activities. Many of the risk-aversion measures commonly found throughout Africa are practiced in famine-prone regions with varying degrees of success (Cekan 1990; Shipton 1990; OFDA 1991).

DIVERSIFICATION OF PRODUCTION. First, smallholders typically try to maintain a diversified portfolio of crops. One or two crops may predominate, but the range is often broad and includes food crops and cash crops, and early-planted as well as late-planted varieties. In Kordofan, for instance, farmers maintained a mix of millet and sesame fields during 1987/88, despite a higher relative factor return to sesame compared with millet (1.4 to 1). This choice was driven largely by a desire to grow some food for consumption so as to not depend entirely on the market.

At the same time, in Kordofan there was a shift in crop mixes away from sorghum and groundnuts toward less-water-demanding millets. For example, taking the average area planted with millet in the province as a whole from 1974 to 1981 as an index of 100, millet production rose to 177 in 1985 (Sudan-MANR 1987a). This was paralleled by a decline in the index for sorghum to 36 in 1985, and for groundnuts to only 21 in the same year.

Crop mixes are also determined by a desire to follow a flexible production schedule that can adjust to variations in rainfall patterns. Staggered planting is common, with crops of different maturation periods being planted successively rather than simultaneously, thereby reducing labor conflicts and protecting against total seed loss from midseason droughts. Also, farmers in western Sudan shift away from millet to other crops (for example, sesame and water-melon) when early rains appear to be inadequate or when rains are concentrated in the later part of the wet season.

Crop diversification also extends to root and tree crops. Although the total area cultivated by root and tree crops may be small in drought-prone regions compared with cereals, noncereals are often essential to the income base and sustenance of many households. Indeed, income from noncereal cash crops (such as gum arabic in Sudan and coffee in Ethiopia) and food from roots and tubers (cassava and yam) often make up for shortfalls in cereal production during brief droughts.

During more severe, extended droughts, however, even these crops often fail to provide income. In eastern Ethiopia, for example, although *chat* (*Catha edulis,* a perennial bush that produces narcotic leaves) is relatively drought resistant, its price fell during 1984/85 because of widespread income collapse and resultant reduced demand. Income from perennial crops was no more dependable in 1984/85 in south-central Ethiopia, where coffee is the traditional cash crop. Coffee-berry disease spread throughout the region in the early 1980s, causing substantial damage to tree stock. During 1985, countless households in one of the most densely populated areas found that their coffee trees did not produce any beans at all because the leaves had dried up or because insects had eaten them (one of the few sources of existing green matter).

This loss of coffee income was particularly hard felt in the southern regions of Ethiopia where the main staple food of the area, *enset* (*Ensete ventricosum*), had also been badly damaged by disease. Indeed, without *enset,* conditions would have been worse still. *Enset* is a starchy tuber containing little protein or fat, but it survives drought well and can be stored underground for long periods. Although bacterial wilt spread rapidly in 1984, few households lost all of their crop. During 1985, most smallholders relied heavily on *enset* (as well as cassava) for both food and income. Nevertheless, losses of *enset* plants (which take several years to mature) were high during the drought, making the region increasingly vulnerable to future droughts and other shocks.

OTHER RISK-REDUCTION STRATEGIES.   Another important strategy in reducing risks is intercropping, widely used as a means of reducing the risk of total loss of any one crop. In Ethiopia, sorghum is planted between *chat* in Hararghe fields, while barley is mixed with lentils and wheat in fields of northern Shewa. In Sudan, millet and sorghum can be interspersed across the same planting area.

Also, because of high local rainfall variability, in addition to crop dispersal it is common for smallholders to disperse individual holdings. In the hilly terrain of Ethiopia's Rift Valley, a distribution of field plots by altitude is favored so that variations in microclimate can be tapped and complete crop failure in a set of contiguous fields can be avoided.

Some farmers also overseed certain favored plots in order to maximize the chance of plant survival, and selectively weed only the most favorable shoots thereby minimizing labor lost on unproductive plants.

Additionally, smallholders in the most risky environments increasingly rely on shorter-maturating cultivars in the search for protection against drought. This practice, which in some ways can keep yields low, is employed in the Sahel, throughout the Rift Valley, and as far south as the dry zones of Botswana, Namibia, and Zimbabwe.

Unfortunately, few private risk-aversion measures can be fully successful against protracted drought or other exogenous shocks. Successive years of below-average or poorly distributed rainfall or both have negative multiplier effects on production, income, and consumption streams. A first drought reduces seed stocks and income for the next year. If a second year of drought again reduces production, food consumption will be affected along with third-year production potential, and so on. The longer a drought sequence lasts, the more human and animal populations will be affected. This was the case across

TABLE 7.2 Area planted, output, and yield of cereals among sample households in Ethiopia and Sudan, 1983–88

	1983	1984	1985	1986	1987[a]	1988
			Area planted			
			(hectare per capita)			
Ethiopia	n.a.	0.08 ·	0.08	0.08	0.07	0.11
Sudan	0.96	1.06	1.07	1.05	0.88	0.99
			Output			
			(kilogram per capita)			
Ethiopia	n.a.	45.69	24.10	33.82	28.65	56.40
Sudan	108.2	20.61	129.41	158.61	75.94	120.70
			Yield			
			(kilogram per hectare)			
Ethiopia	n.a.	294	181	306	320	508
Sudan	160	40	190	221	137	213

SOURCES: Compiled from IFPRI Sudan household survey data 1988/89; IFPRI Ethiopia survey 1989/90.
NOTE: In Ethiopia, cereals include teff, wheat, barley, maize, sorghum, millet, and oats; in Sudan, cereals include millet and sorghum only. n.a. = not available.
[a]Prior to 1987 data are based on respondents' recollections of results recorded during the 1988/89 survey.

much of the Sahel during the early 1970s, and in the Horn of Africa in the mid-1980s.

The primary effect on crops from the droughts of the 1980s was the major decline in output, not only in Ethiopia and Sudan, but also in neighboring Chad, Kenya, and Somalia. In 1984/85, the average output of the households surveyed in Ethiopia was reported to have dropped to only twenty-four kilograms per capita (Table 7.2). However, relatively wealthier households in the highlands of Ethiopia maintained their average output at close to 100 kilograms per capita (more than double that of the lowest-income households), with yields roughly three times greater (Webb 1993). A similar outcome was found in Burkina Faso during the severe drought of 1984/85, when millet yields among relatively wealthy households were, on average, 40 percent higher than those obtained by the poorest households (Webb and Reardon 1992). In such cases the advantage of owning oxen, being able to hire labor, and being able to purchase seed resulted in higher cereal yields and output (in the worst year) than for the poorer, resource-deprived households.

In northern Kordofan, the 1984 harvest was a record low due to the drought. Production of millet and sesame (the two most important staples) fell to less than 14 percent of their average 1974–81 amount. Mohammed (1988) noted that there was total crop failure in 20 villages in eastern Kordofan in 1984/85. And the IFPRI Kordofan survey also confirmed a sizable crop failure during that period (see Table 7.2). The main response to such drastic yield and output failures among smallholders appears to have been a search for alternative sources of income.

Responses with Livestock

Diversification of and adjustments within farm production extend beyond crops into the realm of livestock. Roughly 43 percent of all livestock in Africa are in the sub- and humid tropics; the remaining 57 percent are found in zones more frequently affected by reduced availability of water and grazing, and of increased disease (ILCA 1991).

Ethiopia has the highest ratio of livestock per capita in all of Sub-Saharan Africa. This country alone accounts for 16 percent of all small ruminants, 19 percent of cattle, 8 percent of camels, and 57 percent of equines on the continent (ILCA 1991). In the highlands, where black, volcanic soils predominate, access to a team of plow oxen is one of the prerequisites to a successful harvest (Gryseels and Jutzi 1986). In 1988/89, an average of only 13 percent of the IFPRI survey households owned a pair of oxen, while 79 percent did not own any at all. Of those that did not own any oxen, 91 percent were households in the lowest-income tercile; these households attempted to borrow oxen from wealthier households in return for a share of the harvest or a promised quota of manual labor.[4]

In the lowlands of Ethiopia, fewer oxen are used for cultivation, but small ruminants, equines, and camels are important for transportation, milk, and meat production. The latter also applies to Sudan, which has the highest number of camels and the second-highest number of sheep (after Ethiopia) on the continent (ILCA 1991).

The most common methods of minimizing herd loss through drought are herd diversification and dispersal. *Diversification* involves the husbandry of a mixed animal stock—both small and large ruminants as well as browsers. This permits better utilization of feed resources (because of varied demand) and easier disposal of small stocks before large stocks during times of crisis. Of course, wealthier households tend to have a greater number of more valuable animals—such as oxen, milk cows, and camels—than poorer households, which tend to have a higher proportion of small ruminants in their herds. *Dispersal* involves spreading the risk of herd loss by splitting the herd into semiautonomous groups or arranging for stock to be husbanded by relatives or contracted labor in more distant locations. This option is more commonly pursued by semitranshumant agro-pastoralists.

---

4. While the survey cannot claim to be representative for Ethiopia, it certainly provides information on structural trends. (On survey design, see Webb, von Braun, and Yohannes 1992.)

The African droughts of the mid-1980s caused much loss of livestock, despite extreme measures taken by owners to preserve their herds. As the drought continued in many countries from 1983 into 1985, the ability of most smallholders to feed their animals was increasingly reduced by rapidly declining income. For example, one survey in Kenya conducted during the 1984 drought recorded a 50 percent decrease in the size of goat herds and an almost 60 percent decrease in cattle numbers (Downing, Gitu, and Kamau 1989). Similarly, the national herd of Niger is thought to have been reduced by 50 percent during the same 1984/85 drought (Swinton 1988; Niger 1991).

In Ethiopia, extraordinary measures were taken by surveyed households to keep their most valued animals alive. Some households shared their own food with favored cows and calves. In one village at the foot of the western escarpment of the Rift Valley, 69 percent of surveyed households pulled the thatch off the roof; mixed it with creeper, cactus stems, and vines; and then fed it to their oxen and milk cows (Webb and von Braun 1994). At another survey site in the southern rangelands of Ethiopia (on the Kenyan border), many pastoral households increased the watering frequency of their herd and the frequency of their transhumant cycles by stopping for shorter periods at any one place. This placed greater stress on the human population but was seen as necessary to saving cattle and camel herds.

Yet despite such preservation measures, loss of production and animal stock during the famine years was high. For example, in Ethiopia's southern rangelands, average "normal"-year milk production per cow (of the Boran species) is estimated at roughly 1 liter per day (Holden 1990). However in March 1985, average production had declined to 400 milliliters per cow per day, reaching as low as 150 milliliters per day at the peak of the famine (Donaldson 1986). Milk production from camels during this period did not decline as much as that of cattle, averaging almost 800 milliliters per day. (This underlines the value of camel ownership during years of drought.)

At the same time that animal productivity declined sharply, the stock numbers also decreased. Smallholders disposed of animals in order to fetch the best price possible in a depressed market, or to avoid imminent loss due to livestock death. As a result, herd disposal rates were higher than usual, reaching 35 percent for sheep in northern Kordofan, and 30 percent for cattle (Mohammed 1988).

Such increases were made possible by the sale of animals that had not previously been destined for market. Typically, owners prefer to sell adult males, unproductive cows, and surplus calves. This selectivity diminished in the 1984/85 period in Sudan as herders were forced to dispose of many more of their animals, weakened by starvation and disease, than anticipated.

In Darfur, animal losses were much higher in the north than in the south. For example, 71 percent of the cattle and 40 percent of the goats in the north were lost to emergency slaughter compared to 37 percent of the cattle and 10 percent of the goats in the south. The camel-herding nomads of the north suffered most (Riely 1991). Ibrahim (1990) noted losses of as much as 70–90 percent of camels among the camel herders, particularly the Medub tribe. Sedentary farmers also experienced a sharp decline in herd numbers. Among a sample of sedentary farmers in northern Darfur, 44 percent reported a total loss of sheep and 14 percent reported a total loss of goats (Ibrahim 1990). Less than 10 percent managed to maintain their herds throughout the drought years.

Total livestock mortality during the worst drought year for households surveyed in Ethiopia was, on average, double the mortality experienced in good rainfall years: 0.36 tropical livestock units (TLU) per capita during the famine, compared with 0.17 TLU in 1989/90.[5] The poorest households (with few animals and the most to lose) took some of the most extreme measures to keep animals alive and were, to some extent, successful. For example, wealthier households surveyed in 1989/90 lost more livestock per capita during the mid-1980s than did poorer households—0.23 TLU versus 0.13 TLU, respectively (Webb, von Braun, and Yohannes 1992). This outcome appears to have been linked to the scale of herding operations and to the effectiveness of targeting scarce resources by herd owners. Of course, although relatively wealthier households lost more animals, they survived the famine with more stock left in hand than poorer households. That is, in 1989, the poorest households held an average of 0.17 TLU per capita, while the wealthier households still owned much more.

This differential postcrisis ownership of livestock according to wealth, also observed in Kenya by Downing, Gitu, and Kamau (1989), has important policy implications for the rehabilitation of farming systems devastated by drought. If the poor are not successfully targeted by restocking projects, the goals of increasing food security and stabilizing incomes among the most vulnerable will not be easy to achieve.

Diversification in Household Income Sources

Given the constant threat of shortfalls in crop or livestock production, most farmers adapt by diversifying their income sources. Table 7.3 presents a breakdown of the sources of income for surveyed households in Ethiopia and Sudan by upper and lower terciles. Total net income is calculated as income from agriculture and nonagricultural sources, minus costs.[6]

Based on net annual income per household for 1987/88 in Sudan and 1988/89 in Ethiopia, the calculation includes (1) own agricultural production

---

5. TLUs are defined in terms of female cattle, with small ruminants aggregated on standard weights.

6. Although for Sudan the expenditure survey provides for a comprehensive picture of total resources and was therefore used as a base for classification of households by terciles, the income survey was more comprehensive in Ethiopia and was used for classification there. Still, the correlation between per capita income and expenditure data in Ethiopia is .43 ($p < .001$) and the rank correlation is .53 ($p < .001$).

TABLE 7.3 Sample household income sources in Ethiopia and Sudan, by tercile, 1988/89

Income Source	Ethiopia[a]		Sudan[b]	
	Poorer	Richer	Poorer	Richer
	(percent of net total income)			
Collected products	27.7	15.1	21.4	11.4
Crops and other vegetable products	55.0	42.0	25.4	29.5
Farm wages	1.3	1.4	8.9	5.4
Handicrafts	2.7	1.2	4.6	2.1
Livestock (and derived products)	6.1	24.3	14.2	13.2
Nonfarm wages	0.3	11.2	3.7	2.6
Petty commerce	1.3	0.4	1.1	7.6
Rental income	0.9	0.6	0.6	0.4
Salary/contracts	n.a.	n.a.	3.9	4.1
Tree crops	n.a.	n.a.	1.6	2.6
Transfers (including remittances)	4.1	4.0	14.6	21.1

SOURCE: Compiled from IFPRI Sudan survey data 1988/89; and Ethiopia survey 1989/90.

NOTE: n.a. = not available. Numbers may not add to 100 due to rounding.
[a]Terciles are based on per capita income.
[b]Terciles are based on per capita expenditure.

(main-season crop production, sales of livestock and their products, and income from farm labor); (2) nonfarm labor income (received as wages for nonagricultural work and income from artisanal activity); (3) transfers, remittances, loans, gifts, dowries, inheritances, sales of food aid, in-kind income derived from food for work; and (4) sales income derived from selling own cash crops (gum arabic, cotton, sugarcane, coffee, *chat*), collected fuel products (wood, dung, incense), collected consumables (food collected in the fields), and processed foods and drinks. The calculation of costs includes the purchase of seed, fertilizer, manual labor, and the rental of oxen and tools. Family labor cost is not included. Income groups were calculated after data had been collected.

Although some underreporting of income is inevitable, these figures give a valid indication of the depth of poverty prevalent at the survey sites. Three points should be highlighted. First, absolute total income for all households surveyed was extremely low. Average income for the survey households in Ethiopia stood at only US$41.50 per person per year. This ranged from only US$10 per person among the very poorest households to US$131 in relatively less poor households. In Sudan, households in the lowest-income group earned an average of US$125 per person per year, with the wealthiest group of households surveyed recording an income four times that amount.

By comparison, a household survey conducted in semi-arid Niger (which was, it should be pointed out, ranked as the country with the lowest UNDP human development index in the world in 1995 and 1996) showed poorest households at three rural sites with an average annual income of roughly US$300 per person (Webb 1992; UNDP 1996).

The second point to be noted is that although cropping remains the primary source of income (representing an average of 44 percent for Ethiopian households and 30 percent for Sudanese households), other sources are crucial. No households surveyed depended solely on crop production for survival. The marketing of animals and their products, wage labor, the sale of fuel products, the sale of craft work, and other activities unrelated to the home farm accounted for 34 percent of total net income for households in the upper tercile of the Ethiopian sample, and 39 percent of income in the lower tercile. In the Sudanese samples, nonfarm sources represented 57 percent of total income for upper-income households, compared with 62 percent for households in the lower-income group. Although the relative importance of nonfarm to total income is greater in the poor households, the absolute amount of nonfarm income is substantially higher in wealthier households in both countries.

The importance of nonfarm income also varies by region, season, and also by gender of the household head. For example, the pastoralists of Ethiopia's southern rangelands and Sudan's Darfur Province have almost no tradition of manual labor, but sales of craft work (such as woven baskets) and of collected products (poles, charcoal, and grass) are important. In the Ethiopian and Kenyan highlands (which are more densely inhabited than the lowlands and also have more opportunities for nonfarm employment), sales of animal products (dung cakes and milk) and firewood constitute important income sources, along with manual labor and craft work. Much therefore depends on the availability of raw products and on the proximity of markets.

Wages for farm labor and income from renting land or draft animals can be obtained only during the rainy season. Craft work and nonfarm labor assume greater significance in the dry season when farm activity is low. Income from certain service activities, such as milling grain by waterwheel, is also relatively seasonal since the busiest months are those following harvest. Alternatively, trading, remittances (private transfers from urban-based relatives), and the sale of processed fuel products (such as charcoal and dung cakes) are less seasonal in nature.

However, droughts and other crises tend to affect markets for both agricultural and nonfarm products and services. A drought-induced collapse in demand for nonessential foods and fuel products (cash being conserved for staple foods) sharply reduces the earning options for most households. For example, in a relatively good rainfall year, 1989/90, women in 21 percent of survey households in Ethiopia earned their primary income from the sale of fuel products. In another 8 percent of households, women were dependent on the sale of processed food and beverages. Yet during the mid-1980s famine, less than 1 percent of all households reported that they were engaged in such activities. Instead, women were forced to sell their last remaining valuable asset (labor) alongside the men. Similarly in 1989, wage labor was a major source of income for men in 17 percent of the survey households and for women in only 3 percent of the households. However, during the worst famine year, the percentage of households in which both women and men were working as laborers rose to 25 percent, despite a 50 to 60 percent decrease in wage rates during the famine.

Increased participation of women in the labor force was also found in Sudan. Women in the Kordofan survey villages, for example, engaged in housekeeping in urban areas—a form of work not customary in Sudanese culture. Yet wage rates fell steadily in rural labor markets as demand for labor dried up. The percentage of families working as local agricultural laborers in Kordofan fell from 18 percent in 1983/84 to 3.1 percent in 1984/85 (Mohammed 1988). In the survey area, a day of labor could buy only 2 kilograms of millet in 1984, compared with 6 kilograms in 1983.

These income adjustments among sample households in both Ethiopia and Sudan indicate that the higher their dependency on agricultural activities for income (which implies limited access to alternative income sources), the greater the risk of income failure during a production collapse. Thus households in drier areas, especially asset-poor households headed by women or with a high dependency ratio, are particularly at risk.

The Erosion of Asset Base and Community Support

With crop and livestock output compromised, capital reserves largely exhausted, and the search for nonfarm income assuming a new urgency, asset sales become more common and economic debts and social obligations are called in. Assets (or savings) can take the form of cash or goodwill stores, food stores, real-value stores (household goods of value), and patronage (Swift 1993). The first of these, cash stores, is difficult to quantify. As noted earlier, no household in the Ethiopian survey reported having a bank account, and fewer than 20 percent belonged to local savings groups. However, roughly one-third of households in a village in the highlands did admit to keeping Maria Theresa coins (Austrian silver dollars minted in the late 1700s) for disposal during an emergency. The local market value of such a coin in 1989 was roughly US$15, equivalent at that time to 50 kilograms of maize.

Food stores are easier to verify. Most households attempt to stockpile a portion of their harvest to tide them over until the following year (McCann 1990). Storage methods are similar across the country: sacks or pots kept in the house, freestanding thatch-covered clay or wicker frames, and lined pits in the ground that may be sealed (used in some parts of Ethiopia in 1985 for burying the dead, since few people had the strength to dig graves).

In Ethiopia, only 35 percent of the 550 households interviewed in 1989/90 roughly six months after harvest had grain (food or seed) held in storage. Those that did averaged a mere 14 percent of the harvest. In real terms, this translated into an average grain store of 17.4 kilograms per capita—very little indeed. Over 65 percent of households had nothing stockpiled at all. Furthermore, the ability to store food was not evenly distributed. The proportion of households with at least a few kilograms of stored grain ranged from 54 percent among relatively wealthier households (the top tercile of respondents on the income scale), to less than 2 percent of the households in the lowest-income tercile.

As for household assets, the most valuable held by households in poorer regions of Africa tend to be livestock, followed by housing materials (metal roofs and wooden posts), metal-framed beds, new clothes, and farm equipment (such as plows and plowing harnesses). As expected, wealthier households had more assets to sell than poorer households, and those that were sold tended to be of greater value. Since private ownership and disposal of land was prevented by law, land did not often change hands during the crisis, either in Ethiopia or in Sudan.

Table 7.4 shows the proportion of Ethiopian survey households selling different types of assets, and the value of income gained from asset sales during the famine period compared with assets held in 1988/89, by income tercile. Income earned from reported livestock sales among richer households during

TABLE 7.4 Value of assets sold during worst famine year and held in 1989, by income tercile in Ethiopian sample households

	Income Terciles[a]		
Item	Lower	Upper	Sample Mean
	(mean birr per capita)[b]		
Famine sales			
Farm assets	0.1	0.1	0.1
Household assets	0.0	0.2	0.1
Livestock assets	5.0	30.1	16.3
Assets held in 1989			
Farm assets	2.5	5.4	3.5
Household assets	2.7	15.8	7.8
Livestock assets	107.03	234.4	135.9

SOURCE: Compiled from IFPRI Ethiopia survey data, 1989/90.

NOTES: Data are derived from household recall. The worst famine year varies according to individual household responses for the period 1983–88.

[a]Terciles calculated across all survey sites.
[b]US$1.00 = 2.05 Ethiopian birr.

the famine was roughly six times higher than that earned by the poorest households.

Similar findings apply to Sudan. For example, only 17 percent of poorer households sold nonlivestock assets, and 55 percent sold livestock. Among richer households, these percentages were 45 and 66, respectively.

There were, of course, differences in the quantity of assets sold according to the intensity of the crisis by location. Only 19 percent of highland Ethiopian households surveyed sold any household goods during the famine years— items such as tables, pots, and blankets. In some lowland areas, by contrast, many people sold their clothing and essential cooking utensils. Such actions are not easy. Selling oneself into destitution in order to survive is not an edifying experience.

There appears to have been some degree of substitution between livestock, household, and farm assets. Where fewer livestock were sold, more household or personal assets were often disposed of and vice versa. With livestock, the majority of animals sold were male cattle, calves, and small ruminants. Nevertheless, draft oxen, cows, and donkeys (the principal mode of transport of both people and products) were also disposed of as conditions worsened.

Table 7.5 shows this progression for survey sites in Ethiopia. In 1984, few animals of any type represented "distress sales" (sales specifically for the purpose of obtaining cash to purchase food). However in 1985, distress sales of all three most-valued animals rose steeply, with another rise for various livestock types in 1987 and 1988. The long-term implications of such asset stripping are considerable. Fewer oxen (and plows) are available for the next season, income from animal products disappears, and sales of fuel products suffer because modes of transport are gone.

Although it has been argued that the distress sale of assets is merely a "rational response" or "normal adjustment mechanism" of households facing a crisis, there is little doubt that famine-related asset disposal strongly impairs postcrisis economic recovery (Moris 1974). The loss of productive assets, such as pack animals and carpentry tools, has a long-term negative effect on the

TABLE 7.5 Percentage of Ethiopian sample households selling at least one cow, ox, or donkey to purchase food, 1984–88

Type of Livestock	1984	1985	1986	1987	1988
Oxen	0.5	13.0	4.7	5.2	3.0
Milk cows	0.2	8.7	3.2	2.3	5.4
Donkeys	—	3.3	1.2	1.4	1.6

SOURCE: Compiled from IFPRI Ethiopia survey data, 1989/90.

NOTE: — = a nil or negligible amount.

household's ability to pursue nonfarm income-earning activities. The loss of a donkey makes it much harder for women to collect firewood or manure bricks and transport them to market. Similarly, the sale of craft products, such as spun cotton and woven cloth, is compromised if a means of transport is unavailable.

As noted at the start of this chapter, the one other important asset to be considered is the social support that is enshrined in the concept of "community." No household lives in a social vacuum; most have ties of exchange and reciprocal obligation with other households, either locally or regionally, which form the framework for systems of social investment (Shipton 1990; Ravallion and Datt 1995).

As part of the Ethiopian survey, every household was interviewed by carefully trained enumerators on the qualitative issue of social relations. Using a format of open-ended questions framed by a common list of issues, conversations were held on the suffering experienced, the generosity of individuals, and the competition between households during the famine. Respondents recalled events of four to five years before, but group interaction and repeated interviews triggered key events that became cornerstones for memory. In fact, most responses needed little prompting—only the children were unwilling or unable to explore their pain. Many late-night discussions among adults were cathartic, exposing both the best and the worst of human nature.

In Ethiopia, around 43 percent of the wealthier survey households reported that they exchanged "more than usual support" with relatives during the famine. Among poorer households, the proportion was only 29 percent. Those not reporting mutual assistance argued that things were so bad that they could not help anyone but themselves. In the Ethiopian lowlands, where the famine was most intense, many people did feel a moral obligation to bury a dead neighbor, but that was the limit of mutual expectations. It was hard for respondents to talk about such matters. Sadness, guilt, and fear all mingled in hushed conversation about the still recent death of neighbors, friends, and relatives. Yet the pragmatic demands of survival during crisis became a solid bottom line for all. There was kindness in the darkness; but most individuals averted their eyes from the despair of others.

The diversity of experiences, both by wealth status and by region, suggests that social relationships can evolve as rapidly as the conditions around them. Cultural norms and the changing severity of local conditions both play a part. As Shipton (1990) points out, "Hunger seems to separate the more- from the less-valued ties . . . as sharing becomes more discriminant." Where it was difficult to find access to shared resources, many households sought loans, even on harsh terms. If relatives could not (or would not) give food or cash in the form of a gift, some would give a loan. More than forty-nine percent of loans obtained by Ethiopian households were from relatives, another forty percent were from friends, with only eleven percent coming from professional moneylenders or merchants. Slightly more of the wealthier households borrowed food and cash than did poorer households. They also took out larger loans. This indicates that primarily the poor but, in fact, all households lack access to credit that is crucial to preserving resources during times of stress.

Interest rates ranged from 50 to 300 percent, payable in cash or kind, and where obtained from relatives (rather than from merchants) they usually carried no time limit for repayment. Iliffe (1990) found by researching historical records that three years after the famine of 1912 in colonial Zimbabwe, many households "still had large unpaid debts for food issued on credit." Clearly the long-term debt incurred merely to survive famine can be a major burden to subsequent household development.

Changing Household Food Consumption

Reducing food consumption and adapting household diets overlap considerably and, in certain cases, precede the coping mechanisms outlined above (Kelly 1992). Even during nonfamine years, calorie consumption in famine-prone countries is extremely low. Table 7.6 lists the average per capita calorie

TABLE 7.6 Average calorie consumption in selected famine-prone, low-, and middle-income African countries, 1994

	Daily Calorie Supply (per capita)
Famine-prone countries	
Angola	1,663
Ethiopia	1,234
Mozambique	1,693
Somalia	1,575
Sudan	2,349
Low-income countries	
Sierra Leone	1,911
Tanzania	2,031
Togo	2,046
Zaire	1,913
Zambia	1,841
Middle-income countries	
Botswana	2,326
Côte d'Ivoire	2,304
Congo	2,133
Senegal	2,269
Zimbabwe	2,105

SOURCE: FAO 1997.

consumption for some of the most famine-prone countries of Africa, compared to averages in both poor- and middle-income African countries. It is clear from the table that each of the famine-affected countries (with the exception of Sudan) consume fewer calories than continentwide averages, not to mention the minimum requirements for survival. For example, the average per capita calorie consumption in Angola, Ethiopia, Mozambique, and Somalia was still below 1,700 per day—a full 600 calories below recommended minimum requirements.

It should be stressed that such figures are usually only rough estimates based on fragmentary surveys, food balance sheets (which often exclude roots and tubers from the calculation), and nutritional monitoring data (Kelly 1987; Mulhoff 1988). However in Sudan, a national survey conducted from 1978 to 1980 allowed income- and price-response parameters to be determined for "normal" consumption patterns preceding the 1984–85 famine (Sudan-MFEP 1982; Yohannes 1989). According to the survey, the Sudanese spent about two-thirds of their income on food. There were, of course, variations in these average shares across regions. A comparison between urban and rural Khartoum, for example, shows that the rural population allocated more of its income to food.

Shares across provinces and among income groups within the same province appear to follow the expected inverse relation between income level and food expenditure. In northern Kordofan, for example, households in the lowest-income group allocated, on average, 14 percent more of their income to food than did the upper-income group. In fact, share elasticity estimates for these provinces are very close, ranging between −0.44 for northern Kordofan and −0.45 for northern Darfur. In other words, the share of income spent on food increases by 0.5 percent at the margin for any 1.0 percent decrease in per capita expenditure.

Food expenditure and resultant calorie consumption also vary considerably across regions and income groups in Ethiopia. For example, the highest average food consumption amounts recorded among survey households in 1989/90 were found in the highlands (the least-famine-affected of the surveyed areas): 2,100 calories per capita (based on weekly and monthly data on food acquisition). In the lowlands, average consumption was a little over 1,700 calories per capita per day.

At the same time, there was variation within sites according to income and gender. Table 7.7 shows that higher-income Ethiopian households consumed over 2,400 calories per capita at the sample mean. Among the poor, there were many households subsisting on less than 1,600 kilocalories per capita per day, indicating a high amount of food deprivation even in the good harvest year of 1989/90.

Yet by nutritional standards, even wealthier households were underconsuming. For the Ethiopian sample as a whole, 68 percent of households con-

TABLE 7.7 Sample household per capita expenditure, food share, and calorie consumption, by tercile and gender of household head, Ethiopia and Sudan

	Total Expenditure per Month	Food Share	Kilocalories Consumed per Day
	(US$)[a]	(percent)	
Ethiopia[b]			
Income group			
Lower	10.77	64.1	1,658
Higher	24.40	65.0	2,444
Gender of household head			
Male	16.32	66.0	1,927
Female	17.83	67.0	2,110
Sudan[c]			
Income group			
Lower	34.12	74.3	1,913
Higher	84.20	68.4	2,961
Gender of household head			
Male	54.00	68.4	2,503
Female	59.30	72.7	2,341

SOURCE: Compiled from IFPRI Ethiopia survey data, 1989/90, and IFPRI Sudan household survey data, 1988/89.
[a]Nominal figures in local currency were converted to US$ using conversion factors from the World Bank, *World Tables* (1992).
[b]Terciles are based on per capita income.
[c]Terciles are based on per capita expenditure.

sumed less than 80 percent of the recommended daily allowance of 2,300 kilocalories. This compares unfavorably with surveys in countries such as The Gambia and Rwanda, which found 18 and 41 percent, respectively, of households to be calorie deficient (von Braun and Pandya-Lorch 1991). In other words, in 1988/89, a good year, no less than 68 percent of the households in the Ethiopian communities could be classified as food deficient.

Taking the analysis a step further, although Ethiopia households headed by women (widows, divorcées, or wives of soldiers) usually earned less than male-headed households, the share of income spent on food and their calorie consumption at the time of the survey were roughly the same as that of comparable male-headed households (see Table 7.7). The share spent on food, roughly 67 percent (varying little by income group), was higher than that spent by the poorest income groups of the Gambia in 1985/86: 59 percent (von Braun, Puetz, and Webb 1989), and higher than the 63 percent spent by landless laborers in Kenya in 1984/85 (Kennedy and Cogill 1987).

The most common calorie sources for the sample households in Ethiopia and Sudan are identified in Table 7.8. This shows that in Ethiopia, maize,

TABLE 7.8 Ethiopian and Sudanese sample household calorie sources, by tercile, 1988–90

Source of Calories	Ethiopia[a]		Sudan[b]	
	Poorer	Richer	Poorer	Richer
	(percent of total calories consumed)			
Cereals				
Maize	62.6	38.7	n.a.	n.a.
Millet	0.7	5.2	49.37	42.37
Sorghum	7.8	8.3	12.76	7.49
Wheat and wheat products	7.7	12.2	1.89	4.61
Other cereals	6.5	15.0	n.a.	n.a.
Noncereals				
Meat	0.2	0.1	2.44	4.64
Milk and milk products	1.5	1.6	2.71	3.53
Nuts and seeds	n.a.	n.a.	2.37	3.43
Oil and butter	0.4	1.1	9.54	9.17
Other noncereals	0.5	4.2	0.76	1.21
Pulses	5.8	10.6	5.33	6.27
Roots/tubers	5.5	1.7	0.03	0.25
Sugar and sweets	0.7	1.0	8.57	10.22
Vegetables and fruits	0.2	0.6	4.20	6.81

SOURCES: Compiled from IFPRI Ethiopia survey data, 1989/90, and IFPRI Sudan household sample survey data, 1988/89.

NOTE: n.a. = not available.

[a]Terciles are based on per capita income.
[b]Terciles are based on per capita expenditure.

sorghum, and wheat are the most common cereals at the survey locations, while pulses, roots, and tubers top the list of noncereal foods. Yet consumption of the major staples is not identical across income groups. In general, the wealthier households have a more varied diet than do the poorer households, eating more wheat. Conversely, the poorest households depend predominantly on maize, which is the most abundant and cheapest cereal. Households in the upper-income tercile also consume more pulses, vegetables, and oil and butter than those in the lower tercile. In Sudan, the staple foods are cowpeas, meat, milk, millet, okra, and sugar. A survey from 1978–80 confirmed that expenditure across major food components varies with income level (Teklu, von Braun, and Zaki 1991). The food shares for cereals decreased with income— from 45 percent in the lowest-income group to 23 percent in the highest. The poor therefore relied mainly on cereals. The shares of other food groups, notably meats, milk, sugar, and vegetables, appear to increase with income.

TABLE 7.9 Major foods consumed by sample households in Ethiopia and Sudan, by tercile, during famine year and 1989/90

	Ethiopia[a]		Sudan[b]	
Food Type	Poorer	Richer	Poorer	Richer
	(percent of households)			
Cereals				
Maize	93.4	70.4	n.a.	n.a.
Millet	1.4	10.1	83.3	89.6
Sorghum	17.8	34.1	25.0	16.7
Wheat and wheat products	22.6	37.7	50.0	83.3
Other cereals	13.1	33.9	n.a.	n.a.
Noncereals				
Meat	1.6	3.2	89.6	100.0
Milk and milk products	24.5	29.4	72.9	93.8
Nuts and seeds	n.a.	n.a.	33.3	52.1
Oil and butter	4.3	20.4	97.9	100.0
Others	29.5	77.8	100.0	100.0
Pulses	30.9	61.6	85.4	91.7
Roots/tubers	24.9	13.3	4.2	25.0
Sugar and sweets	9.3	48.1	97.9	100.0
Vegetables and fruits	9.3	48.1	100.0	100.0

SOURCES: Compiled from IFPRI Ethiopia survey data, 1989/90, and IFPRI Sudan household sample survey data, 1988/89.

NOTE: n.a. = Not available.

[a]Terciles are based on per capita income.
[b]Terciles are based on per capita expenditure.

But, do households rely on the same foods during a crisis? There are three main consumption responses to absolute food shortage: (1) diet can be diversified to incorporate food items not normally consumed, (2) the quantity of food consumed per meal can be reduced, or (3) the number of meals per day can be reduced (Webb 1993). All three measures were adopted by the households in the two study countries.

The principal foods consumed in Ethiopia and Sudan during 1988/89 are compared in Table 7.9. This shows that in a good harvest year, the Ethiopian survey households relied considerably on maize for their cereal consumption, supplementing that with varying shares of sorghum, wheat, and "other cereals" (which, in practice, meant teff). The relatively wealthier households consumed a greater share of the more expensive teff, as would be expected; the cheaper maize was consumed more by the poorer households. In Sudan, the principal cereal consumed in 1988/89 was millet, followed by wheat and then sorghum.

Again income played a differentiating role in that wealthier households consumed more wheat and poorer households more sorghum.

Of the noncereals, wealthier Ethiopian respondents reported considerable intake of oils, pulses, sugar, and vegetables. The poorest respondents, by contrast, consumed relatively more pulses, roots, and tubers. Interestingly, the converse was true in Sudan, where many more of the upper-income households consumed roots and tubers than did the poor. The wealthier group also consumed more meat and animal products than the poor.

Of course many households were also forced to eat "famine foods" as conditions became severe. Although certain forage foods are collected as a matter of course even during normal years, the range of items and frequency of consumption rose considerably during the crisis. In northern Kordofan, wild cereals and tree fruits (*aradabe, kursan, nebag,* and wild rice) were widely collected for consumption. Twenty-seven percent of the Sudanese sample households resorted to eating wild rice and tree fruits, 59 percent of these indicated that they would not have consumed these food items in a normal year.

When conditions worsen, the range of "edible" products becomes ever broader—a distressing experience that is not new to Africa. In precolonial Zimbabwe, for example, it was recorded that during the major famine of 1898 (caused by a combination of war with incoming white settlers, epidemic, and drought), many Matabele were "starving, having to eat baboons and monkeys. Others grind up the skins of rinderpest oxen and cook the powder for food, while others are now living on wild fruit such as berries, and roots of trees in the veldt" (Iliffe 1990). Similar conditions were recorded in precolonial Gambia by a pastor from the London-based Methodist Missionary Society. Pastor Thomas Dove reported to his superiors that after two successive years of drought in the upper reaches of the country, locals were "reduced to eating monkey, rats, snakes, dogs, and cats" (Webb 1994).

In Ethiopia during the 1995 famine, more than 95 percent of surveyed households in worst-hit areas supplemented their diets with tree roots, leaves, and even (in extreme cases) grass, dogs, and rats. In less-affected areas, the share of households consuming "famine foods" was close to 35 percent.

Table 7.10 indicates that in Ethiopia, a surprising 58 percent of households in the upper-income tercile increased their consumption of famine foods, compared with only 41 percent of those in the lower tercile. For Sudan, it was also the relatively wealthier households that increased their consumption of famine foods, more so than the poorer households. The other two methods of dealing with food shortage (reduced consumption per meal and reduced number of meals) represent severe hardship and a lack of alternatives, rather than coping. Between 55 and 75 percent of households in Ethiopia reduced the amount of food consumed per meal during the worst famine year (see Table 7.10). Again, more of the households doing so were relatively wealthier, rather than poorer. This is because poor households already start from a lower base.

TABLE 7.10 Consumption responses to famine of sample households in Ethiopia and Sudan, by tercile

Responses	Ethiopia[a]		Sudan[b]	
	Poorer	Richer	Poorer	Richer
	(percent of households)			
Number of meals per day				
One	63	47	43	26
Two	35	41	36	41
Three	2	12	21	31
Reduced quantities	55	75	81	64
Consumed famine foods	41	58	14	19

SOURCES: Webb, von Braun, and Yohannes 1992; Teklu, von Braun, and Zaki 1991.
[a]Terciles are based on per capita income.
[b]Terciles are based on the distribution of livestock ownership in 1984–85.

At the same time, most households also cut back on the number of meals per day. Table 7.10 shows that 63 percent of poorer sample households in Ethiopia consumed only one meal per day during the famine, compared with only 47 percent of richer households. The most extreme cases were recorded in the Rift Valley. In 1989, 67 percent of the households there consumed at least three meals per day; during the famine, 78 percent of households had only one (or fewer) meals per day. "Or fewer" is included because a dozen households reported going for up to four days without any food at all.

The same pattern was also found in Sudan. Families had to cut the frequency as well as the size of meals to ration food consumption in 1985. Roughly 70 percent of sample households reported that they had to cut meal size during 1985, and one in three households survived the worst of the famine on a single meal per day. Inevitably more households suffering malnutrition came from the poorest category—43 percent, compared with 26 percent from the more wealthy.

Nutritional and Demographic Responses to Famine

Prolonged food scarcity coupled with increased incidence of disease cannot be withstood for long without suffering adverse physiological effects (Payne and Lipton 1994). Some people were able to flee the famine. In Ethiopia, thousands of refugees crossed the border into Sudan and northern Kenya (Clark 1986; Kidane 1989; de Waal 1991). However, the number of people relocating *within* Ethiopia (not counting the movement toward feeding camps) was relatively small (Webb, von Braun, and Yohannes 1992). This might be explained by the fact that personal mobility was highly restricted by law during the 1980s, and that, although devastated by famine, each of the villages surveyed was reached by a relief organization before large numbers of people attempted to migrate.

The situation was different in Sudan where internal migration was less restricted. Data on the magnitude of displacements during the famine are patchy, but fragmentary information indicates that sizable movements occurred (KRMFEP 1986; de Waal 1987; Mohammed 1988). By 1984, the population that had already settled in four large feeding camps around Omdurman was estimated to be 46,000 (Economic and Social Research Council 1988). In 1984/85, larger-scale movements began soon after the farmers realized the harvest would be a complete failure.

Early distress migration was also observed among the northern nomads in Darfur in the 1983–85 period. Most of the Medub tribe lost their camels and moved to eastern Darfur to work as agricultural laborers, or to a relief camp in the town of Mellit. The Zaghawa people began to migrate from their tribal land at the end of 1983 and settled south of El Fasher with their relatives who had moved earlier during the droughts of the 1970s. The Zaghawa also migrated to areas south of Darfur and outside the region to Omdurman and Gezira. The Zayadia nomads also moved from Mellit to southern Darfur, as well as to the El Daein area.

High rates of migration were also recorded in the Kordofan sedentary sample. In one village as many as 95 percent of the IFPRI sample families claimed at least one migrant member; the rate of migration per family reached a high of 89 percent; and whole-family migration reached 74 percent (Teklu, von Braun, and Zaki 1991). Large-scale movements involving whole families were also evident in other parts of the region. A study among sedentary farmers in eastern Kordofan revealed that, from a low of 14.7 in 1980/81, the percentage of whole-family households that migrated reached 45.9 in the peak drought year of 1984/85 (Mohammed 1988).

Migration in northern Kordofan was in different directions, but because of diminished farm-employment opportunities the emphasis was generally toward nearby towns and major cities. The percentage of migrants in the IFPRI Kordofan survey who moved to urban areas (mainly Omdurman and Um Ruwaba) peaked at 63.8 in 1984/85, compared with the preceding four-year average of 5.4 percent. Those camped on the outskirts of El Obeid were estimated at 45,000 by March 1985 and by June 1985 there were approximately 25,000 people living in the camps on the outskirts of Kosti. Those without prior experience of migrating for seasonal work opted to move either to areas where they had relatives, access to casual work, or to relief camps.

These variations in migration patterns indicate the importance of proximity to urban areas, ecological variation (the existence of vegetative growth as a source of food and cash income), and availability of water. Distress migration was high in areas where the agricultural resource base was limited, alternative income sources were absent, and survival foods were not easily affordable or accessible. Also, in villages where the social-support network was discriminatory (providing little aid for recent immigrants), the disadvantaged were forced to migrate. However, there were also household-specific factors that contributed to emigration. Statistical analysis of household-level variables through a dichotomous logit decision model indicates that the odds of migrating were higher

1. Among families headed by men than those headed by women (who have fewer options)
2. Among households with few livestock assets
3. Among families with a large number of dependents (indicating distress migration or greater ability to seek labor opportunities or both
4. Where there was no access to clean water within a village

Some of those who stayed behind did survive the famine relatively unscathed, but most were affected by severe food deficits and increased levels of undernutrition and malnutrition.

A number of nutrition surveys were undertaken in Ethiopia and Sudan during the famines of the 1980s. These surveys were usually based on anthropometric measures of changes in weight relative to height of children under five years old. Such measures were compared with standard international references in order to identify groups that qualified for food distribution and supplementary feeding, and to monitor the nutritional effects of food shortage during the drought. In too many instances survey results showed acute levels of malnutrition equivalent to severe marasmus and kwashiorkor. For example, one July 1985 survey by Redd Barna/(Save the Children [Sweden]) covering the densely populated highlands of south-central Ethiopia found that 35 percent of infants were malnourished—that is, at less than 80 percent of the World Health Organization (WHO)/U.S. National Center for Health Statistics standard (Table 7.11). Conditions improved once the agency opened a feeding camp, thereby bringing the percentage of malnourished infants down to only 2.5 a year later. A similar OXFAM/United Nations Children's Fund (UNICEF) survey in the province of the Sudanese Kordofan also found that about 25 percent of the children in northern Kordofan were malnourished in mid-1985 (Table 7.12). The proportion dropped to 11 percent during the 1985 harvest, and stabilized at around 7.5 percent in early 1986.

The relationship between child malnutrition and food prices (reflecting food scarcity and high demand) is illustrated in Figure 7.1. The dramatic deterioration of purchasing power caused by changes in the terms of trade between cereals and livestock was translated into an increased incidence of severe child malnutrition in Kordofan and, in many cases, increased levels of mortality. Death was the last stage of the famine for many people. In Ethiopia, the proportion of surveyed households that lost at least one family member to

TABLE 7.11 Percentage of children severely malnourished in Gara Godo (Ethiopia), selected dates 1985–89

Date	Weight for Height		Sample Size
	< 80 Percent	< 70 Percent	
1985			
March	21.9	6.0	800
July	35.0	7.5	467
December	4.5	0.1	n.a.
1986			
March	6.0	0.5	n.a.
June	2.5	0.1	n.a.
1987			
March	3.5	0.7	2,507
December	4.7	0.8	1,881
1988			
June	10.5	n.a.	3,200
December	8.9	n.a.	2,996
1989			
May	18.3	2.9	234
September	11.7	1.2	343

SOURCE: Webb, von Braun, and Yohannes 1992.

NOTE: n.a. = not available.

famine-related death averaged 40 percent in the lowlands. In the highlands, the average was much lower: 18 percent. At one lowland site on the Rift Valley escarpment, 18 whole families were lost out of 120 households in the village. The immediate cause of death at this site was cholera. Most of the victims were preschoolers and the elderly. Of the 80 or so famine deaths in sample house-

TABLE 7.12 Proportion of malnourished children < 80 and 70 percent of standard weight for height among a sedentary population in Kordofan (Sudan), 1985/86

Time	Sample	North Kordofan	South Kordofan
		(percent)	
Feb./March 1985	< 80 percent	13.1	10.2
	< 70 percent	1.1	0.4
May/June 1985	< 80 percent	25.2	11.5
	< 70 percent	3.4	1.3
Sep./Oct. 1985	< 80 percent	11.0	9.5
	< 70 percent	1.2	0.5
March/April 1986	< 80 percent	7.5	6.0
	< 70 percent	0.7	0.7

SOURCES: OXFAM/UNICEF and Kordofan Regional Government data for 1985 and 1986.

FIGURE 7.1 Price shocks and malnutrition in Kordofan children, January 1981–December 1986

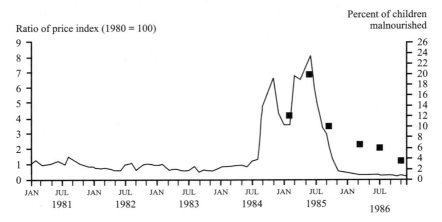

— Terms of trade (sorghum to cattle)

■ Children malnourished (less than 80 percent of weight for height)

SOURCE: Teklu, von Braun, and Zaki 1991.

holds in that village, 46 percent occurred in children less than 5 years old, while the majority of adult victims were over 40.

In IFPRI's Kordofan survey villages, no significant excess mortality rate was evident for 1984/85. The crude mortality rate did increase, but not as much as expected in a period of low food intake and high incidence of disease. Thus the expected intensification of high mortality and low fertility was not evident in the survey villages. Although specific to study areas, these results contrast with de Waal's (1987) findings for Darfur of a decline in the natural growth of village populations due to an excess mortality rate coupled with a decline in birthrate. There certainly was a slowing of the growth rate in many of the IFPRI survey villages, dropping from 2.7 percent per year in 1983/84 to 2.3 percent in 1984/85. However, a high rate of emigration, especially in the short term, was largely responsible for this effect.

Coping with Life after the Famine

The 1984/85 famine in the Horn of Africa ended with a relatively good harvest in 1986, and was combined with improved food aid distribution mechanisms. In October/November 1986, 35 percent of children in Sudan under five years of age were identified as stunted (height for age), 42 percent were underweight (weight for age), and 16 percent were defined as wasted (weight for height) (Teklu, von Braun, and Zaki 1991). The prevalence of malnutrition was higher in rural Sudan, particularly among the nomadic population, but was also high in urban areas. Large regional variations were also observed. The worst areas were in the provinces of Gezira, Kassala, and Red Sea. The country experienced a persistent food security problem after the famine with significant variations across locations (urban/rural), provinces, and seasons (Maxwell 1989).

In Ethiopia, malnutrition continues to be both a chronic and an acute problem even in good rainfall years. Surveys in the early 1990s indicate that approximately 10 percent of infants were identified as wasted (less than 80 percent of the standard weight-for-height ratio), and more than 64 percent were defined as stunted—less than 80 percent of the standard height for age (World Bank 1993; Pelletier et al. 1995).

There is significant variation in these rates across both regions and seasons. For example, the 1992 National Nutrition Survey showed that the proportion of wasting (acute malnutrition) ranged from 4.4 percent in Bale in the southeastern part of the country to 14.2 percent in the province of Tigray in the north (Habte-Wold and Maxwell 1992; Pelletier et al. 1995). Stunting similarly ranged from 57 percent of infants in the northern Shewa region to 75 percent in southern Gondar (in the northwest). In certain areas, seasonal fluctuations in food supply and energy expenditure resulted in an average decrease of 2 kilograms of body mass in both male and female adults during the preharvest ("hungry") season (Kumar Neka Tebeb, and Pastore 1992).

Conclusions Concerning Household Coping Mechanisms

The study of household behavior and individual coping strategies under famine stress demonstrates that famine causes multifaceted economic and social responses in the affected society. A diverse set of market and community insurance systems allows for a variety of household responses. Government and public policies must first understand and then build on these responses in order to achieve the goal of efficient famine mitigation prevention. It must not be forgotten that the study of coping is, in fact, the study of human ingenuity under economic stress. Famine mitigation requires public action to support and strengthen that ingenuity.

8 Policies and Programs to Mitigate and Prevent Famines

This chapter examines a selection of publicly supported initiatives aimed at responding to or reducing the impact of famine. At the outset, a few broader points must be emphasized. First, it must be stressed that famines cannot be effectively dealt with through specific programs alone. Larger policy issues discussed in the preceding chapters must be kept in mind when dealing with events that affect many millions of people over large areas. Insufficient attention to the macropolicy context can undermine programs for famine prevention, leading them to be unsustainable or ineffective or both. This is particularly true in an environment characterized by war and banditry, and without legal recourse (see Chapter 3).

The second point is that appropriate policies for market integration (and possibly also price stabilization) need to be in place if individual projects are to function effectively (see Chapter 6). Appropriate macropolicies should be embedded in a framework of trade and exchange-rate policies that facilitate not only economic growth and domestic agricultural production, but also the effective implementation of targeted project activities (see Chapter 4). Unfortunately, during the 1970s and 1980s, most famine-prone countries, including Ethiopia (Manyazewal 1992) and Sudan (Atabani 1991), did not establish appropriate macroeconomic policies, thereby not only making famine more likely but also hindering effective project-level responses.

Policies aimed at securing adequate household food security are the basic pillars of social security policy. Short-term policies differ from long-run ones in a distinction that Sen has called "entitlement protection" versus "entitlement promotion." Both can be achieved through an appropriate division of responsibilities between the public and private sectors. Such a division of responsibility depends on country-specific capabilities that can be enhanced with external support, with strengthening institutional and human capital development as longer-term goals. So is the economic growth upon which effective policy depends. Given the close relationship between agricultural production and vulnerability of the poor in rural economies, agricultural policy over the medium and long terms should be seen in association with food policies of a more short-term nature.

These broad policy conclusions are reiterated here to avoid any possible misperception that the main emphasis is on the lessons of micro- and program-level interventions. On the contrary, it is argued here that neither famine mitigation nor prevention can be achieved through appropriate grassroots action alone. It is true that in the absence of strong governmental, nongovernmental, and community institutions, some broader policies may fail because of implementation constraints. However, many micro projects also fail where the macrocontext is inappropriate. The two need to be considered in tandem.

For a long time, famine activities have been exempted from even simple economic assessments, applying to both the economics of famine creation (for example, the political economy of violence) and the economics of famine relief and prevention. Strengthening of international policies, possibly sanctions, and conflict resolution is needed to reduce the possibility of the former (see Chapter 3). Some options and cost considerations for the latter are discussed below.

Toward Optimal Program Mixes

When discussing a conceptual framework for public action against famine, at least two dimensions need to be distinguished: First, *what* should be done; that is, what policies, programs, and projects should be implemented? And second, *when* should it be done— that is, at what point will implementation be most effective? The question of how to implement appropriate policies relates to each of the above.

The conceptual framework presented in Figure 2.1 did not explicitly include a time frame that would take account of lags associated with actions and impacts. For instance, a policy of price stabilization (to avoid food price explosions), or the release of publicly held reserve stocks can have an immediate impact. So can feeding schemes. Employment programs, if launched only during a crisis, are likely to have difficulty meeting "output"-based objectives. This is even more true of agricultural development programs. The key is to combine short- and long-term interventions (relief *and* development) in mutually reinforcing ways.

An illustrative picture of these alternative choices is shown in Figure 8.1. The figure depicts the two dimensions of time and relative impact (famine mitigation and prevention). Of course the alternatives considered have different characteristics in terms of sustainability potential. Whereas agricultural technology programs have a high potential for sustainable effects, this is not the case with large-scale feeding schemes.

The policy and program focus of many African countries (and their donors) has increasingly shifted in the 1980s and 1990s to short-term actions.

FIGURE 8.1 Patterns of time-dependent impacts of alternative policies and programs on famine mitigation and prevention

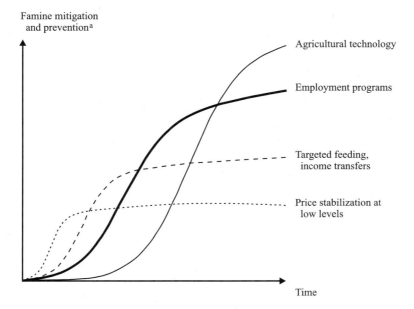

Famine mitigation and prevention[a]

Agricultural technology

Employment programs

Targeted feeding, income transfers

Price stabilization at low levels

Time

NOTE: It is assumed that there is a similar amount of resources spent on each of the alternative programs.

[a]Measured, for instance, in terms of number of people prevented from famine risk.

For instance, in the early 1990s the United Nations WFP largely shifted away from its "developmental" activities in Africa because of pressing immediate relief needs. In 1987, the WFP allocated $175 million to development activities in Sub-Saharan Africa, which represented roughly 65 percent of the institution's total expenditure for the region. By 1995, this amount had reached more than $616 million, of which development projects accounted for less than 20 percent—the lions' share taken up by relief expenditures and extrabudgetary costs (WFP 1991a, 1996b). Similarly, the United States spent more on "relief" than on "development assistance" in the early 1990s, while the World Bank has also begun designing programs that cater to relief as well as to development concerns in Africa (Binswanger and Landell-Mills 1995).

In other words, as the response to short-term needs has become more urgent, the focus of attention has shifted toward the left on the time axis in Figure 8.1. The cost of international peacekeeping operations, for instance, rose from $0.5 billion in 1991 to around $1.5 billion in 1995, not including operations in the former Yugoslavia (OECD 1997). Under prevailing resource limitations, this trend may carry a cost in terms of reduced potential for investments with a developmental impact. Net Official Development Assistance to Sub-Saharan Africa declined steadily after 1992, reaching an amount in 1995 that was lower in real terms than in 1985 ($16.8 million versus $18 million at 1994 prices) (OECD 1997). One consequence of this may be a growing vulnerability of certain countries to large-scale shocks, particularly where donor commitment to supporting external intervention is weak (as it was for Kenya, Rwanda, and Sudan during the mid-1990s).

There is no easy solution to the dilemma. Ignoring short-term needs of malnourished people is not a politically acceptable option for democratic governments in countries with a free flow of information. Thus increased resource mobilization will be needed to ensure that relief interventions can contribute as much as possible to overcoming famine risks in the longer term. At the same time, the potential long-term result of relief actions should not be overlooked; their impact on health and human resources may have very long-term (intergenerational) consequences (WFP 1996b). Only children protected from famines can live up to their potential. Concern for people first is appropriate not only on ethical grounds, but also in terms of sound economics: appropriate relief represents a basic investment in human development.

The Cost of Relief and Rehabilitation

Famine prevention and mitigation require large resources. However, what is the optimal mix of such interventions for achieving an effective reduction in famine vulnerability for populations in the short and long term? Whereas the answer is related to the nature of specific famine conditions and realistic alternatives, an outline of a necessary approach is offered. Each of the actions considered in this chapter works toward the common goal of protecting people against the consequences of famine (mortality, dislocation, destitution), both in the short and the long term. To be sure, there is a potential for complementarity as well as competition between different project approaches that operate under inherently different time frames. Marginal welfare gains (or losses) associated with individual interventions may depend on what other projects have been implemented in the same area; for example, free food aid may compete with food-for-work projects, or the benefits of cash-for-work programs may be compromised by policies inhibiting private trade.

Given limited public resources for famine mitigation and prevention, concern about costs will continue to be a deciding factor. The choice of projects and policies used should be guided by the concern to save life in as rapid and efficient a manner as possible, in ways that reduce future household vulnerability and do not, through short-term action, compromise the benefits of long-run human development. Reestablishing a sustainable livelihood is one of the prime elements of postcrisis rehabilitation activities.

However, quantification of intervention costs is not straightforward. Defining points of reference against which to evaluate a policy or program is complex in crisis situations with their highly uncertain time paths. According to Reutlinger (1988), the cost-effectiveness of an intervention designed to transfer income depends not only on the marginal income transferred, but also on the subsidy component of the scheme. That is, private costs and benefits may differ from social costs and benefits. The marginal income transferred to the individual can be calculated as the difference between income received by project participants and the cost to the participants (such as potential income lost from other sources). And the subsidy component represents the difference between the value of assets or services generated and the cost of the scheme to the public (Reutlinger 1988).

The data required for analyzing projects according to these parameters are rarely generated in practice (Alderman and Kennedy 1987; Reutlinger 1988). Although research into the cost-effectiveness of specific nutritional improvement programs has progressed considerably since the mid-1970s (see, for example, Mateus 1983; Berg 1987; Pinstrup-Andersen, Pelletier, and Alderman 1995), the same cannot be said for research into the cost-effectiveness of relief interventions in famines. Many evaluations do provide detailed audits of input disbursements (food, cash, assets), numbers of beneficiaries, and gross costs (NORAD 1984; Ethiopia-RRC 1985; Jareg 1987; UNHCR 1988). However, few generate the data required for detailed net-cost calculations.

A broad, merely indicative, calculation of the costs involved in choosing alternatives among possible food relief interventions might relate a targeted population's incremental food consumption to total program costs. Total costs would include project costs, private costs, and national overhead costs. Such calculations are to be interpreted cautiously and would have to be performed for different population groups and income strata in order to assess the effectiveness of an activity in reaching the most needy people.

Introducing an economic rationale into famine mitigation and prevention is not meant to promote a static planning approach, but to enhance public awareness of the costs and benefits to alternative famine prevention policies and programs. None of the interventions considered below was able to collate all of the suggested cost-relevant data. Only a broad indication of costs associated with the public works, food distribution, and income transfer projects can be given. An assessment of the comparative costs of intervention types and scales, based on more descriptive net-cost information, as outlined above, remains essential in determining priorities and creating effective counterfamine policies. The interventions considered below are categorized according to time dimensions—short-term mitigation versus long-term prevention of famine.

Information for Early Warning

Effective action against famine has two important prerequisites: first, an adequate capability to detect potential emergencies and alert appropriate organizations of danger; and second, advance preparation by international, national, and local organizations for an effective response to crisis alerts. Where the first prerequisite is concerned, EWSs have grown in number, complexity, role, and relevance during the 1980s and 1990s. There are many versions. Some systems have been developed with the main goal being to inform international agencies about the need for action. These include the FAO's Global Information and Early Warning System on Food and Agriculture (GIEWS) and its Emergency Prevention Systems (EMPRES) for Desert Locust, the U.S. Agency for International Development (USAID)'s Famine Early Warning programme (FEWS), the WFP's Vulnerability Assessment and Mapping (VAM) activity, the WHO's Epidemiological Early Warning System (EEWS), and Save the Children (United Kingdom)'s Risk Mapping Project (supported by the European Union [EU]). Other systems have been developed for national use, such as the Southern African Development Coordination Regional and National Early Warning System (based in Harare), the Intergovernmental Authority on Drought and Development's Regional Food Information System (based in Djibouti), and the Club du Sahel Program for the Sahel (based in Niamey). The latter systems typically collaborate with, and sometimes receive funding from, international donors.

The rapid evolution and spread of such EWSs, particularly in Africa, is one of the success stories of development. There has been important progress in drought alerts (such as the major drought in southern Africa in 1992/93), monitoring locust swarms, and in plotting market-price movements, to name but a few of their benefits. Also, developments in EWS methodologies have intensified debate about the nature of food insecurity and about the most appropriate ways to tackle it. As a result there should be few future droughts or locust swarms that escape the attention of EWS analysts and, through them, policymakers and politicians.

However, that does not rule out future famine. There are still two main problems within the realm of "preparedness." First, most famines are no longer related to environmental vagaries—it is armed conflict that causes the worst of today's crises. Although it was possible to head off famine in Zimbabwe in 1992 thanks to early warning of the likely severity of drought (and a massive international donor response), it was hardly possible to curtail crises in Burundi/Rwanda/Zaire, Liberia/Sierra Leone, or in Somalia in the mid-1990s. In other words, EWSs are well suited to alert against drought or other environmental disasters, but they are poorly equipped to warn of impending civil war or political upheaval.

Warnings of political crises can, of course, be obtained through diplomatic as well as media channels. However, there are as yet few well-established, widely accepted, apolitical systems for the collation and analysis of human- and sociological-crisis data[1]. There remains an absence of agreement on the basics; namely: What are the appropriate data sources? How does one measure conflict risk? What analytical methodologies are appropriate? And how can organizations with universal membership (such as the United Nations) best disseminate "sensitive" information?

A case in point is Rwanda. According to the Joint Evaluation of Emergency Assistance to Rwanda, considerable information about plans and conspiracies had been collected by this UN system by early 1994 (JEEAR 1996). However, there was no structured way of using, interpreting, or responding to it. One of the JEEAR's conclusions was that any useful EWS dealing with sociopolitical stresses must go beyond simply developing a network, building on data-based systems, or creating formal models for anticipating crises. None of these techniques would have been adequate in the Rwandan case. As is evident, this is an area that requires urgent research and action.

The second main problem with most EWSs is that even when warnings are timely and accurate, the relief response may be neither. Although technicians and analysts are increasingly able to offer useful warnings, policymakers often ignore them—with well-known tragic consequences. As Buchanan-Smith and Davies (1995) argue, "There is little point in further improving the ability of EWSs to provide decisionmakers with the certainty they crave, until there are changes in the institutional framework within which they operate." Thus fine-tuning the forecasting is less urgent than upgrading the response. Improvements in early warning have limited value if they are not unequivocally tied to timely responses based on previously prepared technical and economic appraisals of potential interventions. Interministerial coordination that defines actions, lines of responsibility, and funding *before* a crisis point has been reached is essential. For example, during the 1980s Zimbabwe had already established an interministerial drought task force that was able to act when drought struck in the 1990s. Similarly, Ethiopia approved its National Disaster Prevention and Mitigation Strategy in the early 1990s, which established structured guidelines for institutional collaboration and interaction aimed at more effective famine mitigation. And the Botswana government's ability to respond quickly to droughts is due to good bottom-up communication between local rural development councils and relevant ministries.

---

1. A few still nascent examples of systems that may in the future help to fill the gap include the Conflict Alert System (CAS) based at the Georgia Institute of Technology, Atlanta, Georgia; the Computer-Aided System for Analysis of Conflicts (CASCON) based in Cambridge, Massachusetts; and the PIOOM system—Risk of Political and Humanitarian Crises Project at Leiden University, Netherlands (still in the formulation stage).

Of course, no system is perfect. Underfunding remains a problem in many countries. There is the danger of complacency where famines have become rare, leading to an erosion of data collection and analytical capabilities. Such disinvestment in EWSs is extremely dangerous and should be avoided. Most of Africa needs to invest further in the collection and analysis of information at local levels, increasingly with the involvement of local institutions. There is also a need to explore the viability and value of developing community-based EWSs. How can society play a stronger role in local systems for early warning and response that helps the most needy in ways that do not offend their dignity or disrupt existing relations in the local economy? This is another area that requires applied research and urgent action.

Combining Program Options with Policy

Analyses in the earlier chapters illustrated that famine is caused by several interacting factors, which, under unfortunate circumstances, reinforce each other to result in terrible hunger, social disintegration, and mortality. The following sections seek to identify the multifaceted responses required for efficient public action. As already stated, no single instrument can lay claim to being a cure-all. The initiatives discussed below must be appropriately combined and timed. Tailoring programs to policy requires a strategic framework. Its sustainability in the African context would depend on, and need to promote, strong economic growth.

The policies discussed earlier, and the programs reviewed below, address different food risks. Table 8.1 illustrates these risks by linking them with selected food-related policies and programs. A number of generally accepted principles are illustrated in this table:

- First, crop production risks are best addressed directly through technological change and improved commercialization of agriculture—a long-term process. In countries with high risks of fluctuating food access and prices, the joint promotion of technological change in staple foods and an appropriate environment for agricultural commercialization is called for.
- Second, short-term food availability and related food price risks can be addressed through varied and specific actions, including macrolevel policies, stockholding, trade, and aid policies, as well as programs that strengthen the entitlements of households lacking adequate food supply. The latter could include public works, provision of consumption credit, food subsidies, feeding programs, and income transfers. Past experiences with food stamp and price subsidy programs in African famine-prone countries have not been encouraging however (Pinstrup-Andersen 1988).

TABLE 8.1 Famine risks and selected food policy choices

Policy Choices	Crop/Livestock Production Risks	Food Availability and Price Risks	Employment and Income Risks
(Agricultural) production policies			
Technological change	lll	lll	
Commercialization, diversification	ll	ll	
Promotion of behavioral change; education	ll	l	ll
Other income and employment generation policies			
Public works		l	ss, l
Credit		ss	
Macroeconomic policies	ss, ll	ss, ll	s, l
Subsidies and transfer policies			
Feeding programs		sss	
Food stamps (including transfers)		ss	
Food price subsidies; rationing		sss	
Food trade, food aid policies	sss, l		s

SOURCE: Adapted from von Braun et al. 1992.

NOTES: extent of positive impacts:
l, ll, lll = some, moderate, high long-term impact,
s, ss, sss = some, moderate, high short-term impact, and
s,l = mix of short- and long-term impact.

- Third, employment and income risks can be tackled in the long run through agricultural production policies, and in the short run through income-enhancement strategies. Labor-intensive public works would have both short- and long-term risk-reduction effects, the latter through the creation of assets that generate future income streams.

Following this discussion through, the programs examined below fall into four broad categories: (1) direct food and income transfers, (2) labor-intensive public works, (3) asset transfers and credit programs, and (4) agricultural technology development and transfers.

Since only these four program types are examined, the importance of health services needs to be addressed. Food security policies have a limited impact on reducing health risks unless they are integrated with effective nutrition, health, and child-care interventions. Famines make malnourished people more susceptible to diseases, and this often happens just as medical services are declining or collapsing. The immediate cause of excess mortality during famines is largely related to disease (de Waal 1989). Health services, often weak in the first place, are ill equipped to take on additional burdens, such as intensive feeding schemes, which are often added to their functions during times of famine.

The Short-Term Response: Emergency Relief

In Africa, public actions often are initiated only after famines are already in progress. Ideally, there should be an opportunity to design optimal prevention strategies before a crisis begins. In reality, there are few mitigation options available with a famine already under way. Access to food during famine cannot be left to market forces alone (Webb 1997). This does not mean that relief operations cannot make use of general principles of competition during relief operations. For example, competitive bidding for food provisioning or trucking services can mean lower project costs. There may even be competition among relief agencies where feasible. Making food accessible to people where they live (rather than encouraging relocation) is the first order of the day. Feeding camps should always be an instrument of last resort. Nevertheless, the undesired feeding camp, whether the result of refugee movements due to natural calamities or political upheaval, is a reality to be faced. The experiences of feeding camps, and the often unsatisfactory performance of nutritional services provided through them, are briefly discussed below (Keen 1992; ACC/SCN 1993).

Other forms of direct food transfers are reviewed in more depth, with examples from Ethiopia and Sudan. Observing the history of feeding camps and of free-food distribution mechanisms suggests, first, that relief operations in the future must be tailored to local circumstances (including organizational capabilities). Second, a poor utilization of aid resources (including food) tends to result from poorly established or ignored rules of distribution. It seems apparent that weak management and ineffective operation of feeding camps can mean the poorest and most disadvantaged households will not receive the aid they need (Duffield 1994).

Although this generally argues for a stronger local role during intervention and relief, it must be stressed that intracommunity as well as intrahousehold discrimination of vulnerable groups (particularly women) also takes place.[2] The discrimination by ethnicity, gender, and status witnessed in Zaire in the Rwandan refugee camps in 1994/95 is a case in point (Eriksson et al. 1996).

Feeding Camps

When no alternative interventions are being offered, crisis circumstances often foster camp creation. Opening of a feeding camp is more art than science; few hard-and-fast rules or criteria exist. As a result, quickly evolving conditions on the ground, political considerations, and the availability of resources interact to determine the siting and operational capacity of new camps. For instance, in areas with deficient infrastructure where few feeding locations exist, camps tend to form—even if no shelter is provided. People in search of food cluster around food-donating outlets. More than 2 million Rwandese crossed the border into neighboring countries during 1994, most of them ending up in the numerous refugee camps set up in Burundi, Tanzania, and Zaire. Another 2 million or more within Rwanda were displaced (Eriksson et al. 1996).

At the height of the Ethiopian famine of 1984/85, almost 300 camps around the country distributed food rations to the seriously malnourished. Among the IFPRI survey households referred to in Chapter 6, 35 percent had at least one child admitted to a camp. Two-thirds of these households came from middle- and lower-income groups. Most of these camps admitted children who were under intensive care for up to nine months. One child from the survey sample of Ethiopian households remained in the camp for more than a year, returning home only when the camp itself was closed down. Only two sample household children died in the camp.

Such camps were opened at two of the Ethiopian survey sites. These were not large camps on the scale of the highly publicized camp of Korem, where, in early 1985, over 10,000 children were fed each day (Appleton

---

2. Commitments made by the WFP at the Beijing conference on women in 1995 sought to establish operational norms whereby women are the principal recipients and managers of food aid distributed in camps (WFP 1996c).

1988). Nevertheless, they each covered several communities with thousands of malnourished children and mothers. For 1985 as a whole, an average of 105 marasmic children were under critical care and intensive feeding each month in these two camps. More than 70 percent of those admitted to critical care were less than 65 percent of the average weight for height (Jareg 1987). Another 209 less-malnourished children benefited from supplementary feeding. And over 200 family rations (60–75 kilograms of grain, plus 3 kilograms of supplementary food for each child under five) were distributed each month. The principal foods provided were wheat flour and soy-fortified sorghum grits, *faffa,* corn-sugar milk, and fish powder. Palatability problems arose with the fish powder and sorghum grits, which were subsequently targeted only to children less than nine months old (Jareg 1987).

The brunt of the crisis had passed by the second half of 1986. By June, the proportion of children below 80 percent of the average weight for height had fallen to less than 3 percent—from a high of 35 percent in July 1985. Relief activities were suspended in September 1986, and attention was turned to projects aimed at rehabilitation. Unfortunately the improvements were not sustainable. The return of drought in 1987 and 1988, coupled with epidemics of malaria and meningitis raised the rate of severe malnutrition back to 18 percent by mid-1989. As a result, emergency feeding activities were resumed toward the end of 1988 (Redd Barna 1989).

Most parents were satisfied that the intervention had saved lives. Almost 50 percent of respondents noted that "all would be dead" had it not been for the camp. The other 50 percent felt that without the intervention more people would certainly have died, but that there were problems to be confronted. For example, it was felt that too many patients contracted infections while undergoing medical care. Over 56 percent of respondents referred to the danger of contagion resulting from overcrowding in the camp. (It should be noted that an estimated 80,000 Rwandese died in the refugee and IDP camps during the 1994 crisis, mainly from cholera and dysentery. Although many times lower than the number killed as a result of genocide and conflict, many of the disease-related deaths were certainly avoidable [Jaspars 1994; Eriksson et al. 1996].)

Whereas cholera and other epidemics were successfully avoided at the camps surveyed in Ethiopia through mass vaccinations (2,000 children were vaccinated by October 1985), one-half of those admitted did contract some kind of disease during their stay (Jareg 1987; Appleton 1988). Most were of an enteric nature, probably due to poor sanitation facilities. During 1985, water and firewood were collected for the camp by volunteers in the community. It was not until late 1986 that public latrines were dug, and none of the springs was protected from contamination (Jareg 1987).

A second complaint concerned project-community communication. The selection process followed standard anthropometric criteria; however not all project staff had the time (or language fluency) to explain routines, timetables, and rationales to the community at large. As a result, many households suffered from a lack of communication with project staff.

A third problem related to the family rations. Many sample households felt that such rations were too small. Households larger than five people received 75 kilograms of cereals per month. This ration was based on an assumed average household size of six people. However, the average household size in the present survey sample was about eight people. Larger families therefore found it difficult to cope. Most camps closed down as soon as location-specific measures of child malnutrition or extreme destitution reached "acceptable" benchmarks. Anthropometric measures were widely used, but the personal judgment of food aid distributors was also generally accepted as a final call.

Free Food Aid Distribution and Transfers

Relief food aid is a form of transfer. Despite the unresolved debate concerning the potential negative dependency, dietary, and disincentive effects of food aid (which relate primarily to the effects of government-to-government-program food aid), few voices were raised against a mass mobilization of emergency food to Ethiopia in 1984/85 (Puetz, Broca, and Payongayong 1995; ADE 1996). The unprecedented scale of the response is well known, and its impact was widely felt. Households in all seven Ethiopian survey sites received food aid during the famine years, but at different amounts, according to need. For example, at one site in the lowlands (Dinki), 95 percent of survey respondents received some food aid, compared with less than 2 percent in Debre Berhan in the highlands. These differences reflect the divergent famine experiences of the two sites. The frequency and volume of food received also varied by survey site. Food distribution was a common activity in Ethiopia throughout the 1980s. Between 1984 and 1992, many households in drought-prone regions obtained food aid (primarily wheat) for several years in a row.

In most cases Ethiopia's Relief and Rehabilitation Commission (RRC) or an NGO carried out distributions that were conducted, on average, once every two months, although this varied by site according to availability of stocks, transport difficulties (mostly in the rainy season), and local storage facilities. Survey households at the more remote locations received rations only once or twice during the entire worst year of famine. Only the pastoralists in Sidamo received food rations more frequently than twice a month.

Distribution procedures also varied. In some camps, anthropometric measures were used as guidelines for food distribution (Young 1986; Shoham and Borton 1989). In others, food went to people who were, according to NGO staff, "skinny in their appearance and had nothing more to sell" (Erni 1988). In some instances lists of needy people were drawn up by village leaders, and it fell to them to ensure an equitable distribution of the food (Intertect 1986).

There is little evidence from the Ethiopian survey sites that distribution was overtly manipulated in favor of wealthier households. Those that cut their consumption back to one meal per day during the famine received, on average, twice as much food as households still consuming three meals per day. The latter had certainly reduced the amounts eaten per meal, but they were clearly not as badly affected as those only eating once a day.

As a result of uneven distributions and often imperfect targeting based on absolute rather than relative need, the amounts of food aid received were small. Standard rations recommended by the RRC were 15 kilograms of cereals and 600 grams of oil per capita per month, equivalent to roughly 1,700 kilocalories per capita per day (Yitbarek 1988). This ration was rarely provided to sample households for more than a few months. Households received an average of only 180 kilograms in the worst year. In other words, food relief in the survey areas enhanced household consumption for a limited time only. It could not, on its own, have supported households through the entire crisis. Instead, food aid acted as a temporary measure until other interventions could be set in place. At the hardest-hit sample site (Dinki), food aid was distributed for six months in 1985 prior to the implementation of a more complex asset-distribution project. When the latter was established, free food distribution was stopped. (The implications of a lack of overlap between such interventions are discussed later.)

Issues of targeting and ration sizes were also important in Sudan. Emergency operations there (including the large 1989/90 "Operation Lifeline" in the south) had to deal with particularly protracted conflict situations. By 1988, one-half of the population of southern Sudan had been displaced, and deaths resulting from conflict-related famine in that year totaled approximately 250,000 (Deng and Minear 1993).

Deng and Minear (1993) give a comprehensive account of the program and conclude that the experience of the major international interventions "provides striking—and distressing—evidence of the limited extent to which the results of past efforts inform future activities" (p. 123). Among their recommendations is an emphasis on institutional reforms, including the call for a mechanism to ensure high-level international political review of humanitarian emergencies, a code of conduct to encourage higher levels of professionalism among aid providers, a clearer authority for UN agencies to deal with armed insurgencies on humanitarian issues, and attention to indigenous resourcefulness (Deng and Minear 1993, pp. 124–129).

In Sudan's western provinces, there were three principal waves of food aid in the 1980s. The biggest flow was from 1984–86. Another crop failure occurred in 1987, prompting a second relief action in 1988. The good crop year of 1988 was followed by two consecutive years of bad harvest, which called for more food aid. Kordofan received a total of 330,000 tons of cereals from 1984 to 1986, after which the flow dropped to 32,000 tons in 1986/87. The institutional response was organized around a set of administrative committees established in Kordofan at the end of 1984, which included a high-level, policymaking relief committee set up in August 1984. It was responsible for formulating plans, strategies, and policies to mobilize resources, and for guiding and supervising relief work. Technical committees were set up at the regional and local levels to implement the 1984/85 relief operation. The office of Regional Food Aid Administration (RFAA) was created in August 1984 to administer food assistance in collaboration with the technical committees.

The Sudanese RRC, which had been created in mid-1985, was not yet in a position to provide effective institutional support. Thus the donor community took a leading role in relief operations there in 1985/86. Food delivery was undertaken largely by donors themselves, with assistance from foreign NGOs. This parallel structure was abandoned at the end of 1986, and the RFAA office in Kordofan took responsibility for the distribution and management of relief work in 1988 (Buchanan-Smith 1990). Intraregional relief-food allocation was largely based on an assessment of area-specific needs. The RFAA office adopted 450 grams per person as a minimum full quota per day. For 1984/85, districts in Kordofan were ranked according to crop production record, emigration numbers, anthropometric measures of nutritional status, and reported mortality rates. Varying fractions of the full quota were then applied to the districts to reflect these rankings. A maximum allocation per family was set, based on the assumption that no family had more than six members. For 1985/86 and 1986/87, the concept of a "subsistence gap" was applied as a measure of need. Rural councils were allocated a variation of the district-specific quota in accordance with their calculated "gap."

For individual households, allocation within specific target areas was based on the principle of "equal distribution." That is, resident families within specific target areas were equally eligible for rations. Priority was accorded to all who stayed in their place of residence during the operation, including those in towns. Except for a small share of the quota that was sold at a subsidized price, food was largely distributed free.

Food aid reached a high percentage of the rural population in the 1984–86 operation, but there were notable deficiencies. Food arrived at villages at different times. In some, the severity of the food shortage reached its peak in the months preceding the arrival of food aid. Furthermore the original allocation plan of "equal amounts per capita" was not observed. For example, there were significant intervillage variations in actual per capita distribution within the same district. These variations were related to irregularities in the timing and frequency of food aid flows across villages.

Part of the problem can be ascribed to the design of the food aid policy. The food ration was based on two key assumptions: an equal weight for every member in terms of food requirements and a maximum family size of six members. The ration per family thus had an inherent bias against large families, particularly those with a high proportion of adult members. The application of universal eligibility (except for nonresidents) also failed to recognize food aid as one of several household coping mechanisms. Families are unequal in terms of their coping capacity (see Chapter 7).

It can be argued that the Sudanese relief policy was less than favorable to the poor. The original plan to extend relief only to those who had no resources failed for lack of sufficient information as well as political insensitivity. The residence requirement for eligibility excluded significant numbers of the poor from the distribution. Most of those who migrated earlier were probably among the poorest. The two-tier distribution modality (free distribution and cash payment at a subsidized price) was also unfavorable to those most needy. In the absence of a program to augment their income, the poor could not effectively participate in the monetization scheme.

The institutional arrangements hastily assembled under the pressure of crises in the second half of the 1980s (which did provide some services to the at-risk population) were largely dismantled in the early 1990s. As a result, learning from experience and a building up of "institutional memory," were inhibited by political disruptions, delayed or nonrecognition of famine conditions, and a shift to new institutional mechanisms (Zaki, von Braun, and Teklu 1991). Sudan, therefore, was arguably less prepared for emergency operations in the mid-1990s than it had been in the mid-1980s.

Old and New Policies for Famine Prevention in Urban Areas

The types of urban interventions for food security are different from rural ones in design. The following section briefly discusses existing and former urban food subsidy policies and reviews some recent programs enacted in famine-prone countries. Urban-biased food subsidy and rationing systems have a long tradition, and their limitations and potentials have been studied comprehensivly (Pinstrup-Andersen 1988). The present review is therefore limited to observations of some specific features common to famine mitigation programs and then turns to more innovative urban policies and programs.

Urban Food Subsidies and Rationing

Public intervention in the food pricing system dates back to the end of the 1960s in Sudan. A bread price subsidy was the earliest program, which began in 1969/70. The program expanded in the early 1970s to include wheat and wheat flour and sugar. Edible oil was added in the 1980s. These commodities were considered to be basic foods, especially for urban consumers. Public intervention in these commodities was justified as a tool for addressing the rising costs of urban living. Such a concept guided the commodity subsidy program until it was terminated in the early 1990s.

A similar commodity subsidy program was pursued in Ethiopia during the 1970s and 1980s to distribute basic foodstuffs to urban dwellers at fair prices. Government-run corporations were established to achieve this goal. None of the food price subsidies was targeted to the poor either in Ethiopia or Sudan. The poor benefited only to the extent that they were able to purchase food either to consume or resell at a relatively higher price. Even in the 1980s when the two countries faced severe economic crises, there was no realignment of the subsidy program to reach the drought- and famine-prone population.

In fact, the decision to subsidize wheat in Sudan was not an appropriate one for providing income support for the poor, since wheat constitutes only a small proportion of their diet. The continued heavy dependence of migrant families on sorghum and millet also indicates the extent they were unable to take advantage of subsidized wheat prices; the residency requirement for access to subsidized food meant that lower-costing wheat was unavailable to them. Those who had recently arrived and lived in the shantytowns, therefore, were excluded by design.

The problem of access becomes even worse in times of scarcity. For example, as distribution methods break down, bread can be found only in bakeries, cooperatives, and residential retail shops. The shift to residential shops in effect discriminates those residents living on the fringe of urban centers. What is more, the excess demand created through a subsidy program drives up open market prices above official prices.

The commodity subsidy program in Sudan was largely government funded. (The important exception was financing of the wheat subsidy program.) In the 1980s, the relative contribution of domestic wheat production averaged only 39 percent. The government was able to sustain the fiscal cost of the program through concessionaire donor support. However, as became evident in the 1991/92 fiscal year, the government had to bear an increasing cost when such support was withdrawn. Public financing of wheat and wheat flour almost tripled from 1990/91 to 1991/92. With the widening gap between domestic production and consumption, the decline in foreign aid receipts, and shortage of hard currency, the government was faced with the question of whether to maintain the program or not (Shugeiry 1990). This was a key consideration in phasing out subsidies in the early 1990s. Concern with mounting fiscal costs of the subsidy program, and the move toward market reform, prompted the governments of Ethiopia and Sudan to abandon universal commodity price subsidy programs. In Sudan, subsidies on wheat and wheat products were removed in 1991. The subsidy on edible oil followed in 1992. The government also removed the subsidy on sugar, but it has maintained its distribution infrastructure.

*New Urban Programs in Famine-Prone Countries: Examples from Ethiopia,
Mozambique, and Sudan*

In Ethiopia, several donors have shown interest in urban poverty and are
involved in urban relief and development initiatives. Among the agencies
directly or indirectly involved in poverty alleviation in Addis Ababa in the
early 1990s were Concern, the Ex-Soldiers' Rehabilitation Commission, Hope
Enterprise, OXFAM, Redd Barna (Norwegian Save the Children), the RRC,
UNICEF, and the WFP. The primary target groups of these organizations were
the urban destitute, street children, ex-soldiers and former war veterans, beg-
gars, displaced persons, and the homeless.

A promising example of a social welfare program in an urban area using
cash transfers has been tested in Mozambique. In Sudan, two programs based
on religious concepts are being implemented. These diverse intervention
mechanisms have different ways of targeting the poor.

SUBSIDIZED FOOD RATION PROGRAM IN ETHIOPIA.   The EU has financed a program to address the needs of the poorest 30 percent of the population of Addis Ababa. In this program, the main objective is to distribute wheat
during the months when prices are the highest. The idea is to distribute 10
kilograms of wheat per month per individual and 50 kilograms per household,
at subsidized prices. *Kebeles*—neighborhood associations—are cooperating
with the EU in identifying the target groups and creating a list of low-income
households (less than 100 birr per year). According to the plan, the EU will
distribute 50,000 metric tons of wheat per year in 50-kilogram bags at less than
market price. The food aid will be delivered by the AMC. *Kebeles* will be
responsible for collecting the grain from the AMC warehouses and distributing
it to beneficiaries on a monthly basis. One of the major problems in the EU
program has been reaching the poor. In an urban appraisal study, it was found
that some households above the income cutoff had received wheat in violation
of program guidelines (Habte-Wold et al. no date).

FREE FOOD DISTRIBUTION AID IN ETHIOPIA.   Until recently, the Ethiopian RRC had been largely concerned with relief and rehabilitation measures
aimed at addressing the needs of the rural poor. However, the change in
administration in May 1991 and the ensuing massive demobilization, displacement, and dislocation of people aggravated the already existing urban poverty
in the city of Addis Ababa and the RRC has since been assisting recently
arrived vulnerable groups. The RRC has been providing food and other basic
items to people displaced from their homes (mainly from Eritrea), families of
war veterans, ex-servicemen, returnees from resettlement areas, political prisoners and their families, and other groups. Free food rations have been
distributed mainly to ex-servicemen, their families, and immigrants. Every
displaced person is supposed to receive 15 kilograms of wheat every month
(though sometimes the amount is reduced to 12.5 kilograms). Ex-soldiers'

families have so far received five rounds (15 kilograms per person for the first round, 12.5 kilograms for the second round, and since then only 7.5 kilograms per person) of aid. Ex-servicemen have been receiving 15 kilograms per month since March 1992. However, returnees from Sudan received 45 kilograms of wheat (that is, a three-months' ration) only once at the end of 1991. Some who returned from resettlement sites received only a one-month ration (15 kilograms) and transportation fees.

URBAN FOOD AND VOUCHER PROGRAM IN ETHIOPIA. The idea of using an urban food/kerosene voucher program as a safety net for Ethiopia's urban poor was proposed by the World Bank in the early 1990s. The objective of the program was to redistribute income to the poor in order to partially compensate for a reduction in real incomes due to the implementation of Ethiopia's structural adjustment program. The voucher scheme was to be carried out through the *kebele* system in cooperation with the Ministry of Domestic Trade, which had had experience with previous ration and voucher programs. In the program under discussion, the major issue of concern was how to identify the poorest of the poor. Thus a committee established within the *kebele* (which included respected elders and was chaired by the head of the *kebele*) was expected to identify the target group on the basis of household income. Accordingly, households with an income less than 100 birr were considered eligible for assistance.

ASSORTED SAFETY NET PROGRAMS IN ETHIOPIA. In the early 1990s there were some 90 local and international NGOs operating within Ethiopia. The activities of most of them are directed toward rural development, but some operate in urban areas as well. They are involved in food distribution, health services, renovating houses and communal facilities, programs for children, day care and feeding centers, programs for women and the elderly, training programs and skills improvement, and saving and credit facilities. Feeding programs have been the most popular form of aid among vulnerable groups. They have also been popular with the NGOs and other donor agencies working with children.

SOCIAL SECURITY THROUGH INCOME TRANSFERS IN MOZAMBIQUE. In 1990, an innovative social security program with cash transfers was initiated in Maputo, Mozambique (Schubert 1993). The program was financially supported and assisted by the Deutsche Gesellschaft für Technische Zusammenarbeit (GTZ). The monthly cash transfer was US$10 for a two-person household, with a scale of decreasing amounts for larger households. Between January 1991 and December 1992, the program grew from 200 to 29,000 people. It took roughly three years to plan and establish the program and to scale it up to some significant size. Those eligible were individuals and households with a per capita income of less than US$10 a month, that had lived more than 12 months in one of the 13 cities where the program operated, and could be classified according to one of the following groups: (1) households with an underweight

TABLE 8.2 Incidence of targeting with food price subsidies and cash transfer programs in Maputo (Mozambique), by quintile, 1992

	Quintile					
Program	Poorest	2	3	4	5	Total
	(percent transfers reaching quintile)					
Cash transfer	50	30	12	5	3	100
Food price subsidy	5	11	17	33	34	100

SOURCE: Schubert 1993.

child or underweight woman in pregnancy, (2) single and aged individuals, (3) single and disabled individuals, or (4) female-headed households with three or more small children. An administrative screening mechanism identified the eligible persons and households. Comparing the program's effectiveness with a food price subsidy program also operating in Maputo was illuminating (Schubert 1993): although 80 percent of benefits from the cash transfer program reached the two lowest-income quintiles, only 16 percent of the food price subsidy program benefited the lowest-income recipients (Table 8.2). The administrative costs of the program were estimated at 13 percent of total costs in 1992 and were expected to decrease to 5 percent when the program expanded to its full scale of about 60,000 households. A survey (in 1993) of children's nutritional status in comparable households of participating and nonparticipating women showed improved birth weights and a somewhat improved nutritional status for the participants (Schubert 1993).

RELIGIOUS TAX AND SOLIDARITY FUND IN SUDAN.   An innovation in Sudan involves the expansion of two religious-based concepts—*el zakat* (the 10 percent taxation for welfare) and *el takaful* (the solidarity fund for the indigent). *El zakat* is based on one of the eight obligations of Islam, which calls for sharing of wealth with the poor. It is, as such, a religious tax. Funds are collected by *el zakat* Chamber, which is a social and economic organization in Islam. The collected funds are then channeled to the poor, which, according to the definition of *el zakat*, refers to individuals who have no access to food. *El zakat* beneficiaries increased from 41,154 in 1991 to 72,398 in 1992. Eligible families receive a monthly cash allowance of SD£600. Since funds are limited, the chamber gives priority to the poorest groups—widowed women, orphans, divorced or deserted women, the handicapped and mentally retarded, elderly people, and low-income groups. Assistance is also provided to active and retired government employees. Such assistance is irregular and is usually in the form of sorghum grain or wheat. The administration of the program is shared between *el zakat* Chamber and *el zakat* committees. The latter have been established in all residential quarters and consist of 5 to 10 elected members. The head of the committee is the imam of a mosque or his representative. The members are elected by residents and those who regularly attend prayers in the mosque. One of these members serves as the liaison to the *el zakat* Chamber. The main function of the committee is to identify and verify the needy. The screening process involves an assessment of social, economic, and health conditions of potential beneficiaries. The poor can also apply for eligibility consideration. The committee prepares a list of beneficiaries every year and sends it to the Chamber through its liaison member. Those on the list are then targeted for the transfer of *el zakat* funds.

The philosophical tenet of *el takaful* is closely related to that of *el zakat*. It is centered around the belief that it is God's will for society to look after the needy and the weak. *El takaful* thus takes its mission from this mandate. However, *el takaful* has a broader scope and includes the traditional values of community support (*nafeer:* donations of work and *faza:* free assistance) and social security practices. There are key differences between *el zakat* and *el takaful* funds. *El zakat* has a narrow conceptual base, but *el takaful* extends beyond the religious precept and includes social support practices that are often prevalent in the "moral economy." Also the funding of *el takaful* is not limited to a religious tax, but is publicly supported through nontax revenues and income-generating activities. Additionally, *el takaful* is not limited to providing income transfers to the poor but also makes available input and credit subsidies to ensure that the indigent are self-producing and self-reliant. The fund uses four distribution methods. The first is a direct cash payment. In 1992, 500,000 families received direct cash payments from the fund through the *el zakat* Chamber. The second method is payment in kind under the umbrella of "the social solidarity system." This involves free distribution of food commodities to target groups such as lower-income families, poor students, hospitalized indigents, and released prisoners. The third venue is through support of income-generating activities. Special consideration is given to projects involving women's activities within the framework of food security. The fourth method is through distribution of consumer commodities at reduced prices to specific groups, such as government employees and pensioners. The *el takaful* fund faces some operational limits at present. One is identifying the poor. According to the fund, "the poor" are those unable to secure the minimum living requirements—food, health, and shelter. However, identifying these basics requires identifying their characteristics. The fund at present is conducting poverty studies to define those most vulnerable, identify their needs, and appropriately target its programs. Additionally, the fund has limited technical and administrative manpower at present to effectively accomplish its mandate.

Employment Programs for Famine Mitigation and Prevention

Famine mitigation should be as relief oriented as necessary, and as developmental as possible. Indeed, classifying public action into "relief" or "developmental" categories is misleading. A single instrument can be shifted in one or the other direction (at a cost) according to need, and some interventions, such as employment programs, can have a variety of benefits (Maxwell 1993). This section focuses on the targeting aspects of such programs, taking into account their multiple functions and goals. Questions that are explored are: Are people in need reached directly or indirectly or both by the programs? How much are women and children's needs met? What institutional arrangements have worked well? And, what is the place for food assistance in them?

Appropriate labor-intensive employment programs (LIEPs) can, through both wage payments and the investment in asset creation, address problems of short-term food needs and go a long way toward sustainable poverty alleviation (and thereby famine prevention) (Drèze and Sen 1989; von Braun 1995). India's experience has demonstrated this and thereby provides a particularly important lesson for some African countries (Drèze 1988, 1989; Ravallion and Datt 1994, 1995). There are several arguments that favor the establishment of new and expansion of existing employment programs in Africa's famine-prone countries:

- Widespread food insecurity and poverty that is linked to the lack of productive employment (Iliffe 1987)
- Chronic deficiencies in rural infrastructure and asset bases that, if improved, could encourage employment-intensive development (Platteau 1991)
- Rapidly growing labor forces and generally dynamic labor markets with strong interregional connections (Collier and Lal 1986; Collier, Radwan, and Wangwe 1986)
- Familiarity with community-based labor-sharing arrangements (Iliffe 1987), which can be integrated with larger works schemes in countries with weak public institutions

A brief overview of the potentials and drawbacks of a variety of employment programs is presented first. Then, the diverse experiences with such programs in different regions of Africa is reviewed. Finally, some policy conclusions derived from this analysis are given.

Conceptual Issues of Employment Programs

Employment programs are public initiatives that provide employment and, typically, generate public goods, such as infrastructure, through labor-intensive means. Whereas they may be publicly supported, employment programs need not necessarily be implemented by the public sector; implementation may rest with the private sector and community-based initiatives. Thus "public works" may often be "private works" in actual execution. "Food for work" is just one form of employment program that has a specific type of wage payment.

Three household behavioral parameters determine the actual food availability outcome (net effect) of public works: (1) participation in public works programs that substitutes for other employment/income sources (gross income from public works minus foregone income), (2) consumption behavior with regard to employment income versus income earned from other sources, and (3) access to and use of income streams derived from generated assets.

The private costs of labor from the poor are rarely zero because few of the poor subsist only on unearned income (such as rent or remittances). The social costs, however, may be low or even negative; for example, when indigent people are pushed into environmentally damaging behavior such as excessive tree cutting and charcoal production in famine-prone environments. For an appropriate evaluation of the costs and benefits of employment programs, an assessment of the social cost of time for the poor is essential (Ravallion and Datt 1995). The net social benefit of such programs depends on the value of assets created and the potential insurance element of public works, not just the direct income benefits (Maxwell 1993). In the long term, the productivity and sustainability of assets, their direct and indirect employment effects, and the income streams they generate—including their distribution—are central issues. The asset-creating effects, and the benefits to the poor of income streams from these assets, make such programs attractive developmental instruments for food security, aside from their direct income-transfer results. When created assets result in private ownership (for example, irrigation infrastructure), it is legitimate to tax them; thereby generating a public income stream.

The direct effects on poor households that result from employment programs can be felt in three ways:

1. Short-term income enhancement (wages) (Ravallion and Datt 1994)
2. Risk insurance where LIEPs are designed with the desirable feature of employment guarantees (Ravallion 1990)
3. Long-term direct and indirect effects from assets created and improvements in human resources (including skills and nutritional status)

The relative importance of each of the three effects differs by type of household and its specific coping capacity. Regarding the distribution of benefits and burdens of incremental employment, it also matters who actually participates in the LIEP from the household—men, women, or children—and at what cost (Ravallion 1990). Macroeconomic and institutional issues determine the scope of and constraints for LIEPs. Many parameters for determining the success of such programs on famine mitigation and prevention remain country, location, and situation specific. These parameters relate to wage rate policies; methods of payment—cash, in kind, or both; seasonal and regional targeting; and institutional arrangements.

Experiences with LIEPs

Results from a review of 13 African countries suggest that using employment programs to improve food availability is no longer rare in Africa—although published assessments are (von Braun, Teklu, and Webb 1991). In the following review of experiences from Botswana, Zimbabwe, Niger, and Ethiopia, selected issues are focused on in each case: institutional policy issues of combined relief and development in Botswana; community benefits, technical feasibility, and labor intensity in Zimbabwe; gender and operational issues in Niger, including rural-urban contrasts; and aspects of food versus cash payment in Ethiopia. In each case, however, actual households' participation and nutritional outcomes are traced.

COMBINED RELIEF AND DEVELOPMENT IN BOTSWANA.   Botswana has a well-developed drought relief program that includes food distribution, labor-intensive public works, and farm support components (Teklu 1995; von Braun 1995). Its important feature is the strong coordination among government organizations and its integration in mainstream planning. The program began in the late 1970s and was put to the test in the 1978–79 drought. It was later expanded with the addition of a labor-intensive public works component and again evaluated during the drought years of 1982 to 1987. The program was further improved and integrated into the country's long-term development strategy. Efforts are also under way to consolidate social safety net measures, with an emphasis on rural public works. The revised program was further reviewed in the 1992–93 drought relief undertaking.

Institutions that operated during nondrought years expanded their operations in drought periods. The Interministerial Drought Committee, which was part of the Ministry of Finance and Development Planning, coordinated these operations. It was responsible for the development of strategy and policy, coordination and monitoring of relief activities, and control and allocation of resources. The committee reported to the Rural Development Council, chaired by the Vice President. The drought relief program of 1982–87 focused on food distribution and public works. These two components alone accounted for 64.8 percent of the operational costs between 1982 and 1984. Emphasis shifted to the recovery of agricultural production in the 1985–87 period, the latter program absorbing 68.5 percent of costs. Except for the partly donor-supported food relief component, the government fully funded the program at a cost equivalent of 13 percent of total government capital expenditures. Village committees played a significant role in identifying and implementing projects. Wages were fixed by the government, but at rates lower than the still operating regular public works programs in rural areas. The lower rates were set to employ as many drought victims as possible in rural and periurban areas. To ensure a high participation rate, projects were required to allocate 70 percent of their costs to unskilled labor. This was scaled down to 40 percent in 1987/88. A

TABLE 8.3 Comparison of child nutritional status measures in Botswana's employment program versus nonparticipants

Nutritional Measure	Participating Household	Nonparticipating Household
Weight for height (percent < 2 SD ZWH)	7.8	7.9
Weight for age (percent < 2 SD ZWA)	19.6	14.5
Height for age (percent < 2 SD ZHA)	25.5	22.9
BMI (body-mass index of adults)	21.0	22.0

SOURCE: Teklu 1994.

NOTES: This indicates the share of the children that are more than 2 points below the standard z-score for weight for height. SD = standard deviation. ZWH, ZWA, and ZHA = Z-score of weight for height, weight for age, and height for age, respectively.

variety of projects were implemented.[3] The entire work program employed the equivalent of about 30 percent of the total estimated smallholder agricultural labor force in the country.

Access to the project also appears to have improved the relative income position of the participants, particularly at the lower end of the income distribution. The proportion of participating households in the lowest- and middle-income terciles were 24 and 44 percent, respectively. Comparable percentages for nonparticipating households were 36 and 28 percent, respectively. The project thus appears to have contributed to some of the households moving up to the middle-income group. Comparison of the child nutritional status of participating and nonparticipating households shows that those in the project have relatively (although the difference is minor) underweight and shorter children (Table 8.3). Although current participation seems to show improved child weights for height, long-standing malnutrition precludes children of participating families to have comparable weights for age. This suggests that the participating households were poorer (and presumably had less access to food), at least on average, before the project than at the time of survey.

Subsequent evaluations of the 1982–87 program inevitably identified some deficiencies (Hay 1988; Buchanan-Smith 1990; Valentine 1990). The program overly emphasized a pure income transfer at the cost of low labor productivity. Also, the temporary nature of income did not translate into appreciable investments at the household level (Asefa 1989).

ZIMBABWE'S DROUGHT RESPONSE THROUGH FOOD FOR WORK. The major drought of 1981/82 spurred the newly independent Zimbabwean government to set up an ambitious and far-reaching relief program based on food for work. Starting with a simple system of food handouts that lasted until 1989, it

---

3. Major undertakings included the improvement of 10,950 kilometers of roads and construction of 1,521 dams, 6,550 kilometers of drift fence and firebreaks, and 1,787 pit latrines, according to Botswana, Ministry of Local Government and Lands.

subsequently evolved into an interministerial program guided by a task force and support committees. The program was designed to operate from the bottom up as much as possible. Project activities were identified by villagers themselves. Their proposals were submitted to the district administrator's office which, in collaboration with district social welfare officers (SWOs), assessed and approved appropriate plans. Implementation was supervised by district SWOs or personnel from the district development fund, which implemented the cash-paid public works program (see below).

"Appropriateness" was measured in terms of community benefit, technical feasibility, and degree of labor intensity. The latter is important because the government's budget allocation for the program covered only the purchase of food, its transportation, and the salaries of program staff. In other words, the project cannot require substantial material inputs. The most common activities have therefore consisted of gully reclamation, the clearing of bush for agricultural development, erecting fencing for grazing schemes, and brick making (Zimbabwe 1990; Sachikonye 1992).

In some cases, food-for-work labor was allocated to projects being implemented simultaneously by other ministries, such as the construction of classrooms and clinics, or the digging of pit latrines (Lenneiye 1991). However, this kind of symbiotic relationship has been ad hoc since no institutional structures exist to promote or facilitate interministry or interprogram collaboration. In early 1991, the largest number of projects involved brick molding and small-building construction, activities generally completed without additional material inputs. The greatest number of such projects were undertaken in Northern Matabeleland and Midlands. The other principal activities implemented in 1991 were water control projects (dam and weir building or rehabilitation) or the construction and maintenance of rural feeder roads. It is interesting that the most common public works activities of the colonial era (erosion-control and agricultural development projects) are the least favored by participants in the 1990s. As noted by Lenneiye (1991), "Officials are more inclined to promote the building of bridges, roads, clinics, and schools before they embark on environmental work because there are no guiding principles formulated." This points to a lack of regional planning, although it may also relate to a distaste among villagers to engage in activities with a colonial association.

Wages for project work were initially set at 10 kilograms of maize per capita per month (supplemented, where possible, by beans and dried meat or fish). The food was purchased by the Department of Social Welfare (DSW) from GMB depots located in rural areas. The DSW was then responsible for transporting the food to some 1,500 distribution points around the country, from where participants were paid for their work. Only one member of each family was required to work for the wage, the number of days worked per month being discretionary. Prior to 1992, only households *not* owning any

TABLE 8.4 Characteristics of Zimbabwe's Food-for-Work Program, selected months 1989–92

	1989[a]	1990[b]	1991	1992[c]
	(thousands)			
People employed[d]	612	1,130	1,128	2,242
Food wages paid (tons)	5,973	9,938	10,983	20,761
Total costs (Z$)[e]	1,661	3,412	3,733	n.a.
Cost per capita (Z$)	4	3	3	n.a.

SOURCE: Webb 1995b.

NOTE: n.a. = not available.

[a]October through December (the first three months of the program).

[b]January through March and August through December (program was suspended April to July).

[c]January through September (provisional).

[d]Average number of workers per month.

[e]Averaged per months of operation.

livestock were eligible to be registered for participation. In late 1992, this criterion was removed because of the danger of households selling animals at severely depressed prices solely to be accepted as participants. Although most projects have required work to be performed before payment, some distributed wages in advance of project implementation and required labor to be repaid later if food needs were high.

The program has both been praised and roundly criticized. While the self-reliance element, contrasting with the dependency of handouts, has been highlighted (given the political nature of the program), most praise has gone to the program's food availability impact during drought years (*Zimbabwe News* 1989; *Herald* 1990). Sachikonye (1992), for example, argues that "what stopped food shortages in 1990 from escalating into a widespread famine in the rural districts was the availability from the government of 'food for work.'"

Table 8.4 shows the coverage and some of the costs of the program. The number of people employed in food for work has risen since the start of the scheme, and far exceeds that attained by the free-food system. Part of the large expansion in 1992 was supported by a US$23 million grant from the World Bank. The grant, part of a large package of structural adjustment loans, was designed to help improve transport logistics (both road and rail) and the coordination of cross-ministry activities.

Nevertheless, it should be underscored that the food-for-work program has reached more people than the free-food system, both in absolute and in relative terms. Table 8.5 shows that the proportion of food needs met by food for work generally exceeded 40 percent in the first few years of operation, rising to over 60 percent in 1992. Only one province (Masvingo) was not able to satisfy 50 percent of its needs between 1989 and 1992; Matabeleland, by

TABLE 8.5 Percentage of food needs met by Zimbabwe's Food-for-Work Program, selected areas, 1989–92

Area	1989	1990	1991	1992[a]
Manicaland	87	51	49	66
Mashonaland				
Central	44	80	40	76
East	27	21	47	73
West	38	62	47	76
Masvingo	47	46	48	42
Matabeleland				
Northern	19	55	55	61
Southern	40	61	57	59
Midlands	62	24	38	54

SOURCE: Webb and Moyo 1992.

[a]March through August.

contrast, appeared to be receiving as much coverage as most other regions, and more than it did during the free-food program.

However, three important points should be highlighted. First, less than two-thirds of officially recognized need was met by the food-for-work program. Second, productivity enhancement based on structural output of the program was minimal. And third, the 1991/92 drought exposed the static nature of the program. That is, expansion in scale and coverage to meet emergency needs was difficult to achieve. Key obstacles in all three areas can be traced to a lack of funding. In 1990, there was a four-month suspension of the program in most parts of the country due to budgetary constraints at the national level. However, even when the program was in full operation, its effectiveness was hindered by funding restrictions and by delays in actual disbursement.

This lack of funding affected all levels of program operation. The geographical coverage of food needs during nondrought years was, for example, hampered by transportation bottlenecks due to a shortage of vehicles. The program generally relied on access to vehicles operated by other ministries, which were only available for program work on a part-time basis. This led to delays in food payments and a loss of faith in program activities (Lenneiye 1991; Sachikonye 1992). It also limited access of program regional staff to rural project locations for technical supervision. At the same time, there was a widely reported lack of staffing in both field and central offices. In the field, supervision of participant targeting and payment, as well as monitoring of project outputs, was often delegated to local councillors and party officials, leading inevitably to charges of personal favoritism and to the politicization of relief activities (Lenneiye 1991). At the ministerial level, inadequate staffing compromised the government's ability to monitor regional needs, to coordinate program needs with GMB supplies at a subregional level, and to mobilize nonlocal resources according to local project requirements.

A lack of government resources for nonwage inputs also meant a serious obstacle for asset creation. Participants were usually expected to bring their own tools (picks, shovels, axes, and buckets) to the work site. The cement, steel, and stone upon which sound infrastructure typically depends were in even shorter supply. The considerable amounts of labor were therefore largely wasted. More structured interaction with nonprogram technical ministries (such as Health and Agriculture), district planning officials, and particularly with the public works program (discussed below) holds much potential for an increased development impact of the food-for-work program. Each of these limitations was clearly exposed by the 1991/92 drought. As the number of people registered by the DSW quickly rose from an average of 800,000 per month in 1991 to almost 3 million per month in mid-1992, the program had to expand fivefold. It was in essence expected to transform itself from a prototype employment program into a huge emergency relief operation, without being given the necessary resources.

For example, the existing transport fleet was only able to cope with about 40 percent of demand. The lack of advance planning had not permitted the siting of food-for-work grain at GMB depots nearest to the busiest distribution points. Additionally, wages were for a time increased from 10 to 15 kilograms of maize per capita per month, with the addition of dried meat or fish.[4] This raised food-movement requirements in late 1992 to almost 60,000 tons per month. The result was extraheavy vehicle usage—with not inconsiderable achievements under difficult conditions. However, such usage also finally exposed previous underinvestment in spare parts and maintenance.

Staffing needs were also unfulfilled within at the central departments. A small unit in the DSW lacked specialists in transportation, relief commodity movement, and in the technical supervision and assessment of project activities undertaken. It also lacked the basic personnel to monitor and record operations as they unfolded. This made coordination with other ministries, as well as with donors and private volunteer organizations very difficult. The addition of temporary staff in the second half of 1992 alleviated some of the pressure, but long-term improvements in the ability of program staff to plan, administer, and monitor appropriate food-for-work activities remains a high priority. For this to be achieved, further funds will be required from central budgetary resources

---

4. Wages were subsequently dropped to only 5 kilograms of maize per month due to the overall shortage of grain, transportation limitations, and the government's desire to rebuild national grain stocks.

for (1) technical specialists from the DSW to be given responsibility for coordinating key activities in collaboration with other ministries, (2) nonwage inputs to become part of the government contribution to project resources, (3) local field staff to be trained in improved screening and supervisory techniques, (4) transportation resources to be allocated specifically to the program (some of which may be obtained via commercial channels), and (5) improved technical assistance from the districts to mobilize labor more effectively. Although many of these requirements have been recognized by the government, action during a time of reduced public spending remains difficult. However, without action in these areas, the labor resources currently mobilized are not fulfilling their potential. Equally important, a future drought would find the food-for-work program in no better a position to respond to emergency needs than it was in 1991.

RURAL AND URBAN EXPERIENCES IN NIGER.   In Niger, at least 14 donors and NGOs were supporting labor-based works programs at more than 100 sites during 1992 (Webb 1995b). Most of these grew out of emergency projects initiated in response to the 1973/74 drought and subsequent famine. They had only a limited focus on asset sustainability; few were ever properly evaluated. Since the mid-1970s, most projects have gained a development focus. In 1985, 180 small projects were implemented, primarily under NGO management, most of which used food as an incentive for mobilizing labor (World Bank 1988). In addition to this, a large number of projects were funded by international donors, such as the WFP and the World Bank, operating in collaboration with government ministries. Over US$150 million was invested in projects with a high labor content in the decade to 1991 alone. This investment generated more than 22 million days of work, mostly applied to erosion control and improving soil and water management in the semi-arid zones. These numbers represent a significant development input from a single instrument.

Several important points emerge from these experiences. First, there was a distinct rural bias. Nine out of these 10 projects were located in more remote, usually semi-arid, parts of the country. This is partly the result of historical inertia: organizations that responded to previous famines remained operating in areas likely to be vulnerable again. However, it is also because urban food security has only recently become a public concern. Lately the balance has moved in favor of urban activities.

The second point is that most rural projects focused on natural-resource conservation, rather than on road building, livestock projects, or irrigation development. Environmental degradation is one of Niger's greatest problems and Lipton (1989) has argued that "public works programs have probably the best capacity for mitigating environmental degradation." This is so because the most common (and most effective) measures against degradation cannot be implemented by machinery alone. The techniques employed for soil and water management require from 50 to 300 person-days of labor per hectare of "recovered" land (Derrier 1991). It is, therefore, these types of activities that dominate Niger's portfolio of labor-based projects.

The third point is that payment methods and amounts vary across projects. It is clear that food for work predominated in the rural areas, while cash for work has so far been associated with urban projects. Voluntary labor is universally wished for by project managers, and sometimes written into donor-community contracts.

The fourth point to be noted is that, whereas a large share of rural participants are women (60 to 80 percent), urban project participants are predominantly male (more than 99 percent). Most rural projects attempt to avoid direct competition with agricultural operations and, therefore, concentrate their activities during the dry season. Since this is the time of male emigration, projects offering a low (usually food) wage are attractive to the poorest of the remaining workforce, namely women.

In urban areas, by contrast, male participants predominate. The urban schemes were initiated on a pilot basis in 1990. They represented an attempt to organize private implementation of publicly funded projects. The Agence Nigerienne de Travaux d'Intérêt Public pour L'Emploi (NIGETIP) was set up as a private NGO to disburse public funds through a bidding process to private agencies for public works. Its three main objectives have been to generate short-term jobs; stimulate the private sector by funding the implementation of projects through small, local enterprises; and generate public goods and services through labor-intensive technology (NIGETIP 1990; World Bank 1990). Private construction, architecture, and engineering firms submit closed bids; the lowest one from an accredited firm making a commitment to allocate a minimum of 20 percent of total costs to salaried labor wins the contract.

In 1991, six pilot projects were initiated in the capital, Niamey. During their test operation they generated 3,500 workdays, mostly in road construction, drain clearing, refuse collection, and soil conservation works. In 1992, NIGETIP went into full operation and expanded its coverage to include all urban centers in the country. Over 200 firms were accredited for placing bids for over 100 contracts during the year. For example, 27,000 workdays were generated by a dozen projects during the month of April alone (NIGETIP 1992).

At their outset, the urban schemes were overwhelmed by demand for work from the city's long-term underemployed males. Since the projects registered participants on a first-come, first-served basis, underemployed male household heads were usually first in line. Many women (nonhousehold heads) expressed a desire to participate, but their involvement was mostly precluded by the volume of male demand. The projects surveyed achieved a relatively high degree of poverty targeting. For example, Table 8.6 compares selected demographic and wealth characteristics of participants heavily involved in the

TABLE 8.6 Selected demographic and wealth characteristics of Niger households, by participation groups in employment programs, 1990/91

	Participation Groups	
	Low	High
Demographics		
Attended primary school (percent)	10.0	0.5
Mean household size[a]	6.0	3.0
Wealth indicators		
Index of income per capita	100.0	48.0
Livestock assets (TLU per capita)	1.1	0.7
Area cultivated (hectare per capita)	0.3	0.1
Crop income (US$ per capita)	128.0	139.0
Participation		
Days of project work per household	27.0	210.0
Project wages as share of income (percent)	4.0	20.0

SOURCE: Webb 1995b.

NOTE: TLU = total livestock unit.

[a]Members actually present during the previous six months.

scheme, versus those less involved. The table shows a strong correspondence between intensity of participation and selected indicators of poverty. The result is that public works participants had an income that was only 48 percent that of nonparticipant households.

Households with a high child dependency ratio, a high share of female adults, and those headed by a woman (typically the poorest households) were more likely to participate than other households (Webb 1995b). A larger share of surveyed households were headed by women in the high-participation group (22 percent) than in the low-participation group (10 percent) (Webb 1992). In the urban projects, by contrast, few women participated at all. This was because the offer of a cash wage in a low-employment environment brought men into competition with women for limited workplaces—limited because projects were small and cash wages were supplied on a first-come, first-served basis. Underemployed men quickly filled the positions offered, thereby squeezing women out of those projects. Table 8.7 displays the results of anthropometric measurements of almost 1,000 Niger children aged six months to five years taken at the time of a household consumption survey in 1991 (Webb 1992). The findings underscore the persistence of malnutrition among Niger households, even in a good harvest year. There is a tendency for children in high-participation households to be more malnourished than those in low-participation households, and for children in rural households to show more

TABLE 8.7 Z-scores for Niger preschooler weight-for-height, height-for-age, and weight-for-age characteristics, by participation in employment program and location, 1990/91

| | Average Z-Scores[a] | | |
	Weight for Height	Height for Age	Weight for Age
Boys			
Participation groups			
High	−1.44**	−2.12	−2.35**
Low	−0.75**	−1.67	−1.66**
Location			
Rural	−1.35*	−2.13	−2.33*
Urban	−0.53*	−1.60	−1.44*
Girls			
Participation groups			
High	−1.48**	−1.19	−1.93
Low	−0.78**	−1.21	−1.41
Location			
Rural	−1.33**	−1.39	−1.94*
Urban	−0.61**	−1.20	−1.30**

SOURCE: Webb 1992.

NOTES: Preschoolers include children 6–60 months; characteristics are all-round averages.

$$^a\text{Z-score} = \frac{(\text{Actual measurement } - \text{ 50th percentile standard})}{\text{Standard deviation of the standard}}.$$

The standard used is derived from US-NCHS 1977.
* .05 level.
** .01 level.

signs of unsatisfactory nutritional status than those in the towns. The differences between groups are highly significant in terms of weight-for-height characteristics for both genders. Differences in weight for age (a measure of short-term wasting) are also highly significant for boys, but not for girls.

These results suggest that without the 20 percent share of total income derived from public works, children in the poorest households might be more severely malnourished—as long as participation itself does not compromise child health and nutrition as a result of reduced care (Brown, Yohannes, and Webb 1994). Yet children may not be the only ones suffering poor nutrition. The average body-mass index (BMI) of male and female adults was 19.0. However, Table 8.8 shows that men in high-participation households showed a significant tendency to have a lower BMI (18.3) than those in low-participation households (19.7). The same holds true, and is statistically significant, for women. Interestingly, when tested against the gender of household head, no

TABLE 8.8 Niger adult body-mass indexes, by participation in employment program, location, and gender of household head, 1990/91

	Gender of Household Head	
	Male	Female
	(BMI)[a]	
Participation groups[b]		
High	18.3**	18.7**
Low	19.7**	19.5**
Location		
Rural	18.6**	18.8**
Urban	20.1**	19.7**

SOURCE: Webb 1992.

NOTE: "Adult" includes those aged 15 to 65.

[a]BMI = body-mass index; calculated as: weight (height)^2. The "normal" BMI range is 18.5 to 25.0. Individuals below 18.5 are considered to be bordering on undernutrition; those below 17.5 are likely to be considerably malnourished.
[b]Sample was truncated to exclude individuals with a BMI of less than 15 or above 28; included 454 men and 530 women.
** .01 level.

significant difference was perceived between the BMI of women in male- or female-headed households. These findings confirm the effective self-targeting of public works. The poorest and most malnourished did make most use of the employment offered (working more days and therefore earning more income). However, they also raise the issue of net project impact on food security. Since nutritional status is the result of net energy balance, it is determined by energy expenditure as well as by consumption. This means that heavy activity in public works programs may fail to improve an individual's nutritional status if the increased labor effort required offsets the positive nutritional effect of the wage transferred (Higgins and Alderman 1992).

THE LARGEST FOOD-FOR-WORK PROGRAM IN AFRICA: ETHIOPIA. Ethiopia has a wealth of experience in public works. It has hosted the largest food-for-work program in Africa—the large-scale WFP project supporting natural-resource programs across the country. It also served as a testing ground for the first large cash-for-work program in Africa (operated by UNICEF). The food-for-work projects implemented at four of the Ethiopian household survey sites offered food as their wage/incentive, whereas households participating in cash for work at three sites received monthly cash wages. These programs are examined in turn.

In 1986, NGOs ran about 60 food-for-work projects, most of which were relief activities; only 4 percent of these projects were initiated prior to 1985 (Hareide 1986). By 1989, the number of projects had risen to 75, but most had evolved into seasonal employment projects (run by many NGOs as precautionary measures during years of low harvest) or longer-term projects engaged in road building, soil and water conservation, or both (WFP 1989).

The employment provided by such projects differed by site according to type of activity, criteria for participant selection, and local response to the food wage offered. Total average annual number of participation days per household across four project sites considered in 1989/90 was 83 (Webb, von Braun, and Yohannes 1992). This compares closely with 80 to 90 days estimated for other parts of Ethiopia by Holt (1983) and Kohlin (1987). Many projects accepted all households wishing to participate (EEC 1989). This principle assumed that food for work is a self-targeting intervention from which the wealthy voluntarily exclude themselves. If that is the case, who does participate, and why? On the one hand, at no site were female-headed households given any priority access. On the other, at three of the four sites participation by poorest households (often female headed) was not lower than that by wealthier households, even taking household dependency ratios into account.

In general, a picture of rather equal access emerges, with the exception of one site in the eastern province of Hararghe. At Adele Keke, where complaints of unfair selection were strong, only 24 percent of sample participants were in the lowest-income tercile, compared with 36 to 40 percent in the other terciles, despite similar dependency ratios across terciles. Furthermore, the poorest households in Adele Keke worked many fewer days (thereby receiving much lower food payments) than households in the upper tercile, and female-headed households also appear to have been disadvantaged (in terms of days worked) when compared with households headed by men.

The standard food wage was 3 kilograms of grain (usually wheat) and 120 grams of oil per day—a ration established in the late 1960s and adhered to in the late 1990s. This ration was supposed to cover the daily subsistence requirements for six people, offering some 1,800 kilocalories per person (Admassie and Gebre 1985). However, there were deviations from the standard because of availability limitations (international food pledges not always matching requirements) and difficulties in estimating numbers of participants (Hareide 1986; USAID 1987). For example, payments did not vary greatly by gender of household head within projects, but they did vary across income terciles and also between projects. Based on participants' own recall, the poorest households at several sites received payments that exceeded not only the standard payment for a day's work, but also the payments received by households in the middle and upper terciles. By contrast, the poorest households at the pastoral site in southern Ethiopia received payments less than the recommended ration.

The latter's grain payments were low because food for work was seen by the implementing NGO as a means of initiating activities that would become self-sustaining, and because the NGO did not wish to establish a dependency relationship.

Two of the factors most widely blamed for failed projects are poor technical design and implementation, and low community involvement in project selection and subsequent maintenance (Maxwell 1978; Holt 1983; Clay and Singer 1985). On the technical side, design problems may result from a conflict (or at least confusion) between relief or employment-creation goals on the one hand, and development or asset-creation objectives on the other. Most food-for-work activities in Ethiopia were initiated in response to conflicts, food crises, or environmental catastrophes. Thus projects were often organized in an atmosphere of urgency, with limited assessments of community needs or of the projects' technical validity. Brown (1989) argues that most of the larger labor-intensive projects in Ethiopia during the 1990s suffered from a lack of participatory and technical planning. Vallee's (1989) evaluation of 24 projects in Hararghe concurs, noting the lack of adequate planning and anticipation of food payment needs. He concludes that, "Without good planning, a technical project involving food for work leads to total confusion." It also has been argued that the success of public works in terms of development is hindered by low labor motivation, low productivity, and a lack of long-term commitment (Clay and Singer 1985; Drèze 1988). Part of this may be ascribed to the characteristics of the labor attracted by public works—the distressed and disadvantaged. However, much may also be due to a lack of community participation in project selection. Detailed consultation between communities and agencies before projects begin is uncommon. An average of 95 percent of Ethiopian sample households had never been asked their opinions about the project, even by on-site project managers.

There is no doubt that improved consultation between communities and project organizers should be a high priority for future projects (Brown 1989). Without a consensus on the validity of project objectives and a clear understanding of asset ownership rules, few households will be willing to whole-heartedly participate in, and subsequently maintain, food-for-work projects (EEC 1989; WFP 1989). On the other hand, there is little doubt that food for work can be an effective means of transferring income to vulnerable households in times of need, as well as the vehicle for some valuable development activities (Maxwell 1993). The best natural-resource conservation projects in Ethiopia were those that required the least maintenance: vegetated bunds and terraces on common-access (but often enclosed) hillsides used for tree planting. Furthermore, the multiplier effects of road building in certain regions were marked. For example, three years after the food-for-work-built road reached the Ethiopian lowland village of Dinki, two water mills were established, new fruit plantations were started, and a traditional cotton-spinning and -weaving industry was revived—all from improved access to highland markets.

Conclusions Concerning LIEPs

Employment programs are not a cure-all, but they are a versatile instrument that can be applied in a variety of contexts. In theory, it is as easy to design ideal employment programs for poverty reduction as to speculate about design flaws, particularly when adverse institutional or political conditions are also considered. Two parameters—food security issues and labor markets—determine to a large extent the optimal choice and design of LIEPs. Table 8.9 summarizes the potential for employment programs in certain broadly defined labor market and food security environments. Widely varying pictures emerge under different conditions, depending on whether labor markets can operate freely or are severely constrained, and on whether famine conditions are transitory crises or chronic.

Programs have a strong chance of enhancing food access in areas where labor markets can operate fairly freely. Under this condition (and assuming that an appropriate wage rate policy is applied) the poor tend to be "self-targeted" by the employment programs. Free, interregional migration of people to work sites can mean that programs reach a large proportion of the needy. In cases where people are able to migrate, programs need not be situated as close to poorer groups as under restricted labor market conditions. Thus the programs' locations become less important under such conditions and can be situated more for achieving long-term returns on investment rather than to target local poverty. Improved understanding of the targeting potentials of LIEPs demands

TABLE 8.9 Employment program potential under different food-security and labor market conditions

Labor Market Conditions and Characteristics	Food Security Conditions	
	Crises/Famine Risk	Chronic Food Insecurity
Free labor market	++	++
Minimum-wage policy/wage control	+	−
Job sharing/employment pooling/community-works traditions	++	++
Constraints in labor markets (e.g., by gender, ethnic groups, or caste)	+	+
Command systems/work obligations	+	+

SOURCE: Adapted from von Braun 1995.

NOTE: − = little or no potential, + = some potential, and ++ = strong potential.

a better understanding of labor market conditions (Kanbur, Kean, and Tuomala 1994). In fact, an understanding of labor markets in famine-prone countries is at least as important as an understanding of food markets for targeting populations where food supplies are insufficient.

Minimum-wage polices or wage-control measures reduce participation by the poor in employment programs. As a result of effective lobbying by formal labor groups, minimum wages are typically higher than the rural poors' returns to labor. Higher wages attract more than just the destitute, and given the typically limited budgets of employment programs, the supply of jobs cannot meet demand and so leads to job rationing. There is a high likelihood that job rationing works in favor of the richer, more influential members of society. However, the wage rate issue is a double-edged sword: in poverty reduction programs, wages should be higher than what amounts to the poverty line for the working destitute, but below the level that attracts the nonpoor. In this sense, a minimum-wage policy does have its justification (Majeres 1994).

Community-works traditions and employment pooling can help LIEPs reach the poor, as was seen in the Niger examples. Communities with such work traditions are prevalent in many parts of Africa. They assist the mobilization of labor and facilitate the production of public goods, such as local production on common fields for public stockholding or neighborhood-assistance schemes. In labor markets with gender or ethnic constraints, inefficiencies and inequality can grow more pronounced and impair the performance of employment programs. On the other hand, some of the studies suggest that employment programs can serve to overcome such constraints.

Two other factors can significantly affect the extent to which LIEPs succeed. The first is the ability of the public works programs to evolve into stronger institutions with an established political support base. The second is the presence of effective local organizational capacity at the local level, which can assist in program implementation (Dev 1994). A third factor that may be just as important is the extent to which future participants are allowed to have input into the program's design.

None of the African employment programs so far includes the feature of an entitlement, that is, an individual right of employment at a minimum wage that permits maintenance of basic needs (Dev 1994). Only the Botswana program came close to this design, but was not established in a formal sense there either. If the call for a human right to food (FAO 1996) is to be translated into reality, it seems hardly conceivable that this can be implemented without a work obligation for employable adults. Employment programs based on such an obligation may be able to help make the human right to food a reality.

Employment programs consisting of workfare, that is, those that disregard the asset-generation component, are generally undesirable. An accurate economic assessment of them, however, depends on the appropriate point of reference. For instance, during a crisis this option may be preferable to distress

FIGURE 8.2 Employment programs, crises, poverty targeting, and asset quality

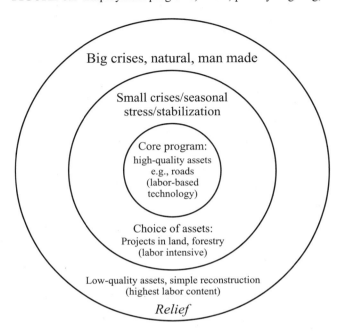

Big crises, natural, man made

Small crises/seasonal
stress/stabilization

Core program:
high-quality assets
e.g., roads
(labor-based
technology)

Choice of assets:
Projects in land, forestry
(labor intensive)

Low-quality assets, simple reconstruction
(highest labor content)

Relief

SOURCE: von Braun 1995, p. 315.

migration and feeding camps. Experiences in East Africa during famines support the judicious use of workfare programs in crisis situations (Webb and Kumar 1994). However, workfare should not be considered a viable option for dealing with chronic food insecurity and poverty. Figure 8.2 outlines the components of a flexible program system designed to provide short-term relief as well as generate high-quality assets.

A core program focuses on the creation of high-quality assets using labor-based technology. This is surrounded by a second set of programs that is aimed at stabilizing and alleviating seasonal stress. In this second circle, the choice of asset creation changes. Here, asset generation is deliberately designed to absorb large amounts of labor quickly to increase short-term transfers. Activities such as land development, forestry, and similar programs are likely candidates for components in this circle. Labor shares in these activities tend to be twice as high as, for instance, road programs. The third circle addresses large-scale relief needs in famine situations. In this outer circle, the priority is maximizing employment. Often the components cannot facilitate the program goal of production of lower-quality assets. The decision to pursue programs located in the outer circle is made after weighing the costs (including human misery) of alternative scenarios during a crisis. These scenarios include relief camps, large-scale migration, or the burgeoning of slums and shantytowns around urban centers that often follows an emergency. Such scenarios are becoming increasingly common in famine-prone areas of Africa (Webb and Kumar 1995).

The initiation of labor-intensive public works entails the acceptance of real trade-offs between such short-term and long-term goals. Accordingly, evaluations of these programs must consider how well they have met their designated goals and the time frame for doing so, compared to program alternatives. For instance, an evaluation critical of a program that successfully reached its short-term objective would be considered flawed if it labeled the program a failure for not generating lasting assets or other longer-term benefits.

Asset Transfers and Credit Programs

Although there is increased recognition of the public potential to mobilize labor for famine mitigation and prevention programs, there still is less recognition of public action in the context of financial markets. That is, use of rural credit for famine mitigation and nutrition recovery, and even (as seen in the Botswana case) effective complementarity with other programs.

It is widely believed that financial markets break down altogether in times of crisis, and that any credit would be "wasted" if used for consumption purposes as there would be no way to pay it back. In the following section it is argued that this notion is based, on the one hand, on an overly simplistic model of rural financial markets, and, on the other, on a too-narrow distinction between "production credit" and "consumption credit." There is little debate over the need for financing in rural areas for recovery after famine, especially to rebuild agricultural capital stock (including reestablishing livestock herds). However, there is much debate over the appropriate timing of public action to recapitalize the rural economy. That is, what role can credit perform both before and after a famine has hit? As with employment creation, there may be considerable flexibility for public action in rural financial markets through appropriate lending programs to the poor. Financial services can contribute much to overcome and possibly prevent the misery of coping with famine-induced hunger (Zeller et al. 1997).

Africa's Undercapitalized Rural Economy: Links to Poverty and Famine

Africa's rural economy is severely undercapitalized. Nonexistent or rudimentary rural financial markets are one symptom of this. Others include the prevalence of subsistence farming, which does little to enhance the coping capacity of smallholders, and unproductive asset holdings, such as large live-stock herds with low output. Often, labor productivity is extremely low because capital is not available. Labor shortage problems (largely seasonal) in parts of Africa are another manifestation of lack of capital and undeveloped financial markets and institutions. The larger problem of rural undercapitalization is revealed by the lack and diversity of rural infrastructure throughout Africa. For example, in the 1980s, estimates of kilometers of road per square kilometer of arable land varied from 2.9 in Zimbabwe, to 2.3 in Kenya, 0.3 in Ethiopia, and 0.1 in Sudan (von Braun, Teklu, and Webb 1991). The amount of capital supplied correlates highly with improved infrastructure. Transaction costs in rural financial markets are a function of information flows and the density of financial institutions in rural areas—both of these are closely related to the quality of the existing infrastructure (Wanmali 1992; Desai and Mellor 1993).

Financing for the poor can have a net positive effect on both income generation and stabilization, and thereby address short- as well as long-term food availability problems. However, it is not always easy to distinguish credit needs for production from those for consumption in poor households. Given the vulnerable position of the needy, food security is an important everyday concern in which credit may play a role as well. Policies addressing this concern aim to improve the ability of households to adjust their consumption and investment through access to savings, credit, and insurance markets. The goal of such policies is to enable households to make periodic adjustments to disposable income for both short- and long-term needs and benefits.

For food-insecure households lacking adequate food supply, savings in the form of cash, food, and other assets are an important means of insurance against both anticipated and unexpected periods of food shortages (see Chapter 7). Credit, on the other hand, increases current disposable income at the expense of income available at a future time. In famine-prone areas of rural Africa, savings and credit options are currently very limited for even average households (Reardon 1997). However, although financial markets are currently very limited and effective systems are rare, this does not deny their potential.

Financial market development has long been based on the assumption that lower-income groups, living predominantly in rural areas, are too poor to save and consequently lack necessary collateral for loans. More recent experience shows that lower-income groups do save, and often have a substantial savings potential (Seibel 1985; Binswanger and Landell-Mills 1995). Flourishing informal institutions (savings/credit groups) in many Sub-Saharan countries (Zeller et al. 1997), suggest that it is quite possible to build rural financial institutions based on the savings potential of the poor.

Credit for Food Security: Informal and Formal Mechanisms

In much of Asia, Latin America, and the Middle East, formal financial markets supply a large proportion of rural financial needs. This is not the case in Africa where only an estimated 10 to 20 percent of farmers obtain credit from formal institutions (Mittendorf 1987). This share has probably declined further in the late 1980s and early 1990s. Thus the majority of small farmers in Africa secure their credit needs, if at all, from informal financial markets. The reality of rural financial markets differs greatly across African countries and is complex within countries. For instance in The Gambia, a survey of household access to credit issued in the informal and formal markets in 1985/86 indicated that the richest households obtained 42 percent of all credit issued for agricultural inputs, whereas the poorest received only 11 percent (von Braun, Puetz, and Webb 1989). The informal-credit sector provided about 80 percent of all credit to the sample households. Friends and relatives were the most important credit source (41 percent), and shopkeepers provided 35 percent, either in cash or as consumer items (von Braun, Puetz, and Webb 1989). Interest rates on informal loans depended on a variety of factors. In 68 percent of credit transactions (58 percent of the loan volume) conducted in 1987/88 in these sample households, no direct interest was charged. Credit within the "moral community" was better characterized as mutual help rather than as commercial-type transactions. For the remaining cases, however, annualized interest rates averaged 126 percent in The Gambia sample. Interest rates on in-kind food loans were lower than for other loans.

A comprehensive analysis of the relationships between access to credit and food consumption in a food-deficient and famine-prone environment is available from Madagascar (Zeller 1993). The analysis revealed that much informal credit is used for food, whereas a lesser amount of formal credit is used as such (Table 8.10). Zeller's (1993) empirical results also show that loans used for production and consumption purposes increase household incomes. In asset-households, family labor is a crucial production factor. Maintenance of and investments in human capital through credit increases household income. These results support the argument that formal credit programs should include consumption loans to food-deficient households. In addition to the indirect credit effect via rising incomes, short-term informal credit significantly increases food consumption. Formal credit used for food consumption, on the other hand, was found to have no significant effect. This indicates that to ensure links between credit and stabilization of food consumption, there need to be institutional arrangements that can disburse small loan amounts and respond to credit demands on short notice.

RECENT INNOVATIVE SCHEMES. The most prominent and uniform characteristic of innovative and successful programs is a provision for voluntary or mandatory savings schemes. This finding is striking, considering the

TABLE 8.10 Use of informal and formal credit by the poor in Madagascar

	Informal (N = 1,355)		Formal (N = 245)	
Category of Credit Use	Mean Share of Amount Used	Average Amount Used	Mean Share of Amount Used	Average Amount Used
	(percent)	(US$)	(percent)	(US$)
Farm inputs	11.3	1.2	57.4	31.7
Farm implements and livestock	3.9	1.0	17.4	11.8
Food	52.2	3.2	11.1	5.0
Health	5.5	0.3	1.3	0.3
Inputs for handicrafts, petty trade	7.9	3.5	3.5	2.4
Reimbursement of other loans	1.2	0.2	3.3	3.5
School expenses	0.5	0.1	0.0	0.0[a]
Social events	4.3	1.1	0.5	1.0[b]
Other uses	13.2	1.3	5.5	3.9
Total	100.0	11.9	100.0	59.6

SOURCE: Zeller 1993.

[a]Amount rounded down from 0.05.

[b]Amount rounded up from 0.95.

different programs, development agencies, and country environments reviewed. In general, potential borrowers needed to accumulate some financial savings in order to gain credit eligibility, although there were exceptions—for example, Caisses Villageoises d'Epargne et de Crédit Autogerées in The Gambia, Madagascar, and Mali (Zeller et al. 1997). Although savings mobilization is part of this institution's financial strategy, the poor may borrow money without having accumulated any savings. The institution also does not discriminate against providing social or consumption loans. In The Gambia and Madagascar, the village committees themselves decide both savings and loan interest rates.

Analysis of financial programs shows that temporary subsidies of institutional buildup frequently precede financial sustainability (Zeller et al. 1997). Nevertheless, innovative financial programs seek to keep costs low through local volunteer management. Transaction and operating costs are kept low in this way.

FAMINE'S EFFECTS ON A FORMAL-CREDIT PROGRAM IN SUDAN. In 1981/82, the Agricultural Bank of Sudan (ABS) initiated a cooperative-based credit program in El Obeid District for production enhancement and consumption stabilization (Teklu, von Braun, and Zaki 1991). The program catered primarily to the credit needs of small farmers in rainfed agriculture. ABS provided loans to finance current production and storage. This program had more formal top-down structures than other schemes. Village-based cooperatives that had a legal status served as a channel for delivery of credit and marketing services to small farmers. Each village formed one cooperative, provided that it had a minimum of 50 members. Membership was open to resident farmers over 18 years of age who had access to land and a sound credit record. Each borrower was allowed to finance a fixed maximum area per crop; ABS determined the loan rate per area. The total loan amount per borrower was based on the loan rate per area and the total area approved for financing. Production loans were disbursed in three installments to ensure that they would be used for designated purposes and to minimize the risk of loan default. ABS also charged an administrative fee on its loaned funds. A maximum of 21 cooperatives covering nearly 2,000 members per season were serviced. A significant number of cooperatives were registered in the 1983/84 and 1984/85 seasons, the two drought and famine years, but only a small fraction of them were subsequently financed. Despite an increase in demand for loans, ABS was unwilling to risk a high loan default rate.

Available statistics covering fund usage show that a large percentage of ABS loans was used for food consumption. Studies by the Kordofan Rainfed Agricultural Project (KORAG) and ABS revealed that 68 and 83 percent of the loans were used for food consumption in the 1986/87 and 1988/89 seasons, respectively (Technoserve/ABS/USAID 1987; Bielen, Crauder, and Rivarola 1989). Another survey showed an average of 73 percent for the 1988/89 season (Teklu, von Braun, and Zaki 1991). No more than 20 percent of the loans were used for the purchase of current agricultural inputs and the cost of labor. Food was thus a top priority of ABS clients. In the end, any comprehensive evaluation of the loans' social costs and benefits would need to establish proper reference points. Distress migration of drought refugees—with all its adverse consequences—would have to figure as one such reference point. Loan default rates alone are not a proper yardstick.

ABS was effective in its early years when loan amounts were small; however, high default rates occurred in the drought years 1982/83 and 1984/85. The lowest level of lending on record was 1984/85, the peak drought and famine year. ABS's strict debt-collection policy (no debt relief, no rescheduling of debts, and no new loans without a settlement of old loans) contributed to a recovery of its past loans in 1986/87, but drove out a large proportion of borrowers.

OXEN AND SEED DISTRIBUTION IN ETHIOPIA.   In Ethiopia, the distribution of farm assets to distressed households became an increasingly common practice during the 1980s (Band Aid 1987; UNICEF 1988). In large parts of Ethiopia, draft oxen are a prerequisite to successful farming (Gryseels et al. 1988). However, in 1983/84 an average of 70 percent of households did not have access to a pair of oxen—and that was prior to the massive livestock losses of subsequent years (Ethiopia-MOA 1984). Farmers not owning their own oxen (usually the poorest households) traditionally engage in sharing, exchange, or rental agreements with (wealthier) oxen owners (McCann 1987). Although such arrangements allow resource-poor farmers access to draft power (albeit only after the owners have finished plowing their own fields), it places them in a position of dependence on wealthier farmers. Ox-distribution projects have tried to help poorer farmers become more independent. Recipients of oxen on credit still need to work within an exchange system, but the exchange is carried out on a more reciprocal basis.

A program aimed at helping poor households build up a stock of draft animals was implemented in the central highlands in 1985. Oxen were distributed on credit, and free seeds, plows, and feed blocks were given away in 26 villages, including one of the Ethiopian household survey sites (Dinki, see Chapter 7). In 1985, the proportion of households without any oxen at all in Dinki was 61 percent. Targeting at the poorest households, roughly half received one ox during 1985 and 1986 (Gryseels and Jutzi 1986).

In 1985, the oxen were purchased in the highlands and walked to the lowlands for distribution. This led to problems of climate adaptability, with many recipients complaining that highland oxen were unsuited to the hotter lowland conditions and were too weak to plow. During 1986, it was therefore decided to give cash instead (300 birr) so that households could purchase their own oxen (McCann 1985). Recipients signed an agreement to repay the loans within two years from September 1987. By 1989 however, no household had repaid its loan and project staff decided not to pursue repayment. The targeting of poorest households was largely successful in Dinki (although loan repayment was not). A greater proportion of households who received an ox (or the cash to purchase one) came from the lower-income tercile (72 percent) than from the upper tercile (50 percent).

On the other hand, there was also some mistargeting in that some recipients already owned one or more animals. For example, 17 percent of recipients in the upper-income tercile were given a second, not a first, animal. Even among the poorest recipient households, 9 percent were already in possession of an ox. However, given that all households justify categorization as "poor" at this extremely deprived location, such limited "mistargeting" is not unduly problematic. More important, 34 percent of households in the lowest tercile tried to be registered for an ox but were turned away. These were told that the quota was full (no oxen left) or that their registration had been lost, or they were promised an ox but never received it. Many of the latter were female-headed households. This oversight was rectified in 1986 through the distribution of cash to households headed by women, mainly for the purchase of milch cows (McCann 1985). Unfortunately, the poorest households had more difficulty in retaining their new assets than did the relatively wealthier households. Forty-five percent of sample recipients from the lower tercile lost the ox soon after they received it (resold or died), compared with only 17 percent from the upper tercile. In most cases, losses were due to feeding problems coupled with the poor condition of animals received.

More than one-third of all respondents complained that the ox was either in "poor" or "very bad" condition when they received it. Many farmers found it very hard to find sufficient feed to maintain the original weight. Almost 20 percent of sample recipients resorted to feeding thatch from their own roofs as well as cactus stems. Consequently, many animals died or had to be sold. Most of the households forced to sell their ox did so during the first harvest season, or less than three months after receiving them. The urgency of distress sales can be ascribed to the fact that immediate food needs were greater than the ability of households to wait three months until the next harvest. In addition to the oxen, many households also received a package of 120 kilograms of seeds. Targeting of the poorest households was effective in this free distribution, with 72 percent of sample households in the lower-income tercile receiving seeds, compared with only 22 percent of households in the upper tercile. However, three problems were observed with this part of the project. First, although the rains had already started, a number of households consumed most of the seed immediately and had none left to plant. Second, although most households did sow their seed on time (distribution took place in May/June 1985), the 1985 rains were sporadic and scant. Thus almost 20 percent of households lost their seed during protracted dry spells in the middle of the rainy season. These households argued that several monthly distributions of seed would have been more advantageous, enabling them to catch the later rains. Third, the maize variety provided (the major portion of the seed package) was less successful than expected. Lack of germination and very low yields from the maize were reported by 36 percent of recipients, most of whom argued that they were given a highland maize variety that was unsuited to the drought conditions of the lowlands.

The above review of experiences with credit and asset redistribution projects suggests at least two lessons: First, formal programs such as the one in Sudan through the ABS have difficulty in adjusting to rapidly changing financing needs under drought and famine stress. They must prepare beforehand institutional mechanisms to deal with such stress situations. Second, ad hoc livestock restocking schemes, if appropriately designed and supervised, can in fact work and provide considerable benefits. However, if a famine is particularly severe, such redistribution programs require complementary action to assure the short-term food security of asset recipients and prevent the poorest from being forced into early distress sales of the newly received assets. More generally, one may conclude that institutional preparedness in financial markets is a precondition for effective program operation. This is true to both maintain the productive asset base of the poor as well as provide timely and effective financial savings incentives at low transaction costs under economic stress situations.

Agricultural Technology and Diversification for Famine Prevention

Famine prevention cannot be addressed effectively and sustainably through redistributive policies alone. Earlier it was argued that famine mitigation and prevention strategies ought to be as developmental oriented as possible without, however, neglecting the short-term urgent needs of at-risk people (Williams 1995; Wahlström 1996). In a narrow economic sense, "developmental oriented" means contributing to increased total factor productivity. This, in turn, calls for technical change and efficiency in factor markets and related institutions. Low productivity of farming and livestock operations needs to be addressed directly through appropriate generation and extension of technology in the smallholder farm sector. Agricultural research, extension services, and timely access to productive inputs are therefore fundamental to famine prevention. In this section, obstacles to food production in Sub-Saharan Africa are briefly considered. It would be beyond the scope of this book to address Africa's overall agricultural production and productivity problems (see Mellor, Delgado, and Blackie 1987; Cleaver and Schreiber 1994). However, it is worthwhile asking the question how do technology improvement programs in agriculture perform in famine-prone areas? Do they tend to collapse under famine-related institutional and market stress and thereby possibly further accelerate instability problems? Would a promotion of subsistence agriculture with minimal external inputs, that is, the farming for sustenance just of the farm family, be the appropriate response to economic, climatic, or political famine risks? General evidence in support of such approaches is not common. Rather, the poor are exposed to risk because of a *lack* of access to technology and commercialization options (von Braun and Kennedy 1994). Before turning to specific program experiences in famine-prone settings, production constraints to national food security are briefly reviewed.

Production Constraints to Country-Level Food Security

In most African countries, there is little question that policies to enhance economic growth, particularly in agricultural productivity, must provide the bedrock for future development, including the removal of famine risk. Agricultural growth can address hunger not only through its potential to increase production, but also by generating rural employment and therefore income. Yet with population growth rates in excess of 3 percent per year in much of Africa and growth in agricultural output during the 1980s rarely surpassing 2 percent per year, the challenge to agriculture is daunting.

Opportunities for bringing new land under cultivation have somewhat compensated the slow yield growth in the past, but continued attempts to expand agricultural land will entail ever larger investments, accelerated deforestation and land degradation, and, ultimately, falling yields. Productivity increases must be sustainable. It is a matter of finding a way to meet growing food needs without compromising the ability of resources (both natural and human) to meet even larger demands in the future (Pinstrup-Andersen 1993b).

To increase agricultural yields in African countries, there is an urgent need for greater investment in agricultural research and technology aimed at yield enhancement and stabilization, particularly of those crops most important to the poor. This calls for investment in local agricultural research and extension capabilities—well connnected to regional and international ones—with a long-term perspective (Eicher and Staatz 1992). As population and food demand continue to grow, failure to develop and implement appropriate technologies in production and marketing will lead either to more food insecurity, for which the current generation of poor will pay, or to further resource degradation, for which future generations will pay (Pinstrup-Andersen 1993a).

Africa's agricultural production potential is far from fully developed. However, a complex set of technological and institutional factors has to be in place if that potential is to be developed in a sustainable and environmentally sound way. Rural infrastructure is essential to facilitate the flow of inputs, outputs, services, and information (Mellor, Delgado, and Blackie 1987; Creightney 1993). A first priority for infrastructural development should be the long-distance connection of high-potential production areas (even across borders) and a good provision of infrastructure within these areas. Whereas the former is a precondition for exploiting gains from specialization, the latter facilitates intensification.

The complementarity between traditional staple-food production and growth of cash crops (food and nonfood) also tends to be underemphasized and their competition overemphasized. Many African countries that fail to expand per capita food production also show negative cash-crop sector growth rates; however, the opposite—growth in both subsectors—is also observed in other African countries (von Braun and Kennedy 1994). Successful development in the staple-food sector (through technological change and appropriate sectoral policies) and growth in the cash-crop sector are not mutually exclusive. Effective programs for input supply, output marketing, and rural infrastructure benefit both sectors and are crucial for that growth.

Lessons from Selected Technology Programs

There may be a fair amount of general consensus on the priority for better agricultural technology promotion; this is less true, however, when it comes to the specifics of technological innovation in famine-prone areas. Given the fact that famines often hit people in marginal agro-ecological zones the hardest, this issue is part of the debate over the role of technology in more fragile ecologies (Vosti and Reardon 1997). However, if the output-increasing efforts of a technology improvement program succeed during a famine period—when output prices drastically increase, as they usually do under famine circumstances— the returns to previous investments accelerate accordingly. There are numerous examples of such successes: a local irrigation project showing its particular benefits during drought periods (von Braun, Puetz, and Webb 1989); another example is a tuber and root-crop project paying off when their prices are elevated by generally rising prices (von Braun, de Haen, and Blanken 1991).

Two country-specific experiences are reviewed in the following section. The first involves a cereal crop productivity program in Sudan; the second deals with cultivation technology and livestock productivity enhancement attempts in Ethiopia. A lesson from both of these is that famine conditions tend to pose severe institutional boundaries on the benefits of technology programs when attempted in isolated areas. However, even such projects can function as islands of hope if their base is strong enough in the period before a famine. This underlines the high costs of development when investment in technology is pushed aside by short-term relief needs.

A CROP PRODUCTIVITY-IMPROVEMENT PROGRAM IN SUDAN: SUC-CESS DURING DROUGHT? Compared with the rest of the western Sudanese province of Darfur, Jebel Marra and its surroundings are areas of relatively high agricultural potential. The region has benefited from a long-term rural development project that focuses on agricultural technology promotion: improved sorghum seeds, fertilizer, some animal-powered mechanization, and agricultural extension services. The use of this technology, plus some promotion of vegetable gardening and fruit-tree planting, has enhanced the production as well as the employment-absorption capacity of the Jebel Marra area in recent years.

In the early 1980s, the region experienced lower than usual rainfall. As in much of western Sudan, in 1984 the drought was severe. The area had to cope not only with food shortages for its own population but also the large number of drought refugees who came from other parts of Darfur and Chad—areas that were even more affected. The drought of 1984/85 led to a total crop failure in many parts of northern Darfur and reduced production in the Jebel Marra Project area. All villages in the project area experienced a drop in grain production, but villages that had access to modern inputs through extension services experienced less of a drop (Table 8.11). Within participating villages, households with access to improved inputs and extension services achieved a higher grain output per capita, producing enough to meet their basic calorie needs.

A comparison of participating and nonparticipating households shows that only a few in the participating group had no male head in the drought year, whereas 50 percent of the nonparticipating households had to manage the drought year without a male head of household (Table 8.12). The relatively small fluctuation in household size and in percentage of female-headed households in the participating group over the years suggests that these households

TABLE 8.11 Per household grain production before, during, and after the 1984 drought, by program participation in the Jebel Marra Project, Darfur (Sudan)

			Participating Villages	
Season (wet)	Participating Villages	Nonparticipating Villages	Participating Households	Nonparticipating Households
		(kilograms)		
1982/83[a]	980	520	1,148	779
1983/84[a]	973	449	1,361	785
1984/85[a,b]	624[c]	220[c]	867	544
1985/86	1,844[a]	1,568[a]	2,082	1,745
1986/87	1,064	1,173	1,498	1,099

SOURCE: Computed on the basis of Jebel Marra project survey data.

[a]The *t*-test mean of participating and nonparticipating groups was significantly different.

[b]Per capita grain production in the 1984/85 season was 178 kilograms for participants and 75 kilograms for nonparticipants. There was no significant difference within participating villages. The same pattern appears when comparisons are made on the basis of proportion of households with less than 1,000 calories per capita per day. The percentage was higher in nonparticipating villages (79) compared to participating villages (41).

[c]The *t*-test mean was statistically lower than previous years.

were in a much more stable position during the crisis year of 1984/85 than nonparticipating households. Those without access to modern inputs produced less and had to manage by adjusting household size through emigration of adult males. Coping was much easier for those who had been participating in the project.

Typically, farmers from northern Darfur came to the project area during the harvest period in search of employment. Also in 1984, most people fleeing drought came to the project area in October and November, around harvest

TABLE 8.12 Household size and percentage of female heads of household in extension villages, by program participation in the Jebel Marra Project, Darfur (Sudan)

	Participating Households		Nonparticipating Households	
Survey Period	Household Size	Female-Headed Households	Household Size	Female-Headed Households
	(persons)	(percent)	(persons)	(percent)
Wet season, 1984/85	5.01	9	3.31	47
Postharvest, 1985	n.a.	16	n.a.	50
Postharvest, 1988	6.65	11	5.78	23

SOURCE: Computed on the basis of Jebel Mara project survey data.

NOTE: n.a. = not available.

TABLE 8.13 Distribution of drought migrants in Jebel Marra area, Darfur (Sudan), by agro-ecological zone, 1984/85–1985/86

Zone	Village Population	Number of Migrants, 1984/85	Number of Migrants, 1985/86
Mountain	1,463	157	52
		(11)	(4)
Upper valley	1,216	209	87
		(17)	(7)
Lower valley	1,542	706	303
		(46)	(20)

SOURCE: Computed on the basis of Jebel Marra Project farm survey data.

NOTE: The numbers in parentheses represent the percentage of migrants in the village population.

time. Many settled near existing villages in the project area, in the fertile lower-valley zone that experienced a significantly better grain harvest than other zones (see Table 8.13). Improved agricultural technology was thus a powerful tool for alleviating the drought crisis. Given the mobility of labor in the region, a concentration of technological change in the comparatively high-potential area provided respite for drought refugees from a large area.

SELECTED TECHNOLOGY PROGRAMS IN ETHIOPIA. Two agricultural programs in Ethiopia were reviewed, one a short-term and the other a longer-term program, both of which provide some insight into reducing vulnerability to famine.

A project designed to have a more lasting effect on the survey village of Dinki's farming system was tied to the oxen-seed distribution program there. Some farmers were given a new type of plow that could be drawn by a single ox rather than by a pair. Designed by the International Livestock Center for Africa (ILCA),[5] this innovation was thought to hold promise for the rapid regeneration of asset-depleted farm economies. Experiments in the highlands indicated that an adequately fed single ox could cultivate up to 70 percent of the area normally plowed by a pair, with no loss in overall yield (Gryseels et al. 1984). It was therefore assumed that farmers with access to only one ox would benefit from reduced dependency on traditional tow-oxen rental arrangements.

The results were disappointing. Most farmers received the plow in June 1985, when the plowing season was already under way, allowing no time for training either people or animals in the new technology. As a result, farmers tried out the plow only during seeding, covering, and weeding. Few were satisfied. Even light tasks, such as soil covering and weeding, required much more time to complete than with a traditional pair (this was, in part, because

5. Now called (ILRI).

many farmers worked their animals only four hours a day for fear of wearing them down). According to 72 percent of recipients, the technology failed because local soils are too dense and stony, and because oxen were too weak to pull a plow alone (Webb and von Braun 1994). The remaining 28 percent stated that they might have used the plow had they not been forced to sell their oxen, or if the ox had not died prematurely. In the event, after a few trials most households never used the plow again. Households in the upper-income tercile, most of which already owned a pair of oxen, also did not use the plow more than a few times. In 1986, farmers in the middle- and lower-income terciles tried to use the plow more often than wealthier farmers, but only for light tasks. Since 1986, only 23 percent of households have used the plow. (Several commented that they had broken up the beam and yoke for firewood.)

Gryseels et al. (1988) found similar results when evaluating rates of use for the new plow in other highland villages. Although preliminary trials were encouraging, "the number of farmers using the system remained a minor fraction of the farm population." The main factors cited for not using it were dense soils, weak oxen, and excessively sloping land. It was concluded that further research into plow adaptation, coupled with a focus on improving the condition of draft animals, was warranted. Clearly a lesson of this experience is that famine conditions are not the time for technological experiments.

A separate project in Ethiopia was conceived not as an emergency intervention, but with long-term household food security in mind. Also designed and implemented by ILCA, the goal of this second project was to raise milk production through the crossbreeding of Friesian bulls with local Boran cows. An attempt was made to upgrade the genetic stock of cattle in the region of Debre Berhan. Between 1982 and 1984, 40 Debre Berhan households purchased cows of 75 percent exotic blood from ILCA (Gryseels et al. 1988). These cost an average of 578 birr, half paid in cash, half given in credit. Farmers had access to veterinary services at a nearby ILCA station, as well as training on how to manage their new resource. Two recommendations made were that farmers should cultivate 0.5 hectare of forage crops (a mixture of oats and vetch) and purchase feed concentrates from Addis Ababa to supplement normal feed.

Of the 40 households that acquired a crossbreed, 32 were included in the Ethiopia household survey. One-third of households purchasing a crossbreed fell into each of the three income groups. The hybrid cattle proved to be highly productive. Between 1984 and 1987, each cow produced an average of 2.5 calves, with no significant difference in calving rates across terciles. On the other hand, the crossbreeds produced up to six times more milk than cows of the local breed (Wagenaar-Brouwer 1986). Between 1983 and 1985, crossbreeds monitored by ILCA yielded an average of 5.5 liters per day (Gryseels et al. 1988). In 1989, these animals were still producing a daily average of 5 liters, compared with 3.5 liters from the Boran cows. Furthermore, although lactation was impaired by a lack of feed during 1987/88 (the worst year of famine in this locality), the crossbreeds continued to maintain much higher milk yields than local cows. Hybrids gave an average of 4 liters per day during the crisis, compared with only 2.5 liters per day from Boran cows. Indeed, many local cows dried up completely after several months of stress, while no crossbreeds ceased lactating.

Income provided by a continued flow of milk was crucial to household welfare during famine years. Household income increased threefold by owning a crossbreed, because of increased milk and butter sales (Wagenaar-Brouwer 1986). Income from milk and butter sales in crossbreed-owning households was almost six times greater than that of owners of local cows during the mid-1980s famine. During famine years, sales of milk products declined along with output, but households in the lower-income tercile still derived a daily cash income from their crossbreeds that was almost three times greater than that obtained by households only owning local cows. However, problems did arise in several areas. First, it proved expensive to feed the crossbreeds. They weighed an average of more than 380 kilograms, compared with local cows that weighed an average of 280 kilograms (Gryseels and Anderson 1983). Farmers owning hybrid cows claimed that they consumed three times more feed than local cattle and had greater water requirements. Although 90 percent of owners did attempt to cultivate special fodder crops as advised, few planted more than 0.1 hectare in oats and vetch (much less than recommended), and neither crop grew well. This caused shortages of seed in ensuing years, leading to complete abandonment of vetch and a decline in the area of oats planted each year.

Instead, farmers increasingly relied on purchased inputs. Monthly costs for the purchase of hay, straw, and grass (both bought and rented as grazing) for consumption by crossbreeds rose in all income groups. For example, in 1986 the average amount spent each month by the lower-income tercile households to feed hybrids was 16.3 birr (few farmers purchased feed for Boran cows). By 1989, this had risen to an average of 33.2 birr (current prices). This trend in increased spending on feed was stalled among the poorest households only during the worst years of the food crisis, namely 1987/88. During that period, the poorest farmers could not afford to spend valuable capital on livestock feed, whereas it appears that the relatively wealthier farmers could.

The other problem was the susceptibility of young cows to disease and starvation. Between 1983 and 1985, calf mortality was estimated at only 16 percent (Gryseels et al. 1988). However, this increased sharply between 1986 and 1989, which covered the worst crisis years at the location. For example, out of a total of over 100 offspring born to the 40 original crossbreeds between 1986 and 1989, only 35 were still on the farms in 1989. The others had either died from sickness and hunger during the crisis (67 percent), or had been sold to purchase food. Although the short-term impact of the crossbreeds was positive (through increased milk yields and associated income), the longer-term sustainability of such an exercise in genetic improvement depends on several factors: better disease control (through greater veterinary support); more reasearch into fodder cultivation (including improved seed availability); analysis of the economic and technical feasibility of feed-concentrate production and distribution in rural areas; and institution building and support within the ministries that take responsibility for the program's long-term management.

In sum, the success of technology programs under famine conditions appears to be mixed. Programs initiated under the severe stress of famine appear to have low success rates. Programs well established before a crisis occurs often show greater than expected results in famine conditions, unless they are vulnerable to input-supply constraints. The plow program in Ethiopia suggests that creating new technologies during times of famine stress may result in less than hoped for benefits. Famine situations are not the time for trial and error. New technologies, if they are to be successful, need to be developed and in place before famine conditions make their use essential for survival.

Policy Conclusions and Priorities

The causes of famine in Africa are diverse and growing ever more so. An analysis of famine's complexities must take into consideration both natural and man-made circumstances in which they occur, in order to prevent and alleviate their worst outcomes in Africa. This book has attempted to increase the understanding of famines:

1. by enhancing the theoretical basis of the debate through a multidisciplinary approach that combines technical, economic, geographic, and political factors;
2. by enriching the theory through empirical fact finding within the realms of production, markets, and—especially—affected households and people; and
3. by assessing famine prevention policies and programs and their performance in the real world.

The policy conclusions discussed in this section are couched within the interaction of these three approaches to the problem.

Although failed projects and programs often attract more attention than successful ones, the international community knows much more about famine prevention and relief in the 1990s than it did a mere decade ago. However, understanding is qualified by the parameters of existing institutional and political arrangements. Political and military conflicts and the absence of personal and legal security are major causes of famine in areas where people are chronically poor and public intervention is weak (see Chapter 3). Without peace, investments in growth and social security are tenuous at best. Little progress can be made in famine relief, and even less in famine prevention, when conflict continues to drain human and capital resources.

However, cessation of armed conflict will not in itself end the risk of famine in Africa. It has been shown that famines are an accumulation of events and policy failures that progressively erode the capacity of the poor to deal with short-term shocks. These shocks often take the form of acute environmental extremes, but the conditions that induce household vulnerability develop over long periods. Those conditions established by past policy failures cannot be rectified overnight. The resource base of the poor in some parts of rural Africa diminished to such an extent in the 1980s that even small events may now result in catastrophic famines.

Thus famine risk is inseparable from chronic food insecurity and poverty at both national and household levels. Without sustainable growth, particularly in rural labor productivity and agricultural output, the risk of famine will persist. Structural economic transformations are necessary to foster a better functioning of capital, labor, and food markets, and to facilitate productivity growth. Yet just as famines do not happen suddenly, the agricultural and economic growth that will prevent famine will not happen overnight.

As a result, famine prevention and alleviation cannot be left to market forces alone—a lesson that should have already been learned through numerous past examples worldwide. Reforming the public sector in Africa will not absolve it of responsibility for famine prevention. Both public and private sectors have a part to play in protecting and enhancing food security, at the same time as pursuing agricultural growth.

Instead of reiterating conclusions stated at the end of previous chapters, the primary focus of this final chapter is on institutional and organizational arrangements. It is in these areas that continued major gaps in knowledge, and thus a need for applied research, are seen.

Comprehensive Policy and Program Action

Famine relief and prevention do not rely solely on optimizing the effectiveness of individual programs, but on combining program components to generate positive multiplier effects. The range of instruments for relief and prevention is broad. Successful policies and programs have been implemented in countries unable to overcome short-term famine risks. These need to be scaled up in order to achieve a more broad-based impact.

The development of rural financial markets and agricultural technology (for both food and export crops) and the dissemination of assets and information remain fundamental for overcoming famine risks. Developing agricultural research and extension facilities is therefore central to long-term famine prevention. Isolated technology promotion and implementation programs cannot solve the problems of larger famine-prone countries. Such programs must be

TABLE 8.14 Key elements of famine mitigation efforts and responses in Zimbabwe, 1992/93, versus Ethiopia in the 1980s

	Zimbabwe 1992/93	Ethiopia 1980s
Conflict	Peace	Conflict
Political recognition	Relatively dynamic press	Constrained press
	Early state emergence	Late recognition
National institutions	Drought task force	Strong RRC
	National public works	No national programs
Targeting	National system	Ad hoc systems
Enabling macropolicies for economic growth	Policy reform under way	Policy constraints
Agricultural growth	Heavy investment	Small investment
Infrastructure	Good road system	Bad roads
Regional framework	SADCC strong	IGADD weak

NOTES: RRC = Relief and Rehabilitation Commission, SADCC = Southern African Development Coordination Conference, and IGADD = Intergovernmental Authority on Drought and Development.

allied with, and indeed protected by, appropriate and timely public actions that involve emergency feeding, health intervention, and income transfers.

In other words, the public capacity and public will to intervene on behalf of disadvantaged people are both crucial to the ability of individuals to cope with the human catastrophe of famine. Some countries are indisputably better equipped to cope than others; the latter will continue to be categorized as "famine prone" until certain crucial investment and institutional decisions are made.

Table 8.14 summarizes the main conclusions of public action concerning famine prevention and underlying conditions in Zimbabwe and Ethiopia. The figure shows that there are several factors at work. Peace or, at the least, minimal conflict is a prerequisite for effective public famine intervention programs. That said, even during times of peace, early recognition of a crisis and rapid institutional responses (facilitated across multiple ministries) are necessary if public action is to be effective. Cross-country coordination may also be necessary where crises are regional in nature, as in the Horn of Africa in the 1980s (where no strong regional institutions existed) and in southern Africa in the 1990s (where regional coordination was strong).

Where specific public interventions are necessary, predetermined and uniform targeting are crucial and could have helped avoid some of the ill will felt by Ethiopian households that were excluded from assistance without knowing why. By extension, nationwide systems that facilitate the timely distribution of assistance in standardized ways (such as Zimbabwe's national Food-for-Work Program) are certainly preferable to the ad hoc creation of projects in direct response to a crisis. It should be underlined that since the 1980s, Ethiopia has learned both lessons, formulating a national emergency code (that goes a long way toward formalizing tasks and responsibilities across its ministries in the event of future crises) and designing a national public works system that seeks to provide an employment-based safety net to all vulnerable people.

Of course, such large-scale public responsibilities have to be supported through economic growth. Policy reforms already under way in Zimbabwe in the early 1990s have now been adopted in Ethiopia, including a greater focus on investment in agriculture and rural road development. Each of these public-led interventions should be based on district or local government knowledge of problems and analyses of appropriate responses. Local NGOs are natural partners in that process. In the end however, the responsibility of national governments to protect the life and well-being of their citizens should not be abdicated. Letting the market "do its job" is essential to the security of Africa's most vulnerable people, but ensuring that markets actually *do* their job is an essential role of government.

Institutional and Organizational Needs

Famine prevention and relief requires an appropriate institutional framework. That is, national laws, international codes of conduct, and systems for response to famine need to be appropriately formulated. The question of "what ought to be done?" must be supplanted by "who should do it and how?" if the prevention of famine is to be successful. It appears that a consensus is developing on the "what" question, but there is much less agreement on the "who" and the "how."

Famine prevention and mitigation policy has a great deal of experience to build upon. The colonial famine programs of Rhodesia and Sudan, for instance, were influenced by earlier experiences from India (Shepherd 1988; Iliffe 1990). In India, detailed famine-related legislation was enacted during the second quarter of the last century. These laws (derived in part from even earlier experiences in England and Ireland) focused on early identification of the risks of famine, the provision of employment and public works schemes for those who could work, and food distribution to those unable to work (Drèze 1988; Webb 1997).

The legal and administrative measures operative in Sudan between 1920 and 1956 were instrumental in preventing major famines. They were applied "almost 50 times in different areas of Sudan" during this period (Pearson 1986). Preventative measures became routine features of famine administration (Shepherd 1988). However, such experiences can also be forgotten; between the mid-1950s and the early 1980s, there were no special institutions that handled famine prevention or relief efforts in Sudan, and coherent action was replaced by improvisation. The Indian and the historical Rhodesian and

FIGURE 8.3 Organization of international and national famine mitigation and relief systems

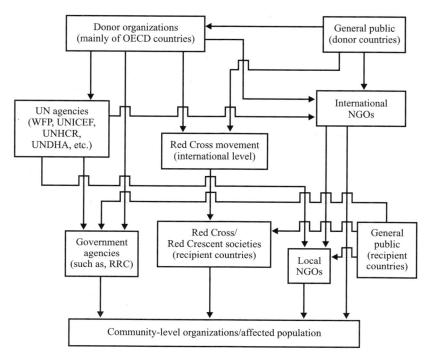

SOURCE: Adapted from Borton 1993.

NOTES: OECD = Organization for Economic Cooperation and Development,
WFD = World Food Program,
UNICEF = United Nations Children's Fund,
UNHCR = United Nations High Commissioner for Refugees, and
UNDHA = United Nations Department for Humanitarian Affairs.

Sudanese experiences therefore remain relevant for famine-prone countries in Africa today.

Famine mitigation and prevention is ever more dependent on the close alliance of local, national, and international relief systems. The means of relief (but not the methods of prevention) have evolved since the end of the Cold War due to the changing nature of emergencies. At the international level, the famine mitigation system is dominated by donor organizations that have different options for providing their assistance. In addition, the general public's contributions to international NGOs and the Red Cross have become sizable:

recent voluntary contributions channeled by NGOs were about US$2 billion per year (Reutlinger and del Castillo 1993). Figure 8.3 shows the principal types of organizations and the direction of resource flows.

The international system of famine relief has changed during the early 1990s in response to new political circumstances and public pressures. More recent innovations include efforts to streamline UN relief-response capabilities (FAO 1996), reorganizing national and supranational donor organizations (the establishment of the European Community Humanitarian Office [ECHO] in 1992 is one such example), and strengthening the role of international NGOs in certain conflict-prone regions where the United Nations or bilateral agencies have difficulties operating. In Ethiopia, for instance, about 80 percent of the relief assistance provided from 1985–91 in government-held areas and areas controlled by the Eritrean and Tigrayan liberation movements was channeled through NGOs, or some combination of NGOs, UN agencies, the Ethiopian government, and liberation organizations (UNEPPG 1989b; Borton 1993).

Within each system there is competition and complementarity, both of which have been underutilized. For each crisis, there are specific characteristics that have to be understood in order to take full advantage of the available relief system. Only with a thorough analysis of these characteristics can a choice of policy instruments be made. Assessment of the famine relief mechanisms used will then depend on how well the systems responded to the short-term crisis as well as laid the groundwork for future developmental improvements.

Local Action and NGOs

The assumption that famine gives rise to generosity only in the industrialized West is misplaced. It was noted in Chapter 7 in relation to Ethiopia that communities supported their members with food gifts, loans, and other assistance. Such local collective action persists in many famine-prone countries (Swift 1993), but displacement, refugee flows, and urbanization have reduced its coverage and relevance (see Chapter 5).

In addition to local action, however, extracommunity NGOs also attempt to mobilize help for distressed communities. In Ethiopia, grassroots initiatives were directed in part by church organizations and in part by regional drought committees. The churches (Baptist, Catholic, Lutheran, Orthodox, and others) were largely coordinated in their relief activities by the Christian Relief and Development Organization, a body comprising over 50 groups. Their apolitical role in distributing food behind lines of conflict was central to successful famine relief efforts during the 1980s (Minear 1988). During 1985, they served as a grassroots outlet for donations from overseas as well as from philanthropic organizations in Addis Ababa. Regional relief committees, on the other hand, were set up under the aegis of local party officials to organize care for destitute migrants as well as to collect voluntary contributions and a famine tax (levied on all peasant associations) for relief activities. Comparable community and local actions were pursued in Sudan, built around locally based voluntary organizations and traditional leadership structures. The implication is that international and government agencies should better identify the existence, strengths, and weaknesses of local initiatives in order to not undermine them; ideally, local actions should be integrated into larger institutional arrangements.

For instance, in Ethiopia in May 1985 there were 48 NGOs operating relief projects. These engaged in activities ranging from relief measures to developmental programs. During the famine, the most common care operations were medical and feeding programs (intensive and supplementary feeding, and dry-ration distribution). However, when the peak of a crisis is over, NGOs are often faced with the question of where to redirect their efforts. The answer for most usually is to go from relief to rehabilitation. This raises questions about long-term dependency relationships between beneficiary populations and local NGOs (Curtis, Hubbard, and Shepherd 1988; Elizabeth 1988). Additionally, the working relationships between international and local NGOs do not always function to everyone's satisfaction (Abdel Ati 1993). It should be evident, however, that continued NGO presence in the field can be crucial to successful aid programs in crisis conditions.

The complex role of NGOs has emerged within the "permanent [state of] emergency" that exists in the countries of the Horn of Africa (Duffield 1993). NGOs clearly are necessary to supplement governmental and international actions during a crisis, but their potential to prevent future crises or enable rehabilitation afterward is limited. Some critics suggest that in specific settings—such as the Red Sea Province of Sudan—NGOs have made no efforts to create an environment conducive to sustained developmental action. Additionally, by refraining from becoming involved in infrastructural projects, their lack of support for local NGOs, and failing to mobilize the traditional organizational systems of local groups, NGOs have planted their own seeds of destruction (Abdel Ati 1993).

Such criticisms must obviously not be generalized. However, two issues concerning their involvement in relief operations need to be addressed. First, when NGOs shift from emergency relief to recovery and development programs, the nature of their relationships with governments and other actors obviously has to change with the circumstances. In that sense, NGOs often have difficulties appointing appropriate (and perhaps different) staff to implement what may be vastly changed program goals.

Second, although NGOs are becoming more involved in famine mitigation, very little comprehensive information on assessing the results of their operations is available. The acute nature of crisis situations may justify the limited information given to evaluate the impact and effectiveness of short-term operations. However, any assessment of famine prevention and relief operations requires comparative costs/benefits analyses between no action versus alternative actions. At present, these analyses are performed sporadically (at best). Thus, concentrating NGO efforts where they have proven their strength and making these operations subject to scrutiny (and hence available for institutional and cross-country adaptation) can only be of benefit to those seeking improved relief and prevention.

Government Interventions

When famines occur, governments are often blamed for not predicting the crisis and providing timely intervention (Gill 1986; Jackson 1990). Some of this blame is often colored by political bias, but the point has merit. Without adequate investment in information gathering and analysis, and in the mobilization of resources for rapid response, famines cannot be adequately dealt with. This applies to the international relief and development community as well as to national governments (Penrose 1987; Fraser 1988).

A generalized answer to the question of whether governments should set up one specific agency or organization to handle famine relief has not been found. Famine-prone countries have often set up specific agencies to deal with such operations. In Ethiopia, the RRC (renamed the Disaster Preparedness and Prevention Committee) is the agency with principal responsibility for operations in the realm of drought and food shortages. Founded in 1974, the RRC was set up to monitor and alleviate the effects of the 1973/74 drought. Its mandate was to provide relief in the worst-affected regions by acting as the central clearing house for all aid activity. Sudan similarly set up an RRC in the mid-1980s which, however, never evolved to the caliber of the Ethiopian model. Country circumstances may argue for or against an RRC-type organization. Countries with a decentralized government might use an arrangement that emphasizes a stronger role of local entities, or might channel all activities through the central ministries, as the circumstances warrant. Its easier to generalize governments' roles in famine mitigation than to identify the specifics of appropriate organizational structures.

The underpinnings of famine mitigation and prevention policies require a legal base. To prevent political influence from hampering famine mitigation efforts, emergency-code legislation (of the Indian kind) should be institutionalized. Such legislation should define three areas of public responsibility: (1) authority and ability to record and diagnose distress signals and to alert appropriate institutions of the danger, (2) development of the local institutional capacity to organize an effective response to such alerts, and (3) design of explicit targeting strategies to cover population groups most at risk. Successful implementation of such legislation requires strong political, financial, and technical empowerment of local government structures. These structures should also bear primary responsibility for the management of regional emergency food stocks.

There is a need for early warning of famine crises, both nationally and internationally. Improvements in early-warning capabilities, however, have limited value if they do not result in timely and effective response.

One of government's roles is to coordinate and integrate administrative bodies, to provide strong administrative linkages between institutions that can identify a problem and those whose responsibility it should be to prevent and, if necessary, remedy that problem. The prepositioning of response measures, combined with monitoring of preventative measures, is essential in alleviating the distress caused by famine. Botswana's experience of coordinating and integrating different food security action—including employment programs—with mainstream public institutions provides an example.

What will be most effective in providing sustained famine relief is to tie the health care systems to the food security systems of government. A strong health care system is a necessity for public action under any circumstances, not just from a famine prevention perspective. Health systems tend to fall apart under famine conditions, as happened in Sudan in the mid-1980s (de Waal 1989; Teklu, von Braun, and Zaki 1991). Not only does better health directly affect child nutrition (see Chapters 5 and 7), it facilitates coping with consumption fluctuations. Also, a strong health care system can be a powerful tool for managing relief operations more effectively, especially for children and mothers.

International Actions

The international donor community has played a critical role in the public response to famine in Africa. As Figure 8.4 shows, the key players in this effort operate through multilateral and bilateral agencies and through NGOs. The inability of states to cope with famine within their own borders has repeatedly led them to seek external assistance. Providing aid to countries with a weak central authority, such as Somalia, is a relatively new challenge, but the probability of such interventions being needed in the future is high. One of the largest internationally guided relief operations, Sudan's Operation Lifeline, revealed the limits of international action when there is a lack of government cooperation, as in Somalia in 1993 and in Sudan in 1998.

Because the severity of famines and their effects is becoming more intense, international awareness has intensified as well. Evidence of this can be seen in opinion and goal-setting meetings, such as the World Summit for Children (1989) prepared by UNICEF; the International Conference on Nutrition (1992) hosted by FAO/WHO; as well as the World Food Summit (1996) prepared by FAO. Each of these efforts stimulated public opinion and led to some country-level actions. Their common problem has been a lack of independent follow-up and related monitoring and evaluation.

Along with greater awareness of the problem, there has been more international response to deal with it, primarily under the auspices of UN organizations. Considerable strides in dealing with famine conditions have been made in the 1980s, but the UN system has found it difficult to establish one strong organization to end hunger. A number of UN groups feel they have a mandate in this field, and this has had the effect of each of them providing only partial responses or working in specific regions. Although the tasks of famine prevention and reducing malnutrition remain complex and certainly require a similarly complex international action network, this cannot be said for the task of famine mitigation, where a strong international organizational setup is long overdue. Famines in many African countries today are the direct result of conflict and oppression. The international capability to address these issues must be strengthened in order to provide realistic aid to those most vulnerable (see Chapter 3). A different legal code, including the rethinking of states' rights versus citizens' rights may be required.

Summing Up

The continued prevalence of famine in Africa represents a general "policy failure" on a worldwide scale, although there have been some success stories. The results of many programs to strengthen household and national security against famine have been positive, and the ability to deal with famines triggered by natural disasters (rather than conflict) is much greater at the end of the 1990s than it was at the start of the decade. There remains, however, a lack of systematic assessment of these programs, which hinders learning and institutional strengthening across borders. That said, progress has been made in a number of key areas:

- The improved performance of EWSs shows that benefits can be great where responses build quickly on early warning (as in Botswana in the 1980s and in Zimbabwe in the early 1990s).
- The improved understanding of the potentials and limitations of market performance under famine conditions reveals where changes must be made in market-oriented mitigation policies.
- More sound transfer and subsidy systems evolved from expensive lessons learned from general price subsidies and rationing systems, in which the poor were served but only at very high costs.
- The refining of targeting mechanisms for emergency aid distribution programs reveals that research into the characteristics, coping limitations, and immediate needs of vulnerable households can pay off.
- There is a better understanding of the role of employment in famine prevention; knowing when and where to initiate labor-intensive, employ-

ment programs, using wages paid in cash or food (depending on local market conditions), is critical.

- The potential of rural financial market development in famine-prone countries is slowly being realized and offers new forms of participatory action.
- The access to and types of agricultural technology needed to alleviate hunger in famine-prone areas have been improved through a greater understanding of the coping strategies used by smallholder farmers.

A number of conclusions can also be drawn. First, present-day famines in Africa are largely the result of military conflicts that arise due to oppressive, unaccountable, and nonparticipatory government (see Chapter 3). There is no doubt that little progress can be made in famine relief, and even less in prevention, while conflict continues to drain human and capital resources. A lasting peace and improved rural participation in governance are the basis for eliminating famine. Yet viewing conflict as the sole cause of famine is misplaced. The genocide in Rwanda was a human tragedy based on ethno-political conflict, which in turn was fostered by population pressure and resource constraints, as well as perceived long-standing economic and political discrimination. In some cases, inappropriate domestic, economic, and international aid policies have contributed to the political climate in which conflicts emerged. Famine prevention policy must, therefore, be concerned with general conflict resolution between and within states, as well as with the human and economic problem of absolute poverty.

Second, famine in Africa is inseparable from chronic poverty and risk. Although famine characteristics differ between countries, the underlying poverty conditions that contribute to famine in Africa are quite similar: lack of employment opportunities; limited household assets; isolation from major markets; low levels of farm technology; constraints to improvement in human capital; and poor health and sanitation environments. Although factors such as political and military conflict and drought contribute to famine, they do so mainly where people are vulnerable in the first place, and where resilience to external shocks has already been worn thin (see Chapter 7).

Third, famines do not happen suddenly. They are an accumulation of events and policies that progressively erode the capacity of countries as well as households to deal with short-term shocks to the economy and food supply. These shocks often take the form of environmental extremes, but the conditions that promote household vulnerability to such extremes develop over long periods (see Chapter 4). Misguided macroeconomic and trade policies have been part of the problem in most famine-prone countries, and conditions established by past policy failures cannot be rectified in the short run. The coping capacity of poor households has substantially declined in the 1980s and early

1990s (see Chapter 7), which suggests that private (market-oriented), short-term solutions alone will not undo years of entrenched poverty.

Fourth, the fact that famines continue to be a threat to life at the turn of the twenty-first century must be ascribed to a failure (both nationally and internationally) to give priority to the conceptualization, analysis, preparation, and implementation of preventative measures. Overcoming the obstacles to food security and famine prevention requires a comprehensive development strategy that places the greatest emphasis on promoting agricultural growth, both of subsistence food crops and crops for sale.

Fifth, one of the main stumbling blocks that prevent turning knowledge into action is the lack of political and financial commitment to create and maintain the legal and administrative frameworks essential to efficient interventions. No long-term progress can be made against food insecurity and famine without the machinery in place to record and diagnose stress signals and to organize swift and effective response to such signals. Relief organizations and systems in famine-prone countries need to be strengthened, their independent operation ensured, their links with local governments emphasized, and their coordination with NGOs streamlined. Basic social security systems for the most vulnerable need to be put in place.

Sixth, to be successful in the fight against hunger and famine, international cooperation must be institutionalized through appropriate incentives. Given the nature of political and administrative processes, the need for integration and coordination between domestic agencies and ministries must be continuously reinforced as well. The UN agencies, such as the FAO, the International Fund for Agricultural Development (IFAD), UNICEF, WFP, WHO, and other development agencies, as well as the Consultative Group on International Agricultural Research (CGIAR), the IMF, and the World Bank, have important complementary roles to play in setting the agenda and in fostering cooperation at country and international levels.

There is no excuse for the continued occurrence of famine in today's world. Famine represents a failure of politics and action at every step, from the local to the international community. Public intervention based on partnerships between communities and government agencies can and does effectively overcome famine. The citizens of famine-prone countries have a right to expect measurable progress toward such a goal. Having enough food to eat is not just an abstract human right, it is the basis of all functioning of society and hence must be the foundation for sustainable development.

References

Abdel Ati, H. A. 1993. The development impact of NGO activities in the Red Sea Province of Sudan: A critique. *Development and Change* 24 (1): 103–130.

Abdou, D., A. G. Katab, M. Damous, and A. G. Rufale. 1991. *Pilot study for food consumption pattern for food insecure groups in Khartoum area.* Khartoum: Ministry of Agriculture and Natural Resources.

ACC/SCN (Administrative Committee on Coordination of the United Nations/Subcommittee on Nutrition). 1992. *Second report on the world nutrition situation.* Vol. 1. *Global and regional results.* Geneva.

———. 1993. *Second report on the world nutrition situation.* Vol. 2. Geneva.

Adams, A. 1993. Food insecurity in Mali: Exploring the role of the moral economy. *IDS Bulletin* 24 (4): 41–51.

Adams, M. E., and J. Howell. 1979. Developing the traditional sector in the Sudan. *Economic Development and Cultural Change* 27 (3): 505–518.

ADE. 1996. European strategy to support food security in Ethiopia. Report to the commission of the European Community, Brussels. Mimeo.

Admassie, Y., and S. Gebre. 1985. *Food-for-work in Ethiopia: A socioeconomic survey.* Research Report 24. Addis Ababa: Institute of Development Research, Addis Ababa University.

Africa Demos. 1992. Vol. 2 (August).

Ahmed, R., and N. Rustagi. 1987. Marketing and price incentives in African and Asian countries: A comparison. In *Agricultural marketing strategy and pricing policy,* ed. D. Elz, 104–118. Washington, D.C.: World Bank.

Alderman, H. H., and E. T. Kennedy. 1987. *Comparative analyses of nutritional effectiveness of food subsidies and other food-related interventions.* An occasional report. Washington, D.C.: International Food Policy Research Institute.

Anderson, J. R., and J. L. Dillon. 1992. *Risk analysis in dryland farming systems.* Farm Systems Management Series 2. Rome: FAO.

Appleton, J. 1988. *Nutritional status monitoring in Wollo, Ethiopia, 1982–84: An early warning system?* Report to Save the Children Fund (United Kingdom), London.

Aredo, D. 1990. The evolution of rural development policies. In *Ethiopia: Rural development options,* ed. S. Pausewang, F. Cheru, S. Brüne, and G. Chole. London: Zed Books.

Asefa, S. 1989. *Managing food security action programs in Botswana.* Michigan State University International Development Working Paper 36. East Lansing, Mich., U.S.A.: Michigan State University.

Ashton, B., K. Hill, A. Piazza, and R. Zeitz. 1984. Famine in China 1958–61. *Population and Development Review* 10 (4): 613–645.

Atabani, F. 1991. Macroeconomic policy perspectives for famine prevention. In *Drought and famine prevention in Sudan,* ed. E. A. Zaki, J. von Braun, and T. Teklu. Proceedings of a workshop held 7 January 1991 in Khartoum, Sudan, by the Ministry of Finance and Economic Planning and the International Food Policy Research Institute, January 7. Washington, D.C.: International Food Policy Research Institute.

Band Aid. 1987. *A review of Band Aid–funded agricultural rehabilitation projects in Sudan and Ethiopia: Summary report.* London.

Bardhan, P. 1997. Method in the madness? A Political-economy analysis of the ethnic conflicts in less developed countries. *World Development* 25 (No. 9): 1381–1398.

Belete, A., J. L. Dillon, and F. M. Anderson. 1991. Development of agriculture in Ethiopia since the 1975 land reform. *Agricultural Economics* 6 (2): 159–175.

Belshaw, D. G. R., 1990. Food strategy formulation and development planning in Ethiopia. *IDS Bulletin* 21 (3), 31–43.

Berg, A. 1987. *Malnutrition: What can be done?* Baltimore, Md., U.S.A.: Johns Hopkins University Press.

Bhatia, B. 1967. *Famines in India.* Bombay: Asia Publishing House.

Bielen, R., R. T. Crauder, and M. A. Rivarola. 1989. Evaluation of the credit component, Kordofan Rainfed Agricultural Project (KORAG). Report submitted to USAID/Sudan.

Binswanger, H. P., and P. Landell-Mills. 1995. *The World Bank's strategy for reducing poverty and hunger: A report to the development community.* Washington, D.C.: World Bank.

Bohle, H., T. Cannon, H. Greene, and F. N. Ibrahim. 1991. *Famine and food security in Africa and Asia: Indigenous response and external intervention to avoid hunger.* Bayreuther Geowissenschaftliche Arbeiten, vol. 15. Bayreuth, Germany: N. G. Bayreuth.

Bondestam, L., L. Cliffe, and P. White. 1988. *Eritrea: Food and agricultural production assessment study.* Final report. Leeds, U.K.: University of Leeds.

Borton, J. 1993. *Recent changes in the international relief system.* Briefing paper. London: Overseas Development Institute.

Boserup, E. 1965. *The conditions of agricultural growth: The economics of agrarian change under population pressure.* London: Allen and Unwin.

Braun, J. von, ed. 1995. *Employment for poverty reduction and food security.* Washington, D.C.: International Food Policy Research Institute.

Braun, J. von, and E. Kennedy. 1994. *Agricultural commercialization, economic development, and nutrition.* Baltimore, Md., U.S.A.: Johns Hopkins University Press for the International Food Policy Research Institute.

Braun, J. von, H. de Haen, and J. Blanken. 1991. *Commercialization of agriculture under population pressure: Effects on production, consumption, and nutrition in Rwanda.* Research Report 85. Washington, D.C.: International Food Policy Research Institute.

Braun, J. von, and R. Pandya-Lorch, eds. 1991. *Income sources of malnourished people in rural areas: Microlevel information and policy implications.* Working Paper 5 on Commercialization of Agriculture and Nutrition. Washington, D.C.: International Food Policy Research Institute.

Braun, J. von, D. Puetz, and P. Webb. 1989. *Irrigation technology and commercialization in The Gambia: Effects on income and nutrition.* Research Report 75. Washington, D.C.: International Food Policy Research Institute.

Braun, J. von, and M. Qaim. 1997. Poverty, hunger and population pressure: A vicious circle? Paper presented to Forum Engelberg. Eighth Conference on Food and Water: A Question of Survival, 18–21 March. Engelberg, Switzerland. Mimeo.

Braun, J. von, T. Teklu, and P. Webb. 1991. Labor-intensive public works for food security: Experience in Africa. Working Paper on Food Subsidies 6. Washington, D.C.: International Food Policy Research Institute.

Bread for the World. 1995. *Hunger 1995: Causes of hunger.* Fifth Annual Report on the State of World Hunger. Silver Spring, Md., U.S.A.: Bread for the World Institute.

Brown, J. B. 1989. Soil conservation, forestry, and food aid in Ethiopia: Some experiences and some current problems. Paper presented at the Sixth International Soil Conservation Conference, 6–18 November, Nairobi, Kenya.

Brown, L., Y. Yohannes, and P. Webb. 1994. Rural labor-intensive public works: Impacts of participation on preschooler nutrition. *American Journal of Agricultural Economists* (December): 1213–1218.

Brown, L. R., and H. Kane. 1994. *Full house: Reassessing the Earth's population carrying capacity.* New York: W. W. Norton.

Brüne, S. 1990. The agricultural sector: Structure, performance, and issues (1974–1988). In *Ethiopia: Rural development options,* ed. S. Pausewang, F. Cheru, S. Brüne, and E. Chole. London: Zed Books.

Buchanan, R. L. 1990. Long-term development aid to Ethiopia: OXFAM America's experience. Statement before the Joint Economic Committee of the U.S. Congress, February 27.

Buchanan-Smith, M. 1990. *Food security planning in the wake of an emergency relief operation: The case of Darfur, western Sudan.* Discussion Paper 278. Sussex, U.K.: Institute of Development Studies.

Buchanan-Smith, M., and S. Davies. 1995. *Famine early warning and response—The missing link.* London: Intermediate Technology Publications.

Campbell, D. J. 1990. Strategies for coping with severe food deficits in rural Africa: A review of the literature. *Food and Foodways* 4 (2): 143–162.

Carlson, B. A., and T. M. Wardlaw. 1990. *A global, regional, and country assessment of child malnutrition.* Staff Working Paper 7. New York: UNICEF.

Cekan, J. 1990. Traditional coping strategies during the process of famine in Sub-Saharan Africa. M.A. thesis, Fletcher School of Law and Diplomacy, Tufts School of Nutrition, Medford, Mass., U.S.A.

Churchill, W. S. 1899. *The river war.* London: Eyre and Spottiswoode.

Clark, L. 1986. *Early-warning case study: The 1984–85 influx of Tigrayans into eastern Sudan.* Working Paper 2. Washington, D.C.: Refugee Policy Group.

Clay, E. J., and H. W. Singer. 1985. *Food aid and development: Issues and evidence.* Occasional Paper 3. Rome: World Food Program.

Cleaver, K. U., and G. A. Schreiber. 1994. *Reversing the spiral: The population, agriculture, and environment nexus in Sub-Saharan Africa.* Washington, D.C.: World Bank.

Cliffe, L. 1989. The impact of war and the response to it in different agrarian systems in Eritrea. *Development and Change* 20 (3): 373–400.

Cohen, J. M., and N.-I. Isaksson. 1987a. *Villagization in the Arssi region of Ethiopia.* Swedish Institute for Development Assistance consultancy report. Rural Development Studies 19. Uppsala, Sweden: Swedish University of Agricultural Sciences.

————. 1987b. Villagization in Ethiopia's Arssi region. *Journal of Modern African Studies* 25 (3): 435–465.

Collier, P. 1993. Demobilization and insecurity—A study in the economics of the transition from war to peace. Center for the Study of African Economies, Oxford. Mimeo.

Collier, P., and D. Lal. 1986. *Labor and poverty in Kenya 1900–1980.* Oxford: Clarendon Press.

Collier, P., S. Radwan, and S. Wangwe. 1986. *Labor and poverty in rural Tanzania.* Oxford: Clarendon Press.

Coppock, D. L., personal communication, 1991.

Corbett, J. 1988. Famine and household coping strategies. *World Development* 16 (9): 1099–1112.

Creightney, C. D. 1993. *Transport and economic performance: A survey of developing countries.* World Bank Technical Paper 232. Washington, D.C.: World Bank.

Curtis, D., M. Hubbard, and A. Shepherd. 1988. *Preventing famine: Policies and prospects for Africa.* London: Routledge.

Cutler, P. 1984. Famine forecasting: Prices and peasant behavior in northern Ethiopia. *Disasters* 8 (1): 48–56.

Daly, M. W., and A. A. Sikainga, eds. 1993. *Civil war in the Sudan.* London: British Academic Press.

Dando, W. A. 1980. *The geography of famine.* London: Edward Arnold Publishers.

Davies, S. 1993. Are coping strategies a cop-out? *IDS Bulletin* 24 (4): 60–72.

————. 1996. *Adaptable livelihoods: Coping with food insecurity in the Malian Sahel.* London: Macmillan.

Degefu, W. 1987. Some aspects of meteorological drought in Ethiopia. In *Drought and hunger in Africa: Denying famine a future,* ed. M. Glantz. Cambridge: Cambridge University Press.

————. 1988. Climate-related hazards: Its monitoring and mitigation. Paper presented at the National Conference on a Disaster Prevention and Preparedness Strategy for Ethiopia, 5–8 December, Addis Ababa.

Deng, F., and L. Minear. 1993. *The challenge of famine relief.* Washington, D.C.: Brookings Institution.

Derrier, J.-F. 1991. *Conservation des sols et des eaux et ressources locales au Sahel: Enseignements et orientations.* Geneva: International Labor Organization.

Desai, B. M., and J. W. Mellor. 1993. *Institutional finance for agricultural development: An analytical survey of critical issues.* Washington, D.C.: International Food Policy Research Institute.

Dev, S. M. 1994. India's (Maharashtra) Employment Guarantee Scheme: Lessons from long experience. In *Employment for poverty reduction and food security,* ed. J. von Braun. Washington, D.C.: International Food Policy Research Institute.

Devereux, S. 1993. Goats before ploughs: Dilemmas of household response sequencing during food shortages. *IDS Bulletin* 24 (4): 52–59.

de Waal, A. 1987. Famine that kills: Darfur 1984–85. Save the Children Fund (U.K.), London. Mimeo.

———. 1991. *Evil days: 30 years of war and famine in Ethiopia.* Washington, D.C.: Human Rights Watch.

———. 1993. War and famine in Africa. *IDS Bulletin* 24 (4): 33–40.

Donaldson, T. J. 1986. Pastoralism and drought: A case study of the Borana of southern Ethiopia. M.Phil. thesis. Faculty of Agriculture and Food, University of Reading, Reading, U.K.

Downing, T. E. 1991. African household food security: What are the limits of available coping mechanisms in response to climatic and economic variations? In *Famine and food security in Africa and Asia: Indigenous response and external intervention to avoid hunger,* ed. H. G. Bohle, T. Cannon, G. Hugo, and F. N. Ibrahim. Bayreuth, Germany: Bayreuther Geowissenschaftliche Arbeiten.

Downing, T. E., K. W. Gitu, and C. M. Kamau, eds. 1989. *Coping with drought in Kenya: National and local strategies.* Boulder, Colo., U.S.A.: Lynne Rienner.

Downs, R. E., D. O. Kerner, and S. P. Reyna. 1993. *The political economy of African famine.* Amsterdam: Gordon and Breach Science Publishers.

Drèze, J. 1988. *Famine prevention in India.* Development Economics Research Program Paper 3. London: London School of Economics.

———. 1989. *Famine prevention in Africa.* The Development Economics Research Program Paper 17. London: London School of Economics.

Drèze, J., and A. Sen. 1989. *Hunger and public action.* Oxford: Clarendon Press.

———. 1991. *The political economy of hunger,* 3 volumes. Oxford: Clarendon Press.

D'Silva, B. C. 1985. Sudan: Policy reforms and prospects for agricultural recovery after the drought. U.S. Department of Agriculture, Washington, D.C. Mimeo.

Duffield, M. 1993. NGOs' disaster relief, and asset transfer in the Horn: Political survival in a permanent emergency. *Development and Change* 24 (1): 131–157.

———. 1994. NGOs, disaster relief and asset transfer in the Horn. *Forum-Valutazione* 7: 107–131.

Duncan, J. S. R. 1952. *The Sudan: A record of achievement.* Edinburgh: William Blackwood and Sons, Ltd.

Economic and Social Research Council. 1988. *Social dimension of adjustment— Khartoum Province: Case study.* Research Report 26. Khartoum: Economic and Social Research Council.

EEC (European Economic Community). 1989. *Evaluation of food-for-work programs in Eritrea and Tigray.* Report to the EEC by Environmental Resources Limited, Addis Ababa.

Eele, G. 1994. Indicators for food security and nutrition monitoring: A review of the experience from southern Africa. *Food Policy* 19 (3): 314–28.

Ehrlich, P. R., A. H. Ehrlich, and G. C. Daily. 1993. Food security, population, and the environment. *Population and Development Review* 19 (No. 1): 1–32.

Eicher, C. K., and J. M. Staatz, eds. 1992. *Agricultural development in the Third World,* 3d ed. Baltimore, Md., U.S.A.: Johns Hopkins University Press.

Eldredge, E., S. el-Sayeed Khalil, C. Salter, N. Nichols, A. A. Abdalla, and D. Rydjeski. 1987. Changing rainfall patterns in western Sudan. UNDP-UNEDS, Sudan Early Warning System. Relief Rehabilitation Commission, Khartoum. Mimeo.

Elhassan, A. M. 1988. The encroachment of large-scale mechanized agriculture: Elements of differentiation among the peasantry. In *Sudan: State, capital, and transformation,* ed. T. Barnett and A. Abdelkarim. New York: Croom Helm.

Elizabeth, K. 1988. *From disaster relief to development: The experience of the Ethiopian Red Cross.* Geneva: Institut Henry Dunant.

Engelmann, R., and P. Leroy. 1996. *Mensch, land!* Study published by Deutsche Stiftung Weltbevölkerung. Hannover, Germany: Balance-Verlag.

Eriksson, J., H. Adelman, J. Borton, H. Christensen, K. Kumar, A. Suhrke, D. Tardif-Douglin, S. Villumstad, and L. Wohlgemuth. 1996. *The international response to conflict and genocide: Lessons from the Rwanda experience: Synthesis report.* Copenhagen: Steering Committee of the Joint Evaluation of Emergency Assistance to Rwanda.

Erni, T. 1988. Report on northern Shewa Relief and Soil and Water Conservation Project in Shewa, Ethiopia, June 1985–June 1988. Lutheran World Federation, Addis Ababa. Mimeo.

Ethiopia-CSA (Central Statistics Authority). 1987a. *Time-series data on area, production, and yield of major crops, 1979/80–1985/86 (1979 E.C.).* Addis Ababa.

———. 1987b. *Agricultural sample survey, 1986/87 (1979 E.C.): Results of area and production by sector.* Addis Ababa.

———. 1988. Report on 1988/89 crops, weather, and food situation. Food Information Systems Project. Addis Ababa. Mimeo.

———. 1989. *Agricultural sample survey, 1987/88 (1980 E.C.): Results on area, production, and yield of major crops by sector and season.* Addis Ababa.

———. Various years. *Report on retail prices of goods and services in rural areas.* Addis Ababa.

Ethiopia-MOA (Ministry of Agriculture). 1979. Area, production, and yield of major crops for the whole country and region in 1974/75–1978/79. Addis Ababa: MOA.

———. 1984. *General agricultural survey: Preliminary report 1983/84,* vol. 1. Addis Ababa.

Ethiopia-Ministry of Economic Development and Cooperation. 1997. Market Analysis Note 2. Addis Ababa, January Mimeo.

Ethiopia-MPED (Ministry of Planning and Economic Development). 1992. *Study on social dimension of adjustment in Ethiopia.* Addis Ababa.

Ethiopia-OXFAM. 1984. *Lessons to be learned: Drought and famine in Ethiopia.* Oxford: Oxford University Press.

Ethiopia-RRC (Relief and Rehabilitation Commission). 1985. *Ethiopia: Review of drought relief and rehabilitation activities for the period December 1984–August 1985 and 1986 assistance requirements.* Addis Ababa.

———. 1990. *Food supply of the crop-dependent population in 1990.* Addis Ababa.

Fafchamps, M. 1992. Solidarity networks in preindustrial societies: Rational peasants in a moral economy. *Economic Development and Cultural Change* 41 (1): 147–174.

FAO (Food and Agriculture Organization of the United Nations). 1984. *Land, food and people.* Based on the FAO/UNFPA/IIASA report Potential population-supporting capacities of lands in the developing world. Rome: FAO.

―――. 1996. *Food supply and utilization data tape.* Rome.

―――. 1997a. FAO yearbook. <http://www.fao.org/FAO STAT Nutrition>.

―――. 1997b. FAOSTAT data bas. <http://apps.fao.org/cgi-bin/nph-db.pl>.

―――. Various years. *Agricultural trade yearbook.* Rome.

―――. Various years. *Food aid in figures.* Rome.

―――. Office for Special Relief Operations. 1985. *Democratic Republic of Sudan, Report of the FAO/WFP multidonor mission, assessment of the food and agricultural situation.* OSRO Report 02/85/E. Rome.

Farah, A. A., and R. K. Sampath. 1993. Poverty in Sudan. Department of Agricultural and Resource Economics, Colorado State University, Fort Collins, Colo., U.S.A. Mimeo.

Farwell, B. 1967. *Prisoners of the Mahdi.* London: Longmans, Green.

Feldbrügge, T., and J. von Braun. 1997. Landminen in Mosambik: Kosten für den ländlichen Raum und Einfluβ auf Nahrungssicherung. University of Kiel, Mimeo.

FEWS (Famine Early Warning System) Project. 1991. How close to famine? *FEWS Bulletin* 5: 2.

―――. 1996. FEWS Special Report 7. November 27.

Fogel, R. W. 1991. The conquest of high mortality and hunger in Europe and America: Timing and mechanisms. In *Favorites of fortune: Technology, growth, and economic development since the industrial revolution,* ed. P. Higonnet, D. S. Landes, and H. Rosovsky. Cambridge, Mass., U.S.A.: Harvard University Press.

―――. 1994. Economic growth, population theory, and physiology: The bearing of long-term processes on the making of economic policy. *The American Economic Review* 84 (3): 369–395.

Fox, R. 1996. Enabling withdrawal from emergency aid. Paper presented at the Senior National Resource Advisers' Conference, 15 July, Sparsholt College, Winchester, U.K.

Frankenberger, T. R. 1991. Indicators and data collection methods for assessing household food security. Office of Arid Land Studies, University of Arizona, Tucson, Ariz., U.S.A. Mimeo.

Fraser, C. 1988. *Lifelines for Africa still in peril and distress.* London: Hutchinson Education.

Gantzel, K. J., and T. Schwinghammer. 1995. *Die Kriege nach dem Zweiten Weltkrieg 1945 bis 1992. Daten und Tendenzen.* Münster, Germany: Lit Verlag.

Gebre, S. 1993. Urban poverty and food insecurity: The case of Addis Ababa. International Food Policy Research Institute, Washington, D.C. Mimeo.

Gedion, A. 1988. Disaster prevention and preparedness plan in the context of the five-year plan. Paper presented at the National Conference on a Disaster Prevention and Preparedness Strategy for Ethiopia, 5–8 December, Addis Ababa.

Gill, P. 1986. *A year in the death of African politics: Bureaucracy and the famine.* London: Paladin Grafton Books.

Girgre, A. 1991. Agricultural policy reform in Ethiopia, 1974 to 1989. International Food Policy Research Institute, Washington, D.C. Mimeo.

Gizaw, B. 1988. Drought and famine in Ethiopia. In *The ecology of health and disease in Ethiopia,* ed. Z. A. Zein and H. Kloos. Addis Ababa: Ministry of Health.

Gonda, S., and W. Mogga. 1988. Loss of the revered cattle. In *War wounds—Development costs of conflict in southern Sudan,* ed. N. Twose and B. Pogrund. London: Panos Institute.

Goyder, H., and C. Goyder. 1988. Case studies of famine: Ethiopia. In *Preventing famine: Policies and prospects for Africa,* ed. D. Curtis, M. Hubbard, and A. Shepherd. New York: Routledge.

Green, R. H. 1987. Killing the dream: The political and human economy of war in Sub-Saharan Africa. Institute of Development Studies Discussion Paper 238.

Greene, W. H. 1990. *Econometric analysis.* New York: Macmillan.

Gryseels, G., and F. Anderson. 1983. *Research on farm and livestock productivity in the Ethiopian highlands: Initial results 1977–1980.* ILCA Research Report 4. Addis Ababa: International Livestock Center for Africa.

Gryseels, G., F. Anderson, G. Assamenew, A. Misgina, A. Astatke, and W. Wolde-Mariam. 1984. *The use of single oxen for crop cultivation in Ethiopia.* ILCA Bulletin 18. Addis Ababa: International Livestock Center for Africa.

———. 1988. *Role of livestock on mixed smallholder farms in the Ethiopian highlands: A case study from the Baso and Worena Woredda near Debre Berhan.* Addis Ababa: International Livestock Center for Africa.

Gryseels, G., and S. Jutzi. 1986. *Regenerating farming systems after drought: ILCA's ox/seed project, 1985 results.* Addis Ababa: International Livestock Center for Africa.

al-Gudal, M. S. 1983. Personal communication with Dr. Mohammed Babiker Ibrahim, Department of History, University of Khartoum, August 19.

Gutu, S. Z., R. Lambert, and S. Maxwell. 1990. *Cereal, pulse, and oilseed balance-sheet analysis for Ethiopia 1979–1989.* Brighton, U.K.: Institute of Development Studies.

Habte-Wold, D., and S. Maxwell. 1992. Vulnerability profiles and risk mapping in Ethiopia. Draft report to the Food and Nutrition Unit, Ministry of Planning and Economic Development, Addis Ababa. Mimeo.

Hansch, S. 1995. An explosion of complex humanitarian emergencies. In *Countries in Crisis . . . Hunger 1996,* ed. Bread for the World. Silver Spring, Md.: Bread for the World Institute.

Hareide, D. 1986. Food for work in Ethiopia. Paper presented at the Workshop on Food for Work in Ethiopia, 25–26 July, Addis Ababa.

Hay, R. W. 1986. Food aid and relief-development strategies. *Disasters* 10 (4): 273–287.

———. 1988. Famine incomes and employment: Has Botswana anything to teach Africa? *World Development* 16 (9): 1113–1125.

Herald, The. 1990. Pledge to help drought victims. October 12.

Helleiner, G. V. 1992. The IMF, the World Bank, and Africa's adjustment and external debt problems: An unofficial view. *World Development* 20 (6): 779–792.

Higgins, P. A., and H. Alderman. 1992. *Labor and women's nutrition: A study of energy expenditure, fertility, and nutritional status in Ghana.* Policy Research Working Paper WPS 1009. Washington, D.C.: World Bank.

Holden, S. 1990. Effects of distance to market, season, and family wealth on dairy sales, and their contribution to pastoral cash income in semi-arid Ethiopia. International Livestock Center for Africa, Addis Ababa. Mimeo.

Holmberg, J. 1977. *Grain marketing and land reform in Ethiopia: An analysis of the marketing and pricing of food grains in 1976 after the land reform.* Research Report 41. Uppsala, Sweden: Scandinavian Institute of African Studies.

Holt, J. F. J. 1983. Ethiopia: Food for work or food for relief? *Food Policy* 8 (3): 187–201.

Holt, P. M. 1970. *The Mahdist state in the Sudan (1881–1898).* Oxford: Clarendon Press.

Horn of Africa Report. 1990. World Bank support continues in Ethiopia. Report 1 (2): 3–4.

Hulme, M. 1984. 1983: An exceptionally dry year in central Sudan. *Weather* 39: 281–285.

Human Rights Watch Arms Project and Human Rights Watch Africa. 1994. *Landmines in Mozambique.* New York and Washington, D.C.

Ibrahim, M. B. 1985. Adjustment to drought hazard in the semi-arid areas of the Sudan. Ph.D. dissertation, University of Alberta, Edmonton, Alberta, Canada.

———. 1990. Drought, famine, and disaster management in Darfur, Sudan. University of Khartoum, Department of Geography, Khartoum. Mimeo.

ICRC (International Committee of the Red Cross). 1996. *Antipersonnel landmines: Friend or Foe?* Geneva.

IFAD (International Fund for Agricultural Development). 1989. *Special programming mission to Ethiopia: Main report.* Rome.

ILCA (International Livestock Center for Africa). 1991. *A handbook of African livestock statistics.* Working Document 15. Addis Ababa.

Iliffe, J. 1987. *The African poor: A history.* Cambridge: Cambridge University Press.

———. 1990. *Famine in Zimbabwe 1890–1960.* Harare, Zimbabwe: Mambo Press.

Intertect. 1986. *An assessment of 1986 food needs for the Catholic Relief Services food distribution network—Ethiopia. Report on the study conducted for Catholic Relief Services.* Baltimore, Md.: Catholic Relief Services.

Jackson, B. 1990. *Poverty and the planet: A question of survival.* London: Penguin Books/World Development Movement.

James, J., ed. 1989. Relief infrastructure study of Ethiopia. Draft report to United Nations Development Program (UNDP)/UNEPPG/WFP. Addis Ababa: Mimeo.

Jareg, P., ed. 1987. *Lessons learned from relief work: Ethiopia.* Addis Ababa: Redd Barna.

Jaspars, S. 1994. *The Rwandan refugee crisis in Tanzania: Initial successes and failures in food assistance.* Overseas Development Institute (ODI) Relief and Rehabilitation Network Paper 6. London: Overseas Development Institute.

Jodha, N. S. 1975. Famine and famine policies: Some empirical evidence. *Economic and Political Weekly* 10 (41): 1609–1623.

Kanbur, R., Kean, M., and M. Tuomala. 1994. Labor supply and targeting in poverty alleviation programs. *World Bank Economic Review* 8 (2): 191–211.

Kates, R., and S. Millman. 1990. On ending hunger: The sermons of history. In *Hunger in history—Food shortage, poverty, and deprivation,* ed. L. F. Newman. Oxford: Bond Blackwell.

Keen, D. 1992. *Rationing the right to life: The crisis in refugee relief.* London: Zed Books.

Kelly, M. 1987. Wollo Nutrition Fieldwork Program. A report. Save the Children Fund (United Kingdom), Desse, Ethiopia. Mimeo.

————. 1992. Anthropometry as an indicator of access to food in populations prone to famine. *Food Policy* 17 (6): 443–454.

Kennedy, E. T., and B. Cogill. 1987. *Income and nutritional effects of the commercialization of agriculture in southwestern Kenya.* Research Report 63. Washington, D.C.: International Food Policy Research Institute.

Kibreab, G. 1995. Eritrean women refugees in Khartoum, Sudan, 1970–1990. *Journal of Refugee Studies* 8 (1).

Kidane, A. 1989. Demographic consequences of the 1984–85 Ethiopian famine. *Demography* 26 (3): 515–522.

Kloos, H. 1991. Health impacts of war in Ethiopia. *Disasters* 16 (4): 347–354.

Kohlin, G. 1987. Disaster prevention in Wollo: The effects of food for work. Report sponsored by Swedish International Development Authority, Stockholm. Mimeo.

KRMFEP (Kordofan Regional Ministry of Finance and Economic Planning). 1986. *The current situation of livestock in north Kordofan—Part 1.* El Obeid, Kordofan.

Kumar, S., H. Neka Tebeb, and G. Pastore. 1992. Investment in nutrition and health for famine prevention in Ethiopia. In *Famine and drought mitigation in Ethiopia in the 1990s,* ed. P. Webb, T. Zegeye, and R. Pandya-Lorch. International Food Policy Research Institute. Famine and Food Policy Discussion Paper No.7, Washington, D.C.

Lancaster, C. J. 1990. The Horn of Africa. In *After the wars,* ed. A. Lake. New Brunswick, N.J., U.S.A.: Transaction Publishers/Overseas Development Council.

Lenneiye, N. M. 1991. Towards a food and nutrition policy for Zimbabwe. A draft inter-ministerial paper, prepared for the National Steering Committee for Food and Nutrition and the University of Zimbabwe/Michigan State University Food Security Project for Southern Africa, Harare. Mimeo.

Lipton, M. 1989. New strategies and successful examples for sustainable development in the Third World. Testimony presented at a hearing on sustainable development and economic growth in the Third World held by the Joint Economic Committee of the U.S. Congress, Subcommittee on Technology and National Security, June 20.

Loveday, A. 1944. *The history and economics of Indian famine.* London: G. Bell and Sons.

MacMichael, H. 1934. *The Anglo-Egyptian Sudan.* London: Faber and Faber.

Macrae, J., and A. B. Zwi. 1992. Food as an instrument of war in contemporary African famines: A review of the evidence. *Disasters* 16 (4): 299–321.

————. 1994. *War and hunger: Rethinking international responses to complex emergencies.* London, N.J., U.S.A.: Zed Books.

Magrath, J. 1991. When farmers take the brakes off. *International Agricultural Development* 11 (2): 15–16.

Majeres, J. 1994. Implementation of employment programs: Key issues and options. In *Employment for poverty reduction and food security,* ed. J. von Braun. Washington, D.C.: International Food Policy Research Institute.

Malthus, T. R. 1798. *An essay on the principles of population, as it affects future improvement of society.* London.

Manyazewal, M. 1992. The economic policy of Ethiopia: Implications for famine prevention. In *Famine and drought mitigation in Ethiopia in the 1990s,* ed. P.

Webb, T. Zegeye, and R. Pandya-Lorch. Famine and Food Policy Discussion Paper 7. Washington, D.C.: International Food Policy Research Institute.

Mateus, A. 1983. *Targeting food subsidies for the needy: The use of cost-benefit analysis and institutional design.* World Bank Staff Working Paper 617. Washington, D.C.: World Bank.

Matiza, T., L. M. Zinyama, and D. J. Campbell. 1989. Household strategies for coping with food insecurity in low-rainfall areas of Zimbabwe. In *Household and national food security in Southern Africa,* ed. G.D. Mudimu and R. H. Bernsten. Harare, Zimbabwe: University of Zimbabwe and Michigan State University.

Maxwell, S. 1978. *Food aid, food for work, and public works.* Institute of Development Studies (IDS) Discussion Paper 127. Brighton, U.K.: Institute of Development Studies.

————. 1989. *Food insecurity in north Sudan.* Discussion Paper 262. Sussex, U.K.: Institute of Development Studies.

————., ed. 1991. *To cure all hunger: Food policy and food security in Sudan.* London: Intermediate Technology Publication.

————. 1993. Can a cloudless sky have a silver lining? The scope for an employment-based safety net in Ethiopia. Paper prepared for a symposium on regional food security and rural infrastructure, 3–6 May, Giessen, Germany.

McCann, J. C. 1985. Social impact report. A paper. Boston University, Boston, Mass., U.S.A. Mimeo.

————. 1987. *From poverty to famine in northeast Ethiopia: A rural history.* Philadelphia, Pa., U.S.A.: University of Pennsylvania Press.

————. 1990. The Socioeconomic context of food storage in highland Ethiopia: Gera Wereda. Report to the American-Jewish World Service and Redd Barna-Ethiopia. Boston, Mass., U.S.A. Mimeo.

Mellor, J. W., C. L. Delgado, and M. J. Blackie. 1987. *Accelerating food production in Sub-Saharan Africa.* Baltimore, Md., U.S.A.: Johns Hopkins University Press for the International Food Policy Research Institute.

Minear, L. 1988. *Helping people in an age of conflict.* Washington, D.C.: American Council for Voluntary International Action.

Mittendorf, H. J. 1987. Promotion of viable rural financial systems for agricultural development. *Quarterly Journal of International Agriculture* 26 (1): 6–27.

Mohammed, A. G. M. 1988. The impact of emergency food aid on traditional agricultural production systems—The case of east Kordofan District. M.S. thesis, University of Khartoum, Khartoum.

Moris, D. M. 1974. What is famine? *Economic and Political Weekly* 9 (44): 1855–1864.

Mortimore, M. 1989. *Adapting to drought: Farmers, famines and desertification in west Africa.* Cambridge, U.K.: Cambridge University Press.

Moyo, S., P. Robinson, Y. Katerere, S. Stevenson, and D. Gumbo. 1991. *Zimbabwe's environmental dilemma: Balancing resource inequities.* Harare, Zimbabwe: Zero Press.

Mulhoff, E. 1988. *Collection of food and nutrition data and its use in Ethiopia, 1979–1988: A review.* Report to the Food and Agriculture Organization of the United Nations. Addis Ababa: Food and Agriculture Organization of the United Nations.

Nicholson, S. E. 1985. Notes: Sub-Saharan rainfall, 1981–84. *Journal of Climate and Applied Meteorology* 24: 1388–1391.

Niger, Ministère du Plan. 1991. *Annuaire statistique: Séries longues. Direction de la statistique et de la démographie.* Niamey, Niger.

NIGETIP (Agence Nigerienne de Travaux d'Interêt Public pour l'Emploi). 1990. Note de présentation. Ministère du Plan, Niamey, Niger. Mimeo.

————. 1992. Rapport d'Activité: Mois d'Avril 1992. Niamey. Mimeo.

NORAD (Norwegian Agency for International Development). 1984. *Report on NORAD-supported health services through Norwegian Lutheran Mission in Ethiopia.* Addis Ababa. Mimeo.

OFDA (Office of U.S. Foreign Disaster Assistance). 1991. *Famine mitigation: Proceedings of workshops held in Tucson, Arizona, May 20–23, 1991, and Berkeley Springs, West Virginia, July 31–August 2, 1991.* Compiled by the Office of Arid Land Studies. Tucson, Ariz., U.S.A.: University of Arizona.

Organization for Economic Cooperation and Development (OECD). 1997. *Development cooperation.* Paris: OECD/DAC.

Organization for Economic Cooperation and Development (OECD)/DAC. 1996. Draft DAC policy orientations for development cooperation in conflict prevention and postconflict recovery. Task Force on Conflict, Peace, and Development Co-Operation. DCD/DAC (96)31. Mimeo.

Osmani, S. R. 1991. Comments on Alex de Waal's "Reassessment of entitlement theory in the light of recent famines in Africa." *Development and Change* (22): 587–596.

Pankhurst, A. 1985. Social consequences of drought and famine: An anthropological approach to selected African case studies. Ph.D. dissertation, University of Manchester, U.K.

Payne, P., and M. Lipton. 1994. *How Third World rural households adapt to dietary energy stress: The evidence and the issues.* Washington, D.C.: International Food Policy Research Institute.

Pearson, R. 1986. Lessons from famine in Sudan (1984–86). United Nations Children's Fund, Khartoum. Mimeo.

Pelletier, D. L., K. Derreke, Y. Kidane, B. Haile, and F. Negussie. 1995. The food-first bias and nutrition policy: Lessons from Ethiopia. *Food Policy* 20 (4): 279–298.

Penrose, A. 1987. Before and after. In *The Ethiopian famine,* ed. K. Jansson, M. Harris, and M. Penrose. London: Zed Press.

Percival, V. T., and Homer-Dixon. 1995. *Environmental scarcity and violent conflict: The case of Rwanda.* American Association for the Advancement of Science (AAAS) Publication 95–235. Toronto, Ontario, Canada: University of Toronto.

Pettengill, T. 1993. International response to famine in the post–Cold War era. M.A. thesis, Dartmouth College, Hanover, N.H., U.S.A.

Pinckney, T. C. 1989. *The demand for public storage of wheat in Pakistan.* Research Report 77. Washington, D.C.: International Food Policy Research Institute.

————, ed. 1993a. *The political economy of food and nutrition policies.* Baltimore, Md., U.S.A.: Johns Hopkins University Press for the International Food Policy Research Institute.

————. 1993b. The food situation in Sub-Saharan Africa and priorities for food policy research and donor assistance. International Food Policy Research Institute, Washington, D.C. Mimeo.

————. 1993b. The food situation in Sub-Saharan Africa and priorities for food policy research and donor assistance. International Food Policy Research Institute, Washington, D.C. Mimeo.

Pinstrup-Anderson, P., D. Pelletier, and H. Alderman, eds. 1995. *Child growth and nutrition in developing countries. Priorities for action.* Ithaca, N.Y.: Cornell University Press.

Platteau, J. P. 1991. Traditional systems of social security and hunger insurance: Past achievements and modern challenges. In *Social security in developing countries,* ed. E. Ahmad, J. Drèze, and A. Sen. Oxford: Clarendon Press.

Puetz, D., S. Broca, and E. Payongayong. 1995. Making food aid work for long-term food security. Proceedings of a USAID/IFPRI Workshop, 27–30 March, Addis Ababa.

Rahmato, D. 1990. Cooperatives, state farms, and smallholder production. In *Ethiopia: Rural development options,* ed. S. Pausewang, F. Cheru, S. Brüne, and G. Chole. Atlantic Highlands, N.J., U.S.A.: Zed Books.

Ravallion, M. 1986. Testing market integration. *American Journal of Agricultural Economics* 68 (February): 102–109.

————. 1987. *Markets and famines.* Oxford: Clarendon Press.

————. 1990. *Reaching the poor through rural public employment: A survey of theory and evidence.* World Bank Discussion Paper 94. Washington, D.C.: World Bank.

Ravallion, M., and G. Datt. 1994. *Income gains for the poor from public works employment. Evidence from two Indian villages.* LSMS Working Paper 100. Washington, D.C.: World Bank.

————. 1995. Is targeting through a work requirement efficient? Some evidence for rural India. In *Public spending and the poor-theory and evidence,* ed. D. van de Walle and K. Nead. Baltimore, Md., U.S.A.: Johns Hopkins University Press.

Reardon, T., C. Delgado, and P. Matlon. 1992. Determinants and effects of income diversification amongst farm households in Burkina Faso. *Journal of Development Studies* (24): 365–377.

————. 1997. *Using evidence of household income diversification to inform study of the rural nonfarm labor market in Africa.* World Development 25 (no. 5): 735–748.

Reardon, T., E. Crawford, and V. Kelly. 1994. Links between nonfarm income and farm investment in African households: Adding the capital market perspective. *American Journal of Agricultural Economists* 76: 1172–1176.

Reardon, T., E. Crawford, V. Kelly, and B. Diagama. 1995. *Promoting farm investment for sustainable intensification of African agriculture.* MSU International Development Paper 18. East Lansing, Mich., U.S.A.: Michigan State University.

Reardon, T., and P. Matlon. 1987. Seasonal food insecurity and vulnerability in drought-affected regions of Burkina Faso. In *Causes and implications of seasonal variability in household food security,* ed. D. Sahu. Baltimore, Md.: Johns Hopkins University Press.

Redd Barna. 1989. Bolosso Woreda Project Area (P.4004). Project background report. Redd Barna-Ethiopia, Addis Ababa. Mimeo.

Reutlinger, S. 1988. Income-augmenting interventions and food self-sufficiency for enhancing food consumption among the poor. In *Food subsidies in developing countries: Costs, benefits, and policy options,* ed. P. Pinstrup-Andersen. Baltimore, Md., U.S.A.: Johns Hopkins University Press for the International Food Policy Research Institute.

Reutlinger, S., and A. M. del Castillo. 1993. Addressing hunger: A historical perspective of international initiatives. Paper for the World Bank Conference on Overcoming Global Hunger, November 30–December 1, Washington, D.C.

Riely, F. Z. Jr. 1991. *Drought responses of the Kababish pastoralists in northern Kordofan, Sudan: Implications for famine early warning.* Rome: Food and Agriculture Organization of the United Nations.

Roberts, S., and J. Williams. 1995. *After the guns fall silent: The enduring legacy of landmines.* Washington, D.C.: Vietnam Veterans of America Foundation.

Rochette, R. M., ed. 1989. *Le Sahel en lutte contre la désertification: Lecons d'expériences.* Eschborn, Germany: Deutsche Gesellschaft für Technische Zusammenarbeit.

Rukuni, M., and C. K. Eicher, ed. 1994. *Zimbabwe's agricultural revolution.* Harare, Zimbabwe: University of Zimbabwe Publications.

Ruttan, V., ed. 1994. *Agriculture, environment, and health: Sustainable development in the 21st century.* Minneapolis, Minn., U.S.A.: University of Minnesota Press.

Sachikonye, L. M. 1992. Zimbabwe: Drought, food, and adjustment. *Review of African Political Economy* 53: 88–108.

Schubert, B. 1993. Soziale Sicherung Mozambik. Report for the GTZ, Berlin. Mimeo.

Seibel, H. D. 1985. Savings for development: A linkage model for formal and informal financial markets. *Quarterly Journal of International Agriculture* 24 (4): 390–398.

Sellström, T., and L. Wohlgemuth. 1996. The international response to conflicts and genocide: Lessons from the Rwanda experience. Study I—Historical perspective: Some explanatory factors. In *Joint evaluation of emergency assistance to Rwanda,* ed. D. Millivood. Odense, Denmark: Strandberg Grafisk.

Sen, A. K. 1981. *Poverty and famines: An essay on entitlement and deprivation.* Oxford: Clarendon Press.

———. 1991. *Wars and famines: On divisions and incentives.* Development Economics Research Program Paper 33. London: London School of Economics.

Shepherd, A. 1988. Case studies of famine: Sudan. In *Preventing famine—Policies and prospects for Africa,* ed. D. Curtis, M. Hubbard, and A. Shepherd. London: Routledge.

Shipton, P. 1990. African famines and food security: Anthropological perspectives. Harvard Institute of International Development, Harvard University, Boston. Mimeo.

Shoham, J., and J. Borton. 1989. *Targeting emergency food aid: Methods used by NGOs during the response to the African food crisis of 1983–86.* Report of a joint study by the Relief and Development Institute and the Human Nutrition Unit, London School of Hygiene and Tropical Medicine. London: Relief and Development Institute.

Shugeiry, S. A. 1990. *Wheat subsidies in Sudan: Policy implications and fiscal cost.* Famine and Food Policy Discussion Paper 3. Washington, D.C.: International Food Policy Research Institute.

Singh, I., L. Squire, and J. Strauss, ed. 1986. Agricultural household models: Extensions, applications, and policy. Baltimore, Md., U.S.A.: Johns Hopkins University Press for the World Bank.

Slatin Pasha, R. C. 1896. *Fire and sword in the Sudan.* London: Edward Arnold.

Stewart, F. 1993. *War and underdevelopment: Can economic analysis help reduce the costs?* Working Paper 56. Oxford: Queeen Elizabeth House.

Stewart, F., S. Loll, and S. Wangwe, eds. 1992. *Alternative development strategies in Sub-Saharan Africa.* London: Macmillan.

Stren, R. E., and R. White. 1988. *African cities in crisis: Managing rapid urban growth.* Boulder: Westview Press.

Sudan-MANR (Ministry of Agriculture and Natural Resources). 1977. *Yearbook of agricultural statistics.* Khartoum.

————. 1984a. *Yearbook of agricultural statistics.* Khartoum.

————. 1984b. *Current agricultural statistics,* vol. 1, no. 4. Khartoum.

————. 1985a. *Agricultural situation and outlook, annual report, 1984/1985.* Khartoum.

————. 1985b. *Agricultural prices in Sudan: A historical review and analysis, 1970–1984.* Khartoum.

————. 1986. *Agricultural commodity prices, 1985 summary.* Khartoum.

————. 1987a. *Agricultural situation and outlook, annual report, 1986/87.* Khartoum.

————. 1987b. *Agricultural commodity prices, 1986 summary.* Khartoum.

————. 1988. *Current agricultural statistics: 1984/85 and 1985/86.* Khartoum.

Sudan-MFEP (Ministry of Finance and Economic Planning). 1982. *Household income and expenditure survey, 1978–80, northern Sudan.* Khartoum.

Swift, J. 1993. Understanding and preventing famine and famine mortality. *IDS Bulletin* 24 (4): 1–16.

Swinton, S. M. 1988. Drought survival tactics of subsistence farmers in Niger. *Human Ecology* 16 (2): 123–144.

Takavarasha, T. 1994. Agricultural pricing policy. In *Zimbabwe's agricultural revolution.,* ed. M. Rukuni and C. K. Eicher. Harare: University of Zimbabwe Publications.

Technoserve/Agricultural Bank of Sudan/USAID. 1987. *KORAG—Credit component baseline study.* El Obeid, Sudan.

Teklu, T. 1993. Labor-intensive public works: The experience of Botswana and Tanzania. In *Employment for Poverty Reduction and Food Security,* ed. J. von Braun. Washington, D.C.: IFPRI.

Teklu, T., J. von Braun, and E. Zaki. 1991. *Drought and famine relationships in Sudan: Policy implications.* Research Report 88. Washington, D.C.: International Food Policy Research Institute.

Thompson, W. S. 1992. Where history continues: Conflict resolution in the Third World. In *Resolving Third World conflict: Challenges for a new era,* ed. S. J. Brown and K. M. Schraub. Washington, D.C.: United States Institute of Peace Press.

Timmer, C. P. 1974. A model of rice marketing margins in Indonesia. *Food Research Institute Studies* 13(2): 145–168.

Torry, W. I. 1984. Social science research on famine: A critical evaluation. *Human Ecology* 12 (3): 227–252.

————. 1988. Famine early-warning systems: The need for an anthropological dimension. *Human Organization* 47 (3): 273–281.

Tucker, C. J., H. E. Dregnes, and W. W. Newcomb. 1991. Expansion and contraction of the Sahara desert from 1880 to 1990. *Science* 253: 299–301.

UN Interagency Task Force. 1989. *South African destabilization: The economic cost of frontline resistance to apartheid.* New York: Economic Commission for Africa, Africa Recovery Program.

UNDP (United Nations Development Programme). 1992. *Human development report.* New York: Oxford University Press.

————. 1996. *Human development report.* New York: Oxford University Press.

UNEPPG (United Nations Emergency Preparedness and Planning Group). 1989. Summary of 1985–1987 emergency operations. UNEPPG Briefing Paper. Addis Ababa. Mimeo.

————. 1990. Briefing notes on United Nations emergency relief and preparedness activities in Ethiopia Addis Ababa.

UNHCR (Office of the United Nations High Commissioner for Refugees). 1988. *Ethiopia: Health and nutrition assessment of southern Sudanese refugee camps in Kefa, Illubabor, and Wolega Awrajas.* Technical Support Service Mission Report 15/88, March 8–22. Geneva.

UNICEF (United Nations Children's Fund). 1988. *Quick assessment: Cash for food in Ethiopia. UNICEF/RRC emergency intervention evaluation.* Draft report. Addis Ababa: UNICEF/RRC.

Unruh, J. D. 1995. Pastoralist resource use and access in Somalia. In *Disasters and development in the Horn of Africa,* ed. J. Sorenson. London: Macmillan.

UNSG (United Nations Secretary-General). 1995. *Supplement to an agenda for peace: Position paper of the secretary-general on the occasion of the fiftieth anniversary of the United Nations.* A. 50/60/S/1995/I. New York.

USAID (U.S. Agency for International Development). 1987. *Final disaster report. The Ethiopian drought/famine. Fiscal years 1985 and 1986.* Addis Ababa: USAID/ American Embassy.

————. 1992. Drought in southern Africa. U.S. Mission, Harare, Zimbabwe. Mimeo.

U.S. Arms Control and Disarmament Agency. 1989. *World military expenditures and arms transfers.* Washington, D.C.

USNCHS (U.S. National Center for Health Statistics). 1977. *NCHS growth curves for children; birth–18 years.* Vital and Health Statistics Series II, No. 165.

Valentine, R. T. 1990. Drought, transfer entitlements, and income distribution: The Botswana experience. Gabarom, Botswana. Mimeo.

Vallee, M. 1989. *Assessment of WFP assistance in the Hararghe region. A report.* Addis Ababa: World Food Program.

van Lierre, M. J. 1993. Coping with household food insecurity: A longitudinal and second study among the Otamuan in northwestern Benin. Ph.D. thesis. Wageningen, Netherlands.

Vosti, S. A., and T. Reardon, ed. 1997. *Sustainability, growth and poverty alleviation: A political and agroecological perspective.* Baltimore, Md., U.S.A.: Johns Hopkins University Press for the International Food Policy Research Institute.

Wagenaar-Brouwer, M. 1986. Nutrition and health of Ethiopian mixed smallholder farmers in relation to the use of crossbred cows. Draft report for the International Livestock Center for Africa, Addis Ababa. Mimeo.

Wahlström, M. 1996. Developmental relief: What is it and why bother? Paper presented at the Overseas Development Administration Senior Natural Resource Advisers Conference, Winchester, 15–17 July.

Walters, H. 1989. Agriculture in Ethiopia—The banks' strategy. A draft report of the World Bank. World Bank; Washington, D.C.

Wanmali, S. 1992. *Rural infrastructure, the settlement system, and development of the regional labor economy in southern India.* Research Report 91. Washington, D.C.: International Food Policy Research Institute.

Watkins, S. C., and J. Menken. 1985. Farming in historical perspective. *Population and Development Review* 11 (4): 647–675.

Watts, J. 1988. Regional patterns of cereal production and consumption. In *The ecology of health and disease in Ethiopia,* ed. Z. Ahmed Zein and H. Kloos. Addis Ababa: Ethiopian Ministry of Health.

Webb, P. 1992. Food security through employment in the Sahel: Labor-intensive programs in Niger. International Food Policy Research Institute, Washington, D.C. Mimeo.

———. 1993. Coping with drought and food insecurity in Ethiopia. *Disasters* 17 (1): 33–47.

———. 1994. Guests of the Crown: Convicts and liberated slaves on McCarthy Island, The Gambia. *Geographical Journal* 160 (2): 136–142.

———. 1995. Employment programs for food security in rural and urban Africa: Experiences in Niger and Zimbabwe. In *Employment for poverty reduction and food security,* ed. J. von Braun. Washington, D.C.: International Food Policy Research Institute.

———. 1997. Famines disprove Hegel: We do learn from the past. University of Hohenheim, Stuttgart, Germany. Mimeo.

Webb, P., and S. Moyo. 1992. Food security through employment in southern Africa: Labor-intensive programs in Zimbabwe. Report to the Deutsche Gesellschaft für Technische Zusammenarbeit, Eschborn, Germany. International Food Policy Research Institute, Washington, D.C.

Webb, P., and T. Reardon. 1992. Drought impact and household response in east and west Africa. *Quarterly Journal of International Agriculture* 31 (3): 230–246.

Webb, P., and J. von Braun. 1994. *Famine and food security in Ethiopia: Lessons for Africa.* London: John Wiley.

Webb, P., J. von Braun, and Y. Yohannes. 1992. *Famine in Ethiopia: Policy implications of coping failure at national and household levels.* Research Report 92. Washington, D.C.: International Food Policy Research Institute.

WFP (World Food Programme). 1989. *Midterm evaluation by a WFP/FAO/ILO/UN mission of Project Ethiopia 2488/(Exp. II): Rehabilitation of forest, grazing, and agricultural lands,* vol. 1. Draft report. Addis Ababa.

———. 1990. *Appraisal of Project Ethiopia 2488/(Exp. III): Food-assisted land improvement project.* Draft report. Main Report. Addis Ababa.

———. 1991. *Status 1991 minimum-emergency food requirements and availability (as of 15 July 1991).* Internal file FDRE Q91. Addis Ababa.

———. 1996a. *Tackling hunger in a world full of food: Tasks ahead for food aid.* Rome.

———. 1996b. *Annual report 1995.* Rome.

———. 1996c. *Commitments for women.* Rome.

Williams, C. 1995. *Agriculture, food and nutrition in postemergency and rehabilitation—issues, needs, and interventions.* Discussion Paper 1 of the ACC/SCN Ad Hoc Working Group on Household Food Security. Rome: FAO.

Winer, N. 1989. Agriculture and food security in Ethiopia. *Disasters* 13 (1): 1–8.

Wohlmuth, K. 1987. *Sudan's national policies on agriculture.* Sudan Economy Research Group Discussion Paper 10. Bremen, Germany: University of Bremen.

Wolde-Mariam, M. 1984. *Rural vulnerability to famine in Ethiopia, 1958–1977.* Addis Ababa: Vikas Publishing House and Addis Ababa University Press.

Wolde-Meskel, G. 1990. Famine and the two faces of entitlement: A comment on sen. *World Development* 18 (3):

Wolde-Michael, H. 1985. The history of famine in Ethiopia. Mimeo.

Wolkeba, T. 1985. Hydrological and meteorological aspect of natural disaster in Ethiopia. Paper presented at the Disaster Prevention Symposium, Ethiopian Red Cross Society, 4–7 September, Addis Ababa.

Wood, C. A. 1977. A preliminary chronology of Ethiopian droughts. In *Drought in Africa,* ed. D. Dalby, R. J. Harrison Church, and F. Bezzaz. London: International African Institute.

World Bank. 1988. *Niger: Small, rural operations project.* Staff Appraisal Report 6910-NIR. Washington, D.C.

———. 1990. *World tables 1989/90.* Washington, D.C.

———. 1991. *World development report 1991.* Washington, D.C.

———. 1993. *World development report 1993.* Washington, D.C.

———. 1994. *Adjustment in Africa: Reforms, results, and the road ahead.* World Bank Policy Research Report. Oxford: Oxford University Press.

Wörz, J. G. 1989. *State farms in Ethiopia.* Diskussionsschriften 14. Heidelberg, Germany: Lehrstuhl für Internationale Entwicklungs- und Agrarpolitik.

Yitbarek, K. 1988. General distribution. In Report on relief workshop, ed. the Christian Relief and Development Association. Addis Ababa. Mimeo.

Yohannes, Y. 1989. Food consumption patterns in western Sudan—1978/80. International Food Policy Research Institute, Washington, D.C. Mimeo.

Young, H. 1986. *The evaluation of the OXFAM energy biscuit and other imported foods in selective feeding programs in Ethiopia and eastern Sudan.* London: OXFAM.

Zeller, M. 1993. Credit policies for food security for the poor: Country case Madagascar. Part 2, Credit for the rural poor in Sub-Saharan Africa. Final report to the GTZ. International Food Policy Research Institute, Washington, D.C. Mimeo.

Zeller, M., G. Schrieder, J. von Braun, and F. Heidhues. 1997. *Rural finance for food security of the poor: Implications for research and policy.* Food Policy Review 4. Washington, D.C.: International Food Policy Research Institute.

Zimbabwe Ministry of Local Government, Rural and Urban Development. 1990. Public sector investment: Public works programme 1991/92. District Development Fund. Harare. Mimeo.

Zimbabwe News. 1989. Masses show enthusiasm in food for work and self-reliance projects. December.

Zolberg, A. R., A. Suharke, and S. Aguayo. 1989. *Escape from violence—Conflict and the refugee crisis in the developing world.* Oxford: Oxford University Press.

Index

Page numbers for entries occurring in figures are followed by an *f;* those for entries occurring in notes, by an *n;* and those for entries occurring in tables, by a *t.*

Abdel Ati, H. A., 182
Abdou, D., 65n, 66, 68
ABS. *See* Agricultural Bank of Sudan
Absolute prices, 71, 78
Adams, A., 93
Adams, M. E., 26
Addis Ababa, 56, 65–66, 140–41, 181
Adele Keke, 157
Admassie, Y., 157
AFC. *See* Agricultural Finance Corporation
Afghanistan, 22
Agence Nigerienne de Travaux d'Interêt
    Public pour L'Emploi (NIGETIP), 153
Agency for International Development,
    U.S. (USAID), 128
Agricultural Bank of Sudan (ABS), 165–
    66, 168
Agricultural diversification, 99–100, 169–
    76
Agricultural employment, 33, 60, 61t
Agricultural Finance Corporation (AFC)
    (Zimbabwe), 34
Agricultural Marketing Corporation (AMC)
    (Ethiopia), 86–87, 140
Agricultural technology, 130, 132, 169–76;
    lessons from selected programs, 170–76;
    population pressure and, 54
Aguayo, S., 11, 65
Ahmed, R., 83
AIDS, 23
Alderman, H., 127, 156
AMC. *See* Agricultural Marketing
    Corporation
Anderson, F., 175
Anderson, F. M., 29
Anderson, J. R., 92
Anemia, 67
Angola, 3t, 10; calorie consumption in,

111t, 112; conflict in, 15, 18, 23;
    democracy and, 19; military expenditures
    in, 21t, 22; production in, 32t; refugees/
    displaced people and, 64t
Antiregime wars, 15
Apartheid, 22
Appleton, J., 134
Aradabe, 116
Aredo, D., 28
Arms imports, 22
Arssi, 43t, 86
Asefa, S., 147
Asela, 84t, 85t
Asia, 7, 12, 62, 71, 86, 164
Asset accumulation, 93
Asset prices, 70
Asset sales, 70, 94, 107–10
Asset transfers, 132, 162–69
Atabani, F., 26, 123
Authoritarian regimes, 19
Awasa, 84t, 85t

Bale, 38, 46, 86, 122
Bangladesh, 3t, 71
Bantu people, 25
Bara, 96
Bardham, P., 19
Barley, 46, 47t, 83, 100
Barré, Siad, 22, 24
Belete, A., 29
Belshaw, D. G. R., 29
Benin, 19, 32t
Berg, A., 127
Biafra, 15
Bielen, R., 166
Binswanger, H. P., 125, 163
Birthrate, 121
Blackie, M. J., 169, 170

About the Authors

Joachim von Braun is director of the Center for Development Research and head of the center's Economics Department at the University of Bonn, Germany. He formerly held the chair for Food Economics, Food Policy, and World Food Issues at the University of Kiel, Germany, and was director of the Food Consumption and Nutrition Division at the International Food Policy Research Institute. He holds a doctoral degree in agricultural economics from the University of Göttingen, Germany. His research has centered on food and agricultural policies, food security, employment, finance, and trade. He is president-elect of the International Association of Agricultural Economists.

Tesfaye Teklu was formerly a research fellow at the International Food Policy Research Institute. He received a Ph.D. in economics from Iowa State University. His research focuses on food demand estimation; famine prevention; and interactions between land, agricultural technology, and poverty.

Patrick Webb is on the faculty of Tufts University's School of Nutrition Science and Policy in Boston, Massachusetts, U.S.A. He formerly held the position of Joseph G. Knoll Visiting Professor for Developing Country Research at the University of Hohenheim, Stuttgart, Germany. He earned his Ph.D. in economic geography from the University of Birmingham, England. He spent several years as a policy analyst with the United Nations' World Food Programme in Rome and as a research fellow at the International Food Policy Research Institute, where his work focused on analysis of early-warning systems for famine prevention, rural employment, and irrigation policy.

LIBRARY OF CONGRESS CATALOGING-IN-PUBLICATION DATA

von Braun, Joachim, 1950–
    Famine in Africa : causes, responses, and prevention / Joachim von Braun, Tesfaye Teklu, and Patrick Webb.
        p. cm.
    Published for the International Food Policy Research Institute.
    Includes bibliographical references (p.   ) and index.
    ISBN 0-8018-6121-7 (alk. paper)
    1. Famines—Africa. 2. Food supply—Africa—Case studies. 3. Famines—Prevention—Government policy—Africa. 4. Africa—Economic conditions—1960– .
I. Tesfaye Teklu. II. Webb, Patrick, 1959– . III. International Food Policy Research Institute. IV. Title.
HC800.Z9F388   1999
363.8′096—dc21   98-8734
                                                                                                            CIP